ECONOMICS IN A CHANGING WORLD
Volume 3: Public Policy and Economic Organization

This is IEA conference volume no.109

ECONOMICS IN A CHANGING WORLD

Congress Editor: Anthony B. Atkinson

Economics in a Changing World

Proceedings of the Tenth World Congress of the International Economic Association, Moscow

Congress Editor: Anthony B. Atkinson

Volume 3
PUBLIC POLICY AND ECONOMIC ORGANIZATION

Edited by

Dieter Bös

St. Martin's Press

First published in Great Britain 1993 by
THE MACMILLAN PRESS LTD
Houndmills, Basingstoke, Hampshire RG21 2XS
and London
Companies and representatives
throughout the world

A catalogue record for this book is available from the British Library.

ISBN 0–333–60125–4

Printed in Great Britain by
Ipswich Book Co Ltd, Ipswich, Suffolk

First published in the United States of America 1993 by
Scholarly and Reference Division,
ST. MARTIN'S PRESS, INC.,
175 Fifth Avenue,
New York, N.Y. 10010

ISBN 0–312–10182–1

Library of Congress Cataloging-in-Publication Data
International Economic Association.   World Congress (10th : 1992:
Moscow, Russia)
Economics in a changing world : proceedings of the Tenth World
Congress of the International Economic Association, Moscow /
congress editor, Anthony B. Atkinson.
   p.   cm. — (v. 3: IEA conference volume : no. 109)
"[Published] in association with the International Economic
Association."
Includes bibliographical references.
Contents: v. 1. System transformation / Abel Aganbegyan, Oleg
Bogomolov and Michael Kaser, editors — v. 2. Microeconomics / Beth
Allen, editor — v. 3. Public policy and economic organization /
Dieter Bös, editor — v. 4. Development, trade and the environment
/ Edmar L. Bacha, editor — v. 5. Capital and labour markets and
economic growth / Jean-Paul Fitoussi, editor.
ISBN 0–312–10182–1
1. Economic policy—Congresses.   I. Atkinson, A. B. (Anthony
Barnes)   II. Series: I.E.A. conference volume ; no. 109.
HD73.I575   1993
330—dc20   93–1789
                                                     CIP

Contents

Contents

PART III   DISTRIBUTIONAL EFFECTS OF SOCIAL
          POLICY

7   **The Western Experience with Social Safety Nets**   121
    Anthony B. Atkinson

8   **Economics of Ageing**   140
    Dieter Bös

9   **Payment of Medical Providers and the Public Provision
    of Medical Care**   153
    Mark V. Pauly

10 **The Dynamics of Housing Prices: An International
    Perspective**   175
    Peter Englund and Yannis M. Ioannides

11 **Non-cash Income, Living Standards and Inequality:
    Evidence from the Luxembourg Income Study**   198
    *Peter Saunders, Timothy M. Smeeding, John Coder,
    Stephen Jenkins, Johan Fritzell, Aldi J.M. Hagenaars,
    Richard Hauser and Michael Wolfson*

12 **Gender Inequality and Economic Development**   218
    Jane Humphries

Preface

Anthony B. Atkinson

The World Congress of the International Economic Association held
in Moscow in August 1992 was the tenth in a series which began in
Rome in 1956 and which had been held most recently in New Delhi in
1986 and Athens in 1989. Each of the previous congresses has had its
distinctive features, but the Tenth Congress was undoubtedly special
because it took place against a background of historic changes in the
Russian economy and society. To quote from the letter sent by
Jacques Delors, President of the Commission of the European Com-
munities, which co-sponsored the Congress:

> The former Soviet society is facing a period of enormous changes,
> the results of which are of global significance. The huge and urgent
> tasks to be accomplished call for a sound analysis of the process of
> economic transformation, to be carried out by Eastern as well as
> Western experts. The Tenth World Congress of the IEA will offer
> the opportunity for them to have discussions together, start
> collaboration and develop a common language.

Those who were present at the Moscow Congress will know that
there was indeed lively discussion of the choices facing Russian
economic policy, and that it provided first-hand insight into the
problems of transition to a market economy. The Congress represented an unprecedented opportunity for contacts, both formal and
informal, between economists from East and West.

At the same time, the 1992 Congress was not solely concerned with
the problems of economic transformation. Like the Ninth Congress
in Athens, it covered in principle all fields of economics. While the
historic changes taking place in Russia and Eastern Europe were in
the forefront of everyone's mind, the Congress was not limited to this
subject. There are several reasons for this. The first is that, with a
meeting only every three years, it is important that all economists
should feel free to attend, whatever their fields of specialism. As my
predecessor, Amartya Sen, remarked in his Preface to the Athens
Congress volumes, 'it seems unreasonable to make economists of

particular specialisation wait many multiples of three years for their turn to come up'. Secondly, while there were indeed important sessions on economic transformation, it was the hope of the Programme Committee that sessions in all areas would be of interest to Russian economists and others whose economies are in transition. Subjects such as Public Finance, the Economics of Financial Markets, Business History and the Economics of Health, just to take some examples, are very relevant to what is happening in the Russian economy and in Eastern Europe.

Thirdly, the IEA is an *international* association, and while meeting in Russia it was most important that we did not lose sight of the economic issues which confront other parts of the world. It would be easy for the economics profession to become immersed in the issues of transition from communism to a market economy and to neglect the enduring problems of Africa, Asia and Latin America. In this context I should draw attention to the sessions on the development problems of Latin America, China, on economic policy with particular reference to Africa, and on the Indian economy. The last of these sessions was organized in honour of Sir Austin Robinson. Unfortunately he could not attend the Congress, but until his death in June 1993, at the age of 95, he continued to play an active role in the Association's affairs, as he had ever since its creation more than 40 years ago

The Congress programme consisted of five plenary lectures (those by Professor A. Blinder, Academician O. Bogomolov, Professor B. Grodal, Professor D. Patinkin and the Presidential Address), of four panel sessions (chaired by Professors K.J. Arrow, B. Csikos-Nagy, J. Drèze and Mr S. Wright), twenty-nine half-day sessions and seventeen full-day sessions, with invited and contributed papers. The programme was organized on a decentralized basis, as was perhaps appropriate in the new Russian circumstances, with each session being organized by one or two Programme Committee members. To them were sent the more than 400 papers submitted, and they arranged for the Invited Speakers. On the final programme were 67 invited papers and 241 contributed papers. Those taking part were drawn from more than 50 countries.

The full list of the Programme Committee is as follows:

A.G. Aganbegyan, Academy of National Economy, Moscow, Russia
B. Allen, University of Minnesota, USA
M. Aoki, Stanford University, USA
K.J. Arrow, Stanford University, USA

E.L. Bacha, Pontificia Universidade Catolica do Rio de Janeiro, Brazil

K. Basu, Delhi School of Economics, India

O. Blanchard, Massachusetts Institute of Tecnology, USA

O. Bogomolov, Academy of Sciences, Moscow, Russia

D. Bös, University of Bonn, Germany

B. Csikos-Nagy, Hungarian Economic Association

J.-P. Danthine, University of Lausanne, Switzerland

P.A. David, Stanford University, USA

A.S. Deaton, Princeton University, USA

J.-P. Fitoussi, Observatoire Français des Conjonctures Economiques, Paris, France

M. Germouni, Rabat, Morocco

J. Le Grand, London School of Economics, UK

J.-M. Grandmont, Centre d'Études Prospectives d'Economie Mathématiques Appliquées à la Planification, Paris, France

L. Hannah, London School of Economics, UK

A. Heertje, University of Amsterdam, Holland

M. Hoel, University of Oslo, Norway

B. Holmlund, Uppsala University, Sweden

J. Humphries, University of Cambridge, UK

Y.M. Ioannides, Virginia Polytechnic Institute, USA

A.P. Kirman, European University Institute, Florence, Italy

A. Krueger, Duke University, USA

D. Kumar, University of Delhi, India

Y. Luo, Beijing University, China

M.I. Mahmoud, African Centre for Monetary Studies, Senegal

P. Maillet, University of Lille, France

J. Malcomson, University of Southampton, UK

E. Maskin, Harvard University, USA

J. Melitz, Institut Nationale de la Statistique et des Études Economiques, Paris, France

P.-A. Muet, Observatoire Français des Conjonctures Economiques, Paris, France

I. Musu, Venice University, Italy

T. Negishi, University of Tokyo, Japan

L. Phlips, European University Institute, Florence, Italy

R. Portes, Centre for Economic Policy Research, London, UK

B.M.S. van Praag, Erasmus University, Holland

J. Sachs, Harvard University, USA

P. Saunders, University of New South Wales, Australia

C. Schmidt, Laboratoire d'Economie et de Sociologie des Organisa-
tions de Défence, Paris, France
S. Scotchmer, University of California, Berkeley, USA
A.K. Sen, Harvard University, USA
M.R. Sertel, Boğaziçi University, Turkey
T. Smeeding, Syracuse University, USA
K. Stahl, University of Mannheim, Germany
O. Stark, Harvard University, USA
P. Temin, Massachusetts Institute of Technology, USA
H. Tulkens, Centre for Operations Research and Econometrics,
Belgium
J. Vinals, Committee of European Community Central Bankers,
Switzerland
A.D. Woodland, University of Sydney, Australia
R.D. Worrell, Central Bank of Barbados
S. Wright, University of Cambridge, UK
S. Zamagni, University of Bologna, Italy

The plenary lectures and invited papers are being published in five
volumes. Each of the volumes has a separate editor and IEA editor:

Vol. 1: *System Transformation: Eastern and Western Assessments*,
edited by Abel Aganbegyan, Oleg Bogomolov and Michael Kaser
(M. Kaser editing for IEA);
Vol. 2: *Microeconomics*, edited by Beth Allen (N. Watts editing for
IEA);
Vol. 3: *Public Policy and Economic Organization*, edited by Dieter
Bös (R. Maurice editing for IEA);
Vol. 4: *Development, Trade and the Environment*, edited by Edmar
Bacha (M. Hadfield editing for IEA);
Vol. 5: *Economic Growth and Capital and Labour Markets*, edited by
Jean-Paul Fitoussi (L. Cook editing for IEA).

I take this opportunity of thanking the editors of the volumes,
Michael Kaser, who is the Association's General Editor, and the IEA
editorial team, for their work in producing these conference
proceedings.

The situation of the Russian economy in 1992 undoubtedly made
the Congress of great interest. It also added to the difficulties of
organization, and I should like to put on record the Association's
deep appreciation to all those who made it possible. First of all, our

Russian hosts. Academicians Aganbegyan and Bogomolov invited the Association and inspired us with their confidence that the Congress could be achieved. The Local Organizing Committee, headed by Vice Prime Minister A. Shokhin, and managed by Vice Rector A.A. Modin, have done all the hard work to make the Congress a reality in very difficult circumstances. We appreciate the hospitality of the Academy of National Economy and the Russian Academy of Sciences, and the participation of other institutions. It is not possible to refer to all of the Academy staff by name, but I would like to assure them that all the participants from outside Russia were very grateful.

The organization has also involved much work for the Association's staff. I would like to thank the Secretary-General, Jean-Paul Fitoussi, whose contribution has been absolutely essential in ensuring that the Congress took place. In Paris, the Administrative Secretary, Elisabeth Majid, has worked tirelessly, together with her colleagues, on travel, visa and financial aspects. For Elisabeth, it is her last IEA Congress, and I would like to put on record the Association's appreciation of all her work. In London, Jacky Jennings as Programme Secretary has taken a great deal of responsibility, and it has been a pleasure to work with her. Alistair McAuley of the University of Essex helped with initial contacts in Moscow. My predecessor, Amartya Sen, and other members of the IEA Executive Committee have been a constant source of help and sound advice.

Before concluding these prefatory remarks, I should express my warm gratitude to the bodies which have funded the Congress. In addition to the co-sponsorship of the European Community to which reference has already been made, the generosity of (in alphabetical order), the Austrian National Bank, the Bank for International Settlements, the British Academy, the Carnegie Corporation, the European Bank for Reconstruction and Development, the Ford Foundation, the Credit-Anstalt, Vienna, the Deutsche Bundesbank, the McArthur Foundation, and the Soros Foundation (which made possible the participation of Eastern European economists) is very much appreciated.

The International Economic Association

A non-profit organisation with purely scientific aims, the International Economic Association (IEA) was founded in 1950. It is a federation of national economic associations and presently includes fifty-eight such professional organisations from all parts of the world. Its basic purpose is the development of economics as an intellectual discipline. Its approach recognises a diversity of problems, systems and values in the world and also takes note of methodological diversities.

The IEA has, since its creation, tried to fulfil that purpose by promoting mutual understanding of economists from the West and the East, as well as from the North and the South, through the organisation of scientific meetings and common research programmes, and by means of publications on problems of current importance. During its forty years of existence, it has organised one hundred round-table conferences for specialists on topics ranging from fundamental theories to methods and tools of analysis and major problems of the present-day world. The ten triennial World Congresses have regularly attracted the participation of a great many economists from all over the world.

The Association is governed by a Council, composed of representatives of all member associations, and by a fifteen-member Executive Committee which is elected by the Council. The Executive Committee (1989–92) at the time of the Moscow Congress was

President: Professor Anthony B. Atkinson, UK
Vice-President: Professor Luo Yuanzheng, China
Treasurer: Professor Alexandre Lamfalussy, Belgium
Past President: Professor Amartya Sen, India
Other Members: Professor Abel Aganbegyan, USSR
Professor Kenneth J. Arrow, USA.
Professor Edmar Lisboa Bacha, Brazil
Professor B.R. Brahmananda, India
Professor Wolfgang Heinrichs,
  German Federal Republic
Professor Edmond Malinvaud, France
Professor Takashi Negishi, Japan

The Association has also been fortunate in having secured the following outstanding economists to serve as President: Gottfried Haberler (1950–3), Howard S. Ellis (1953–6), Erik Lindahl (1956–69), E.A.G. Robinson (1959–62), G. Ugo Papi (1962–5), Paul A. Samuelson (1965–8), Erik Lundberg (1968–71), Fritz Machlup (1971–4), Edmond Malinvaud (1974–7), Shigeto Tsuru (1977–80), Victor L. Urquidi (1980–3), Kenneth J. Arrow (1983–6), Amartya Sen (1986–9). Professor Michael Bruno took office at the conclusion of the Moscow Congress.

The activities of the Association are mainly funded from the subscriptions of members and grants from a number of organisations, including continuing support from UNESCO.

List of Contributors

Professor A.B. Atkinson, Faculty of Economics and Politics, University of Cambridge, UK

Professor D. Bös, Institute of Economics, University of Bonn, Germany

Dr J. Coder, Bureau of the Census, Washington DC, USA

Professor P. Englund, Department of Economics, University of Uppsala, Sweden

Mr J.S. Flemming, European Bank for Reconstruction and Development, London, UK

Dr Johan Fritzell, Swedish Institute of Social Research, University of Stockholm, Sweden

Professor A.J.M. Hagenaars, Department of Economics, Erasmus University, Rotterdam, The Netherlands

Professor P.J. Hammond, Department of Economics, Stanford University, California, USA

Professor R. Hauser, Department of Social Policy, University of Frankfurt, Germany

Professor D.M. Hausman, Department of Philosophy, University of Wisconsin-Madison, Madison, Wisconsin, USA

Professor C.J. Heady, School of Social Sciences, University of Bath, UK

Professor Dr. A. Heertje, Department of Economics, University of Amsterdam, The Netherlands

Dr. J. Humphries, Faculty of Economics and Politics, University of Cambridge, UK

Professor Y.M. Ioannides, Department of Economics, Virginia Polytechnic Institute and State University, Blacksburg, Virginia, USA

Professor S. Jenkins, Department of Economics, University of Swansea, UK

Professor P.R. Kleindorfer, Department of Economics, University of Pennsylvania, Philadelphia, Pennsylvania, USA

Professor M.S. McPherson, Department of Economics, Williams College, Williamstown, Maryland, USA

Professor M.V. Pauly, The Wharton School, University of Pennsylvania, Philadelphia, Pennsylvania, USA

.

.

Dr P. Saunders, Social Policy Research Centre, University of New South Wales, Australia

Professor M.R. Sertel, Department of Economics, Boğaziçi University, Bebek, Istanbul, Turkey

Professor T.M. Smeeding, Maxwell School of Economics and Public Policy, Syracuse University, New York, USA

Dr M. Wolfson, Statistics Canada, Ottawa, Canada

Abbreviations and Acronyms

AFDC	Aid for Families with Dependent Children
BASYS	Beratungsgesellschaft für Angewandte Systemforschung (Council for Applied Systems Research)
CES	constant elasticity of substitution
CPE	centrally planned economy
CSD	Capitalism, Socialism and Democracy
DWE	discriminating workers' enterprise
EBRD	European Bank for Reconstruction and Development
EC	European Community
EF	entrepreneurial firm
GATT	General Agreement on Tariffs and Trade
GDP	gross domestic product
GNP	gross national product
GSP	General System of Preferences
HMO	Health Maintenance Organization, USA
IMF	International Monetary Fund
LIS	Luxembourg Income Study
LMF	labour-managed firm
MIT	Massachusetts Institute of Technology, USA
NBER	National Bureau of Economic Research, USA
NDWE	non-discriminating workers' enterprise
OECD	Organization for Economic Co-operation and Development
OLG	overlapping generations
OPEC	Organization of Petroleum Exporting Countries
RMI	Revenu Minimum d'Insertion
RSE	reforming socialist economy
SSI	Supplemental Security Income
UN	United Nations
UNICEF	United Nations International Children's Fund
UNIDO	United Nations Industrial Development Organization
VAT	Value Added Tax
WE	workers' enterprise
WIDER	World Institute of Development Economics Research
WPM	worker-partnership market

Introduction: Challenges for Public Economists

Dieter Bös[1]

This volume contains twelve papers on 'public policy and economic organization' which were presented at the Tenth World Congress of the International Economic Association. As the table of contents shows, the volume spans a wide variety of problems: from ethics and welfare as basic principles, to the transition of post-communist economies and the problems of how to help the poor by distribution policies. An introduction to such a volume should explain the inherent logic and coherence in the selection of papers. I shall use this occasion to highlight some recent developments in public economics and to lead the reader to a recognition of particularly challenging areas of research, as reflected in the contributions in this volume.

First, one has to 'take ethics seriously', as Hausman and McPherson indicate in the title of their paper which opens Part I of the book. If other economists underestimate the importance of ethical principles in economics it is up to public economists to be more open minded. The neglect of environmental problems by pure technocrats in the former communist countries clearly revealed how important it is to evaluate and consider potential environmental damages before accepting any public project. Hausman and McPherson's central idea, that individuals do not necessarily rank situations according to their pure egoistic interest, shows that economists, and in particular public economists, should be willing to reconsider even the basics of economic terminology.[2] We should also rethink the basics of welfare economics in a time when former communist countries are in transition to market economic structures and when liberalization has become extremely popular in the USA and in the EC. Hammond, in his paper, stresses that liberalizers do not need 'outdated doctrines based on the classical theorems of welfare economics. That is how they have been misled into neglecting the distributional questions associated with economic reform. The theorems are elegant. The liberalizing policies they suggest may even raise gross domestic product in many cases. But often they also cause needless suffering, and not just because of protest action by those who are the first to become clearly worse off'.

The above quotation reveals two areas in which the expertise of public economists is particularly desirable: namely, with respect to economic organization in transition and to the distributional impact of public policy measures. In Part II of this book some papers on transition are presented. It begins with expressions of surprise about the sudden breakdown of the communist central planning systems. Heertje, in his paper, considers the question of how so farsighted an economist as Schumpeter could err in his forecast of the eventual breakdown of capitalism. Heertje considers it a paradox that Schumpeter, who in all of his earlier writings stressed the importance of entrepreneurship and of innovation, dismissed this idea too easily in his late work on *Capitalism, Socialism and Democracy*. His very own ideas should have led Schumpeter to forecast the breakdown of communism not of capitalism. Indeed, the breakdown of communism is the starting-point of the transition to market oriented economies. Even if a gradualistic approach to transition is chosen instead of a big bang policy,[3] one of the obvious problems during a period of transition is the distributional hardship caused, in particular, by rapidly rising unemployment (which was unknown in the communist countries, so that the experience of unemployment is particularly traumatic for any citizen who is affected). Many theoretical and practical proposals attempt to mitigate the distributional problems which arise in the period of transition. Wage or employment subsidies is one of these[4] and Flemming's paper in this volume addresses this question. Flemming shows that in fairly reasonable 'second best' frameworks, these subsidies may be Pareto-improving, investment-improving or welfare-improving. However I personally must admit that I am not convinced of the appropriateness of the short run modelling of such subsidies on the assumption that the potential output of the economy is unaffected in the period of transition. What is needed instead is a medium term analysis in which the typical reduction in potential output is explicitly considered.

Wage or employment subsidies are not the only instruments to cope with income or wealth redistribution in economies in transition. 'Popular capitalism', that is a policy of widespread share ownership, is often chosen. Management buy-outs are also a much discussed policy (Poland) and often are actually employed ('spontaneous privatization' in Hungary and many cases in East Germany). Workers' enterprises, discussed in Kleindorfer and Sertel's contribution to this volume, offer another alternative. They are distinguished from labour-managed enterprises in that shares in the equity of the firm are sold to both present and future employees competitively. The authors show that workers' enterprises are an efficient form of internal organization, in contrast to labour-managed firms. Finally a paper by Heady addresses the economic transitions which developing countries undergo under the auspices of international organizations like the International Monetary Fund and the World Bank. Heady pleads for a careful evaluation of the special situations of developing countries. It is often sub-optimal to impose Western policy mreasures on developing countries, for instance, forcing on them privatization campaigns, reduction in government expenditures or Western-type tax policies.

The discussion of economies in transition has already hinted at the importance of distributional considerations in public policy. It is a pleasure for me to emphasize the importance of distributional policy in a volume of the *International* Economic Association: I have often obtained the impression that caring about distributional problems is a *European* attitude, and that it is next to impossible to persuade *US* economists of the importance of income distribution.[5] It is even better that a leading European in the theoretical and empirical analysis of the distribution of income and wealth, namely Atkinson, became president of the IEA! A good example of his deep insight into the topic is given in his presidential address, which opens Part III of this volume.

Part III of this volume is biased in a very interesting way. When an international programme committee decided to invite those speakers whose papers are presented in this volume, they made a surprising omission: they did not invite anyone to speak about income redistribution by means of taxation. The only topics on redistribution by public policy measures included in the programme related to income redistribution by means of public expenditures. I must admit that I myself did not realize this omission before writing this introduction, which forced me to think about the coherence of the several papers brought together in this volume. How can the omission be explained? In my opinion there are two explanations. First a deficiency in the theory of taxation with respect to its relevance to income distribution. Twenty years ago this topic was explored by Mirrlees (1971) for non-linear direct taxation and by Diamond and Mirrlees (1971) for indirect taxation. In subsequent years extensions of the basic approaches appeared, but a new breakthrough has not occurred since then. Quite a few economists at the moment find the topic of optimal direct taxation simply boring. The models are typically very complicated and not very productive. From the theoretical point of view, the efficiency results are always fairly similar; from the practical point of view, the applicability of the results seems not to be feasible. But perhaps this view reflects my own frustrations: for some time I tried to no avail to find a theoretically convincing answer to the question: 'why should an income tax be progressive?'ᵇ I finally had to accept that a generally convincing answer to my question does not exist, and that even the importance of my question can be challenged. A second explanation for the omission from the papers selected for this volume could be empirical. Sah (1983) showed that the redistributive capabilities of indirect taxation are low; he derived ceilings on the possible redistribution by transforming the Ramsey-Rawls tax rules. For West Germany Recktenwald and Grüske (1980) claimed that the overall redistributive effect of all public revenues (taxes, public sector prices) was zero; only public expenditures were effective instruments of personal redistribution.

The most important distributional instruments, which are treated in several papers in this volume, are cash transfers (Atkinson), non-cash benefits (Saunders *et al.*), public old age insurance (Bös) and public health insurance (Pauly). Of course, this is only a selection of interesting topics: others are missing, such as the distributional effects of education expenditure or public unemployment insurance. The latter is particularly relevant to income distribution in economies in transition. Income redistribution by public expenditure always raises complicated problems of measurement. For the provision of medical care, Pauly shows in his paper how cross-national comparisons of medical care spending should be corrected for the various governmental influences on input prices: the USA spends 1.56 per cent of its GDP on medical doctors, Norway only 0.43 per cent; but if re-calculated using US wages, Norway spends 1.83 per cent of its GDP on medical doctors. Moreover any measurement of income distribution should take account of the personal characteristics of economic agents which influence their well-being. It is necessary to differentiate according to these characteristics, for instance, according to gender, as shown in this volume by Humphries. Age, race and religion also play an important role. This has often been dealt with in empirical studies, in particular of older women, and poverty studies of the elderly and of disadvantaged ethnic and racial groups. Unfortunately, in neoclassical theoretical analyses, the principle of anonymity of individual agents presents a sort of mental barrier to the explicit modelling of such personal characteristics.

To summarize, the challenges for public economics can be seen from this treatment of the contents of the present volume to be the following:

- take ethics seriously;
- do not fall for elegant models which fail to take account of the most important economic and political facts;
- try to construct a theory of the transition of former communist economies which combines both efficiency and distributional elements – and, I would like to add, which combines the best of typical public economics and industrial organization models;[7]
- do not be afraid of concentrating on income distribution; all recent political experiences have shown that distribution matters in practice and since public economics is not art for art's sake, distribution should also matter in public economics,
- never forget the personal characteristics of the economic agents involved, like gender, race or age.

Notes

1. For careful discussions of an earlier draft of this introduction I am grateful to Peter Hammond, Lorenz Nett and Wolfgang Peters.
2. A good example of such a reconsideration is a recent paper by Amiel and Cowell (1992), in which the basic axioms of income inequality are scrutinized. The authors show, for instance, that the 'transfer principle' is often not accepted in questionnaire experiments.
3. A big bang policy seems to be successful in East Germany because West Germany is there to pay the bill. (However some other countries feel that there is some beggar-thy-neighbour policy involved.) The Czech (and Slovak) voucher privatization has elements of a big bang. The big bang policy obviously did not work in Poland. A gradualistic policy is claimed to be successful in Hungary and in China, but in these countries the gradualistic transition had already begun before 1989.
4. Particularly well known is the proposal by Akerlof *et al.* (1991) for East Germany. For criticism of the Akerlof proposal, see Bös (1992).
5. Hammond, whom I quoted earlier in this introduction, is English, although he is a professor at Stanford.
6. See, for instance, Bös and Tillmann (1989a), with a fairly aggressive comment by a philosopher, Gray (1989), and the reply in Bös and Tillmann (1989b).
7. Public economics can often be effectively blended with industrial organization. See, for instance, my recent book on privatization, (Bös, 1991).

References

Akerlof, G.A., Rose, A.K., Yellen, J.L. and Hessenius, H. (1991) 'East Germany in from the Cold: The Economic Aftermath of Currency Union', *Brookings Papers on Economic Activity*, vol. 1, pp. 1–87.

Amiel, Y. and Cowell, F. (1992) 'Measurement of Income Inequality. Experimental Test by Questionnaire', *Journal of Public Economics*, vol. 47, pp. 3–26.

Bös, D. (1991) *Privatization: A Theoretical Treatment* (Oxford: Oxford University Press).

Bös, D. (1992) 'Privatization in East Germany', International Monetary Fund, Fiscal Affairs Department, Washington, D.C.

Bös, D. and Tillmann, G. (1989a) 'Equitability and Income Taxation', in Bös, D. and Felderer, B. (eds) *The Political Economy of Progressive Taxation* (Berlin–Heidelberg: Springer) pp. 75–99.

Bös, D. and Tillmann, G. (1989b) 'An Economist's View of Equitable Taxation', in Bös, D. and Felderer (eds) *The Political Economy of Progressive Taxation* (Berlin–Heidelberg: Springer) pp. 107–9.

Diamond, P.A. and Mirrlees, J.A. (1971) 'Optimal Taxation and Public Production, Part I: Production Efficiency', *American Economic Review*, vol. 61, pp. 8–27; 'Part II: Tax Rules', *American Economic Review*, vol. 61, pp. 261–78.

Gray, J. (1989) 'A Political Philosopher's View of Equitable Taxation', in Bös, D. and Felderer, B. (eds) *The Political Economy of Progressive Taxation* (Berlin–Heidelberg: Springer) pp. 101–5.

Mirrlees, J.A. (1971) 'An Exploration in the Theory of Optimum Income Taxation', *Review of Economic Studies*, vol. 38, pp. 175–208.

Recktenwald, H.C. and Grüske, K.-D. (1980) 'Justitia Distributiva durch Umverteilung. Eine Analyse der personellen Budgetinzidenz' (Distributive Justice by Redistribution. An Analysis of the Personal Incidence of the Budget), *Kyklos*, vol. 33, pp. 16–62.

Sah, R.K. (1983) 'How Much Redistribution is possible through Commodity Taxes?', *Journal of Public Economics*, vol. 20, pp. 89–101.

Part I

Welfare Economics and Ethics

1 Why Economists Should Take Ethics Seriously[1]

Daniel M. Hausman
UNIVERSITY OF WISCONSIN–MADISON

and

Michael S. McPherson
WILLIAMS COLLEGE

1 INTRODUCTION

This paper arises out of a project we have been working on for the past two years concerning the relationships between economics and moral philosophy. The impetus for the project was an invitation from John Roemer to write a survey essay on the subject for the *Journal of Economic Literature*. That essay is now complete and will be published shortly (Hausman and McPherson, 1993), but we have hardly exhausted the subject. In this paper, we will mention some of the conclusions we have reached, though there is no good way to condense a survey of contemporary moral philosophy into a brief essay.

Our goal in writing about economics and ethics has been to show clearly and precisely how moral philosophy is relevant to economics and, though perhaps to a lesser extent, how the tools and theories of economics can contribute to moral philosophy. Our objective is ultimately practical. We want to show how knowing some moral philosophy can help economists to do economics better. We are not claiming that moral philosophy has a great deal to add to every branch of economics. Those exclusively concerned with the elasticity of demand for herring may have little to gain from thinking about ethics. But we think moral philosophy has a great deal to contribute to many branches of economics.

In our survey of contemporary moral philosophy, we found a surprisingly large amount of useful work. But it is hard to say a great deal about what we found, for it is really in the details that the value of moral philosophy for economics lies. So rather than attempt to summarize our survey, we would like instead to motivate the whole endeavour of investigating the interrelations between economics and ethics and to develop a theme that has struck us with increasing force as we have pondered this literature. That theme is the considerable normative importance of the theory of rationality that lies at the heart of theoretical economics. We want to suggest that right at the core of economics lies an ethical theory.

We are sure that our readers have heard it said that economics is a moral science, that it embodies moral propositions, and that it cannot be value-free. Such claims are often supported by arguments that make used car contracts sound clear and straightforward. Though we do not want to deprecate previous work on economics and ethics, to which we owe an enormous debt, it seems to us that few of the large scale attempts to show how understanding ethics contributes to doing economics have been convincing. Most economists, we suspect, shrug their shoulders at such talk and return to their work. Even if these claims were true, so what? In our view, the world is not in need of more strained and unconvincing arguments concerning how impregnated by values economics is. In this paper, we will attempt to defend some precise theses concerning exactly how economics involves ethics.

First we shall clear out some underbrush by considering two familiar objections to the idea that ethics has anything useful to contribute to economics, and then we shall clarify and defend the thesis that a fragment of moral theory is central to contemporary economics.

2 OBJECTION 1: ECONOMISTS ARE POSITIVE SCIENTISTS AND ENGINEERS

The suggestion that ethics has anything to contribute to economics gives rise to an immediate objection, which has probably already occurred to many readers. It goes as follows:

Objection 1: Economics is, of course, relevant to policy. But its relevance is purely technical. It provides causal knowledge of the consequences of policies. That knowledge helps policy makers to choose effective means toward their ends. Ethics is relevant to policy, too. It determines the ends and constrains the means that may be employed. But though economics and ethics are both important in policy making, they have nothing to do with one another.

There is some truth in this picture of the economist as an engineer, who provides purely technical information. Although it is a caricature, it is a useful one. It fits some economic activities well: consider, for example, work devoted to estimating how much revenue would result from the imposition of a new value added tax. But, as Fritz Machlup (1969) pointed out, the political process rarely formulates its economic problems so clearly. When economists are called on to give 'purely technical' advice about how to accomplish certain ends, they are rarely given a purely technical problem. The current plight of economists asked to advise governments on how to transform command economies into market economies is a particularly obvious example. But the same difficulties arise when economists are asked for advice on narrower questions, such as how to lower inflation or control pollution. To give advice, economists need to know what other objectives policy makers have and how to weight them. At some point economists will have to rely on some of their own values to fill in the gaps. Similar problems arise when economists select problems to investigate. The moral commitments of economists also suggest new lines of research. Consider, for example, work on the economics of property rights or John Roemer's models of exploitation (Roemer, 1982, 1988). If economists refuse to muck about with messy moral matters, they will not know what questions to ask.

Economists also need to know something about morality to grasp the terms in which policy questions are cast. When politicians and non-economists think about problems of welfare, they employ concepts that do not easily translate into the language of standard economic theory. In his Presidential Address at the Tenth World Congress of the International Economic Association, Professor Atkinson (1993) examined what policy makers mean when they speak of a 'safety net.' Notions of safety nets, needs, fairness, opportunity, freedom and rights are as important in policy making as are concerns about welfare. Insofar as economists want to assist in the formulation of policy, they must link economic theory to such concerns. Doing so requires understanding what these vague things are that people apparently value so much. Economists need to be aware of their understandable tendency to play down moral distinctions that do not translate into the preference-satisfaction framework of theoretical economics.

Consider, for example, the question of whether government should provide food or health care in kind, or whether it should instead provide a cash supplement to those in need. Many economists are tempted by an overly simple argument as to why the government should supply cash.[2] The argument is as follows: construct an indifference map for an individual with quantity of health care on one axis and some composite consumption commodity on the other. Increased income raises the budget line. If the income increase is as large as the value of the in-kind health care provision, then the individual can purchase what the government would have provided if he or she prefers, or the individual can instead consume more of something else. The cash supplement makes individuals at least as well off as does the in-kind provision. Cash supplements are not only Pareto-superior to in-kind provision, but they also serve freedom by increasing the range of individual choice. Furthermore, simpler administration means smaller, less intrusive and cheaper government, which makes possible more freedom and either lower taxes or greater benefits.

Although this analysis brings in the value of freedom, it works mainly within the terms set by orthodox economic theory. Even in these terms, the argument is faulty, for it leaves out of consideration (among other things) the preferences of the donors. Asymmetric information also gives rise to serious problems (Blackorby and Donaldson, 1988). If cash rather than medical care is provided to those in poor health, people will have an incentive to pretend to be sick. But even if these flaws could be remedied, the terms within which the argument addresses the question are too narrow. There is no mention of needs, of the presuppositions of individual dignity, of opportunity, of rights or of fairness. There is no concern with the moral reasons that make individuals willing to pay taxes to provide such benefits (Hochman and Rogers, 1969; Kelman, 1986). Are people motivated by a general benevolent desire to satisfy the preferences of others, or do they instead see themselves as obliged to help others in *need*? Might they regard people as having *rights* to food or medical care which justify taxing others? These are hard questions even to ask within the framework economists employ.

Furthermore many, though not all, of the arguments against substituting cash for in-kind provision are openly paternalistic. A crude version runs, 'If you give the poor money, they'll spend it on drugs and junk instead of food and medicine.' Paternalism is not a popular doctrine, but one should not foreclose discussion of people's ability to promote their own welfare by equating welfare with the satisfaction of preferences by definition.[3]

The view of the economist as a value-free social engineer cannot be sustained. In deciding what to study and in thinking about how to apply economics to practical problems, economists must think about ethical matters.

3 OBJECTION 2: POSITIVE ECONOMICS IS VALUE-FREE

But there is a more moderate second objection, which has again probably occurred to many readers. It goes as follows:

> Objection 2: The first objection exaggerated. One must grant that ethics has a role in determining what problems to study and in policy applications of the results of economic analysis. It is not really surprising that ethics is relevant to people's interests and to normative economics. But the role of ethics ends there. Ethics may pose questions for economists, but it cannot contribute to their answers. Ethics has nothing to contribute to positive economic analysis itself.

Notice first how much the second objection concedes. It confesses that economists may need to understand the concepts and the criteria that are and ought to be applied to the evaluation of economic outcomes *and* processes. Since a very large part of economics is done with a view to its possible policy application, it concedes that ethics has a very important part to play. All this second objection insists on is that positive economics itself – that part of economics that is concerned with the properties, outcomes and mechanisms of actual economies – is independent of ethics.

We have no wish to deny that there is a good deal of truth in Objection 2. Some work in economics is largely independent of all ethical concepts and theories. But a good deal of positive economics is in practice unavoidably penetrated by ethical concerns. For ethical commitments are among the causal factors that influence people's economic behaviour, and consequently they are among the factors with which economists need to be concerned. If people did not generally tell the truth and keep their promises, economic life would grind to a halt. As many theorists who study labour markets have noted, employees and employers have moral beliefs that affect the wage and employment bargains they make. People's moral dispositions affect economic outcomes.

The causal factors just cited might be regarded as sociological rather than moral. What matters is people's behavioural dispositions and their *beliefs* about what is fair, not what is 'in fact' fair. But in practice it is difficult if not impossible to avoid all questions about the adequacy of the moral commitments of economic players. Economists may be able to advance their work by appraising people's moral dispositions as well as by tracing their causal consequences. It is natural, illuminating and virtually unavoidable for economists to inquire whether people's observed (or alleged) moral commitments 'make sense.' If, as Richard Titmuss argues (1971), the gift of blood seems to many people less valuable when blood may be sold as well as donated, one needs to understand *why*. Understanding moral beliefs can rarely in practice be separated from appraising them and hence from understanding ethics. Descriptions of individual motivation and judgment are likely to be evaluations too, and are not less useful for that. We are not (at least here) defending some deep philosophical claim about the inseparability of describing and evaluating moral commitments. Ours is the more mundane but, we think, no less significant observation that, however separable these may be in principle, in practice they are inevitably intertwined.

This evaluative element in positive economics is not only unavoidable, it is also itself causally significant; for the moral convictions of economic agents, unlike causal factors such as rainfall, can be influenced by the way in which they are analysed and described by economists. Saying that human behaviour can be modelled as if it were entirely self-interested legitimizes and fosters self-interested behaviour. Indeed there is some evidence that learning economics may make people more selfish (Marwell and Ames, 1981). Similarly the values and beliefs of influential actors in labour markets are to some degree shaped by the moral and intellectual setting in which they operate. They vary between countries and over time, and may well be shaped by prevailing views about economics. Even if individual workers and personnel managers do not read theoretical monographs concerning, for example, gift exchange or efficiency wages, the staff of legislative committees and consultants to unions and firms do. In popularized form, wage theories reach newspapers and magazines and consequently shop floors and corporate conference rooms. How economists think about labour markets depends on their moral values as well as their theoretical training, and it has moral consequences.

The facts that economists can rarely describe moral commitments without evaluating them and that economists affect what they see by the way they describe it, provide even purely positive economists with reason to think about both the morality that is in fact accepted in the society they study and the morality they think should be accepted. Moral reflection has a role in both positive and normative economics. Positive economics may, as Objection 2 maintains, be separable in principle from all evaluative propositions, but positive economists will be influenced by their moral values and their attitudes toward the values of the agents they study.

Though these reflections about the role of ethical considerations in positive economic theorizing are, we believe, correct, they are beginning to sound too much like the sort of strained and abstract account of the relevance of economics to ethics that we hoped to avoid. More detailed discussion of examples, which we cannot provide here, would, we believe, dispel this impression. Fortunately there is another way to show how ethics is relevant to standard economic theory, for, at the very heart of standard economics, at the very centre of the theoretical citadel, stands an ethical theory! This theory is regarded as a positive theory, that just so happens also to be a theory of rationality. It is not regarded as a moral theory, but it is a moral theory just the same.

4   RATIONALITY, MORALITY AND THE POSITIVE THEORY OF CHOICE

At the foundation of both positive and normative economics lies a thin normative theory of individual rationality.[4] An agent A chooses (acts) rationally if A's preferences are rational and A never prefers an available option to the option chosen. Preferences are rational only if they are complete and transitive. If an agent's preferences are rational, one can assign numbers to the objects of preference. These numbers, which are arbitrary apart from their order, merely indicate preference ranking. They are 'utilities', and the theory of rationality may be restated: agents are rational if and only if their preferences may be represented by ordinal utility functions and their choices maximize utility.[5] We intentionally avoided saying that they act 'in order to maximize utility'. For in contemporary economic theory, utility is merely an index or indicator. It is not a substantive aim or an object of preference. Maximizing utility is just doing what one most prefers to do. Rationality is having complete and transitive preferences and choosing what one most prefers.

Rationality is a normative notion. One *ought* to be rational. One is foolish or mistaken if one is not rational. But it might reasonably be contended that rationality is not a moral notion. One can be a rational villain. What one ought rationally to do need not coincide with what one ought morally to do. The standard 'thin' theory of rationality as utility maximization is not *itself* a moral theory. The wicked can have complete and transitive preferences, and the preferences of saints may not be complete. But the standard theory of rationality does not stand by itself. On the contrary, it is embedded in both normative and positive economics, and via this embedding it smuggles crucial elements of moral theory into positive economics.

The relationships between positive economics, normative economics and the theory of rationality are intricate. Consider first how positive economics and the theory of rationality jointly determine the character of normative economics. One can in fact virtually derive normative economics from the theory of rationality and components of *positive* economics! This is how: start with the theory of rationality and add a standard (though not universal) assumption of positive economics, that individuals are self-interested. This further assumption need not be regarded as itself a part of the theory of rationality, although economists often associate rationality and self-interest. Next notice that it is part of the meaning of the term 'rational' that a rational individual does not knowingly and intentionally choose what is worse with respect to whatever objectives the individual has. So rational and self-interested individuals never knowingly and intentionally choose what is worse for themselves. For self-interested individuals, the theory of rationality is the theory of prudence. Someone who is self-interested is rational if and only if he or she is prudent.

According to the theory of rationality, intentional choice follows preference. So rational and self-interested individuals never knowingly prefer what is worse for themselves to what is better. Add, then, a second common assumption of positive economics, that individuals have perfect knowledge. It then follows that what is best for an individual is what the individual most prefers. How well off an individual is is just the same thing as how well satisfied an individual's preferences are. Orthodox normative economics consequently identifies an individual's welfare or well-being with the satisfaction of an individual's preferences. This identification is usually made in a flash, without its crucial significance being noticed. We will return to discuss the importance of this identification in a moment.

Once one has made the step of identifying well-being with the satisfaction of preferences, the central features of normative economics follow naturally. Just add a further (and much less controversial) moral principle of *minimal benevolence*: other things being equal, it is a morally good thing if people are better off. Then it is, other things being equal, a morally good thing to satisfy an individual's preferences. The main issue in standard normative economics is accordingly to what extent economies enable individuals to satisfy their preferences. Hence the importance of Pareto optimality. Although a Pareto optimum is typically defined as a state of affairs in which it is impossible to make anyone better off without making someone worse off, this purported definition is misleading. Indeed, it shows how completely economists identify well-being with the satisfaction of preferences. In fact R is a 'Pareto improvement' over S if nobody *prefers S* to R and somebody *prefers R* to S. R is a Pareto optimum if and only if there are no Pareto improvements over R. If and only if one identifies preference and well-being, then this last definition implies the misleading standard definition.

Given minimal benevolence, Pareto improvements are (other things being equal) moral improvements and Pareto optima are (other things being equal) morally desirable. Add in the first welfare theorem (that perfectly competitive equilibria are Pareto efficient), and one can conclude that, other things being equal, perfectly competitive equilibria are morally desirable and market imperfections that interfere with the achievement of competitive equilibria are morally undesirable. Note that this is a theoretical defence of *perfect competition*, not a defence of actual markets or of a *laissez-faire* policy.

A consideration of the 'other things' that are morally relevant leads to ethical controversy, which economists would like to avoid. Indeed we conjecture that economists rarely make the case for markets on the grounds of individual liberties and rights, because they believe (mistakenly, in our view) that arguments based on premises concerning liberty or rights are more philosophically controversial and ambitious than is the benevolence argument.

Among the 'other things' that must be equal is justice, and a Pareto improvement that leads to distributional injustice may be morally undesirable. But the argument above may be continued. Given the second welfare theorem (that all Pareto optima can be obtained as competitive equilibria from the right initial distribution of endowments), one can conclude plausibly, although not validly, that all other moral concerns, including concerns about justice, can be satisfied by adjusting initial holdings. The conclusion does not follow, because there may be no Pareto efficient state of affairs that satisfies all other moral constraints.

Whether defenders of *laissez-faire* or of extensive government intervention to address market failures, most economists share a moral commitment to the *ideal* of perfect competition. It is this commitment that gives point to the analysis of market failures. (For why should they matter if market successes are not a good thing?) The fact that this commitment appears to presuppose nothing more controversial than minimal benevolence helps solve an apparent paradox. For, on the one hand, economists do not see themselves as moral philosophers and they attempt to steer clear of controversial ethical commitments when doing theoretical welfare economics. Indeed economists have sometimes supposed that theoretical welfare economics was independent of all value judgments. Yet, on the other hand, when welfare economists address policy questions, they speak with apparent moral authority. They purport to know how to make life better.

What explains how economists can feel themselves possessed of moral authority without the trouble of doing moral philosophy? The answer, we think, is that economists do not regard the identification of well-being with the satisfaction of preferences as a controversial ethical judgment. It seems to be just a part of the standard view of rationality. Once one accepts this identification, one need only add an uncontroversial principle of minimal benevolence to get the argument for perfect competition sketched above. Yet, as we noted a moment ago, this identification of well-being with preference satisfaction is anything but uncontroversial. On the contrary it is mistaken, and it is important to understand both how serious this mistake is and why economists so readily make it. What people prefer may not be good for them, because people make mistakes, and they may prefer to sacrifice their own well-being in pursuit of some other end. Satisfying Gertrude's desire for wine in the last act of *Hamlet* failed to make her better off, probably for one of these reasons.[6]

Yet economists typically go on casually identifying well-being with the satisfaction of preferences. Why? To some extent they just paper over these difficulties by appropriating the evaluative term, 'rational', which in ordinary speech is often used as a synonym for 'prudent'. In addition, since most economic models assume that agents have full information and are self-interested, they exclude the above difficulties. Most positive theory also treats preferences for commodities and services as just and given, and not themselves subject to theoretical inquiry or explanation. There is little work on preference formation, on 'adaptive preferences' (Elster, 1982), on 'cognitive dissonance' (Akerlof and Dickens, 1982) or on other grounds for the criticism of actual preferences. Markets are not a political forum in which one's *reasons* matter. All of this makes it easier to accept the view that what people prefer is what is good for them. Because of these features of *positive* economics, into which the model of rationality is also incorporated, economists feel little discomfort in identifying well-being with preference satisfaction.

These sketchy remarks show how central the theory of rationality is to the normative theory of welfare economics and how much moral reflection is needed to make sense of theoretical welfare economics. But the theory of rationality also plays an important role in positive economics. If one adds to the theory of rationality the generalization that real people are to some extent rational, then one has the central lawlike principles of the positive theory of economic choice. More is added, of course, concerning for example the objects of preference and rates of substitution. But in economics the theory of rational choice is simultaneously the theory of actual choice.

Positive economics can be formulated without using the word 'rational'. Rather than first defining 'rational' and then stating that individuals are in fact to some extent rational, one can instead assert that the preferences of individuals are in reality (to a considerable extent) complete and transitive, and that individuals in fact usually choose whatever they most prefer. But the identification of the actual with the rational remains. It does not depend on any particular formulation. It is, rather, a reflection of the fact that economics simultaneously provides a theory of the causes and consequences of people's economic choices *and* of the *reasons* for them. For a theory of choice that cites *reasons* automatically opens the possibility of evaluation and criticism.

Furthermore, the fact that the theory of actual choice is simultaneously a theory of rational choice increases the credibility of positive theory. Suppose one finds evidence that people's preferences are not complete and transitive. Psychologists claim to have found such evidence. For example, with a bit of experimental trickiness, one can get individuals to judge that a bet or investment J is definitely better than another bet or investment K, but to express a willingness to pay *more* for the inferior bet, K. This preference reversal phenomenon is well established in experimental settings. People's preferences are thus not complete and transitive.[7] Such solid evidence failing to confirm central theoretical propositions of positive economics ought to be worrying.

But most economists are not worried. Why not? One reason is that choice phenomena such as preference reversals are not only in conflict with the positive theory of choice, but they are also in conflict with the normative theory of choice. Preference reversals are *irrational*. Consequently they are *unstable*. For irrational preferences can be exploited. Indeed, in recent work, Chu and Chu (1990) sold K bets to experimental subjects for the price they stated they were willing to pay, had them exchange the K bets for the J bets, which the subjects claimed to prefer, and then purchased back the J bets for the lower price subjects claimed the J bets were worth. At the end of the series of transactions the subjects were, of course, poorer. It did not take many times through such a transparent money-pumping cycle for subjects to figure out that they were being made fools of and to adjust their stated preferences or the prices they were willing to pay for the bets.[8] Because the theory of actual choice is simultaneously a theory of rational choice, there must be limits to how far wrong it can be.

A defender of the standard theory might then go on to claim that, although not perfectly correct, the standard theory of choice must be the best first approximation. For irrational behaviour is unstable and a theory of actual choice that portrayed it as irrational would thereby reveal opportunities for exploiting this irrationality. But people will learn not to be exploited. Acting on such a theory would consequently undermine it. We do not want to endorse this argument fully, but if, as we suspect, you feel it reverberating within you, you should recognize how important it is that the positive theory of choice is simultaneously a theory of rational choice and thereby serves to evaluate even as it predicts and explains agents' conduct.

The above discussion sketches some of the complicated ways in which positive and normative economics are linked via the theory of rationality. But does this linkage show what we claimed, that a moral theory lurks within the core of positive economics? Not as a matter of logical necessity – the theory of rationality conjoined with assumptions of self interest and perfect information need not *necessarily* constitute a moral theory. But, in practice, this conjunction functions as an important fragment of moral theory at the very core of orthodox economics. Standard economic models depict prudent individuals interacting. Since prudence is a virtue and since nothing else is said about the characters of economic agents, they and their lives are not subject to moral criticism. The actual, the rational and, other things being equal, the moral, too, all coincide within economic models.

5   THE INFLUENCE OF MORAL COMMITMENTS ON POSITIVE ECONOMICS

Recognizing the moral commitments implicit in the theories of rationality and self-interest to which economists are wedded can help one to understand why positive and normative economics are so often intermingled. To illustrate, consider an interesting case that one of us has discussed at length elsewhere (Hausman, 1992, ch. 7). One striking and fruitful theoretical contribution of the 1950s was Paul Samuelson's (1958) model of overlapping generations. In his celebrated paper, 'An Exact Consumption-Loan Model of Interest with or without the Social Contrivance of Money', Samuelson addressed the following problem: suppose individuals want to save for their old age, when they cannot produce anything, and there is nothing imperishable that they can lay by. All people can do is to strike a bargain with younger workers to support them later in exchange for some current consideration. In a world of endlessly overlapping generations of workers and retirees, what will the pattern of interest rates be? To isolate the effect of this desire to provide for one's old age from other factors that influence the rate of interest, such as technological productivity or time preference, requires a number of heroic assumptions. Samuelson formulates an *extremely* simplified model in which everyone lives exactly three periods. In the first two periods of their lives, all people produce one unit of a completely perishable consumption good, while, in the third period of life, people produce nothing. To simplify further, Samuelson considers first an absolutely unchanging economy and then one growing eternally with an unchanging rate of growth and an unchanging rate of interest. In these models a rate of interest equal to the rate of growth clears all markets and is, moreover, Pareto optimal. To achieve such a rate of interest requires, however, either fiat money or some sort of social contract, because the consumption goods transferred to the retirees by the working generations can only be repaid by generations still to come.

All this is highly idealized, yet fruitful, positive theorizing. But if one looks carefully at Samuelson's original essay and the immediate responses to it by Abba Lerner (1959a, 1959b) and William Meckling (1960a, 1960b) one is in for some surprises. For, half way through his essay, Samuelson more or less forgets the question he began with concerning the effects on the rate of interest of the desire to save for one's retirement. Instead his focus shifts to the fact that the 'biological' rate of interest (equal to the rate of growth) cannot be obtained without fiat money or some sort of social contract. If the economy never ended, the rate of interest that would be sustained by a competitive market in the absence of money or a social contract would be sub-optimal. In a finite model, the competitive rate of interest would make everyone except the last two generations worse off. Although these are positive theoretical claims, their interest is almost entirely normative. For a fixed point of welfare economics is that perfectly competitive markets are Pareto efficient. But other things being equal, perfect competition is not a good thing here.

Although both Meckling's and Lerner's comments purport (erroneously[9]) to find analytical mistakes in Samuelson's work, both are driven by normative concerns. From a utilitarian perspective, Lerner criticizes Samuelson's view of retirement consumption as financed by savings and denies the ethical desirability of a rate of interest equal to the rate of growth. Meckling, on the other hand, cannot accept the conclusion that a perfectly competitive market, even in such utterly unrealistic and idealized circumstances, does not lead to an efficient allocation; and he criticizes one of Samuelson's assumptions essentially because it permits this conclusion.

Obviously this example is not representative of all work in theoretical economics. But it does show how positive and normative are sometimes intermingled in even the most highly regarded theoretical economics (and in this case by an author who defends a positivistic view of science, with a sharp positive/normative distinction). Understanding how rationality and self interest jointly constitute a fragment of moral theory enables one to understand why positive and normative are so interlinked.

6 CAN MORAL PHILOSOPHY HELP?

Even if economics is heavily interpenetrated with moral concepts, and even if its application requires that economists have moral views of their own and grasp the moral distinctions and commitments of policy makers, it does not follow that economists have anything to gain from studying moral *philosophy*. For moral philosophy might be abstruse, abstract and arcane gobbledygook. We do not think this is the case, and indeed we conjecture that many economists would be surprised at how comprehensible and useful contemporary moral philosophy can be. One reason is that a good deal of contemporary moral philosophy has been influenced by the work of economists such as Professor Sen, the organizer of the session on welfare economics and ethics in which this paper was presented.

In our survey essay we emphasize particularly the large body of work that has been devoted to clarifying specific ethical concepts or particular *dimensions* of evaluation. Though such work, unlike global theories such as utilitarianism, does not purport to answer all ethical questions, it can be extremely useful nevertheless. Given the difficulties with grand theories in ethics, such narrowly conceived work concerning, for example, equality, exploitation or liberty, may indeed be the most useful part of contemporary moral philosophy. We cannot survey contemporary moral philosophy now, and we have to end with nothing more than a teasing promise of its considerable worth.

7 CONCLUSIONS

If we have succeeded in demonstrating that strong and contestable ethical principles are woven into standard economic theory, we may have persuaded economists that they cannot do much economics without facing moral questions. There is no way completely to divorce the explanation and prediction of human choices from their rational and moral evaluation. Economists are stuck with moral problems, not only in their overt efforts to evaluate economic outcomes and processes, but also in their attempts to understand them. But perhaps to say economists are 'stuck' with these problems is too negative. Not only are moral problems unavoidable in much of economics, reflection on them is also instructive, illuminating and even (dare we say it?) satisfying.

Just as philosophers need to know some mathematics to do logic or some psychology to do philosophy of mind, so economists, especially those who hope to illuminate issues of public policy or institutional reform, need to know some ethics. We are not saying, of course, that economists need to become moral philosophers, just that they need to reflect about those moral questions that are relevant to the particular issues and analyses with which they are concerned. They will not find the answers neatly listed in any compendium of moral philosophy (nor, we fear, in our survey essay either). Economists will in most cases have to provide their own answers. But moral philosophy can, we believe, clarify the questions and, sometimes, help to answer them.

Notes

1. The authors are indebted to Frank Hahn for his comments at the Congress session where this paper was presented and to Amartya Sen for inviting us to present this essay at the Tenth World Congress. The work was supported by the National Endowment for the Humanities (Grant no. RO 22362–92) and Daniel Hausman's part was also supported by a Vilas Associate award from the University of Wisconsin–Madison.
2. For criticisms of this argument, see Okun (1975) and Thurow (1977).
3. Paternalism is the view that it is sometimes justified to coerce individuals for their own good. Merely denying that individuals are always the best judge of what is good for them is not paternalism. Mill's classic critique of paternalism in *On Liberty* (1859) does not identify an individual's good with whatever satisfies an individual's preferences, and it specifically allows that individuals may make mistaken choices. For assessments of apparently paternalistic interventions, see Dworkin (1971) and Feinberg (1986).
4. The view of economics sketched over the next few pages is developed at length in Hausman (1992). See particularly chapters 1, 2, 4 and 15.
5. If there is an uncountable infinity of options, then the existence of a continuous utility function also presupposes that an agent's preferences are continuous. See Debreu (1959) pp. 54–9.
6. The problem is not that a utility function may fail to represent preferences by leaving out some of the variables upon which preferences depend, but that what individuals prefer may not make them better off. First, we can distinguish those things we want because we think they will make us better off from those things we want for other reasons. Second, we can see that others (especially children) sometimes want things that are bad for them and we know that in the past we sometimes mistakenly wanted things that were harmful. We can also be pretty sure that next week or next year we will find out that some of the things we currently want for ourselves are not good for us. So well-being is not the satisfaction of preferences. Apart from these two difficulties, there are subtler philosophical objections which we shall not comment on. See Griffin (1986) Part I and Arneson (1990). An early and influential critique of the identification of preference satisfaction and welfare is Sen (1973).
7. Actually the most recent work has shown that preference reversals are not due to intransitivities, but to the absence of any context-free preference ordering at all. See Tversky, Slovic and Kahneman (1990).

8. But it has to be obvious that one is being pumped. See Berg *et al.* (1985).
9. See Samuelson (1959) and (1960).

References

Akerlof, G. and Dickens, W. (1982) 'The Economic Consequences of Cognitive Dissonance', *American Economic Review*, vol. 72, pp. 307–19.

Arneson, R. (1990) 'Liberalism, Distributive Subjectivism, and Equal Opportunity for Welfare', *Philosophy and Public Affairs*, vol. 19, pp. 158–94.

Atkinson, A.B. (1993) 'The Western Experience with Social Safety Nets', this volume, pp. 121–39.

Berg, J., Dickhaut, J. and O'Brien J. (1985) 'Preference Reversal and Arbitrage', in Smith V. (ed.) *Research in Experimental Economics*, vol. 3 (Greenwich, Conn.: JAI Press) pp. 31–72.

Blackorby, C. and Donaldson, D. (1988) 'Cash Versus Kind, Self-Selection, and Efficient Transfers', *American Economic Review*, vol. 78, pp. 691–700.

Chu, Y. and Chu, R. (1990) 'The Subsidence of Preference Reversals in Simplified and Marketlike Experimental Settings: A Note', *American Economic Review*, vol. 80, pp. 902–11.

Debreu, G. (1959) *The Theory of Value* (New York: Wiley).

Dworkin, G. (1971) 'Paternalism', in Wasserstrom R. (ed.) *Morality and the Law* (Belmont, CA: Wadsworth Publishing Company) pp. 107–36.

Elster, J. (1982) 'Sour Grapes – Utilitarianism and the Genesis of Wants', in Sen, A. and Williams, B. (eds) *Utilitarianism and Beyond* (Cambridge: Cambridge University Press) pp. 219–38.

Feinberg, J. (1986) *Harm to Self* (Oxford: Oxford University Press).

Griffin, J. (1986) *Well-Being: Its Meaning, Measurement and Moral Importance* (Oxford: Clarendon Press).

Hausman, D. (1992) *The Inexact and Separate Science of Economics* (Cambridge: Cambridge University Press).

Hausman, D. and McPherson, M. (1993) 'Taking Ethics Seriously: Economics and Contemporary Moral Philosophy', *Journal of Economic Literature*, vol. 31, pp. 671–731.

Hochman, H. and Rogers, J. (1969) 'Pareto Optimal Redistribution', *American Economic Review*, vol. 59, pp. 542–57.

Kelman, S. (1986) 'A Case for In-Kind Transfers', *Economics and Philosophy*, vol. 2, pp. 53–74.

Lerner, A. (1959a) 'Consumption-Loan Interest and Money', *Journal of Political Economy*, vol. 67, pp. 512–18.

Lerner, A. (1959b) 'Rejoinder', *Journal of Political Economy*, vol. 67, pp. 523–5.

Machlup, F. (1969) 'Positive and Normative Economics', in Heilbroner, R. (ed.) *Economic Means and Social Ends: Essays in Political Economics* (Englewood Cliffs, NJ: Prentice-Hall) pp. 99–124.

Marwell, G. and Ames, R. (1981) 'Economists Free Ride. Does Anyone

Else? Experiments on the Provision of Public Goods, IV', *Journal of Public Economics*, vol. 15, pp. 295–310.

Meckling, W. (1960a) 'An Exact Consumption-Loan Model of Interest: A Comment', *Journal of Political Economy*, vol. 68, pp. 72–6.

Meckling, W. (1960b) 'Rejoinder', *Journal of Political Economy*, vol. 68, pp. 83–4.

Mill, J.S. (1859) *On Liberty*, reprinted 1978 (Indianapolis: Hackett Publishing).

Okun, A. (1975) *Equality and Efficiency: the Big Tradeoff* (Washington, DC: Brookings Institution).

Roemer, J. (1982) *A General Theory of Exploitation and Class* (Cambridge, Mass.: Harvard University Press).

Roemer, J. (1988) *Free to Lose: An Introduction to Marxist Economic Philosophy* (Cambridge, Mass.: Harvard University Press).

Samuelson, P. (1958) 'An Exact Consumption-Loan Model of Interest with or without the Social Contrivance of Money', *Journal of Political Economy*, vol. 66, pp. 467–82.

Samuelson, P. (1959) 'Reply', *Journal of Political Economy*, vol. 67, pp. 518–22.

Samuelson, P. (1960) 'Infinity, Unanimity and Singularity: A Reply', *Journal of Political Economy*, vol. 68, pp, 76–83.

Sen, A. (1973) 'Behaviour and the Concept of Preference', *Economica*, vol. 40, pp. 241–59.

Thurow, L. (1977) 'Cash vs. In-Kind Redistribution', in Dworkin, G., Bermant, G., and Brown, P. (eds) *Markets and Morals* (Washington, DC: Hemisphere Publishing Corporation; New York: Halsted Press) pp. 85–106.

Titmuss, R. (1971) *The Gift Relationship: From Human Blood to Social Policy* (New York: Random House).

Tversky, A., Slovic, P. and Kahneman, D. (1990) 'The Causes of Preference Reversal', *American Economic Review*, vol. 80, pp. 204–17.

2 Credible Liberalization: Beyond the Three Theorems of Neoclassical Welfare Economics

Peter J. Hammond[1]
STANFORD UNIVERSITY

1 INTRODUCTION

The world economy is undergoing startling change. Almost every country has been moving towards freer markets and extensions of the private enterprise capitalist system. Of late the process has been most marked, I suppose, in China during the early 1980s and the more recently in the amazing transformation of the formerly communist nations of Eastern Europe. But nations belonging to the Organization for Economic Co-operation and Development (OECD) have also privatized state-owned industries, deregulated private industry, freed international trade and capital movements, and seem intent on further liberalizations. Meanwhile the aid, loans and debt relief to developing countries provided by the World Bank, the International Monetary Fund (IMF) and other lending agencies appear to be tied more and more to schemes that extend the influence of competition in world markets upon each nation's economic system.

This drive towards global economic liberalization is not without its good features. The world economy probably has much to gain from the increased efficiency that is being brought about. Yet there are important limits to what market systems can achieve on their own. By themselves they do not guarantee distributive justice and can even exacerbate extreme poverty. By themselves market systems will not protect us from any adverse effects of global warming, industrial pollution or other ecological hazards. It is far from clear that market systems by themselves will provide future generations with good economic prospects, or even ensure adequate old age pensions for many of those currently alive. And in the United States, which still

21

clings to the myth of a free market for the provision of medical care and health insurance, the result is increasingly being regarded as both unduly expensive and appallingly inadequate. In fact, not only do markets on their own fail to resolve some of these economic problems satisfactorily, but they may also make it harder to create alternative non-market institutions which could resolve them.

So the effectiveness of markets as good allocators of resources remains an issue worth discussing. As a theorist, I shall try to provide a picture of what economic theory currently has to say about this topic. A surprisingly large proportion of the relevant writing turns out to be based upon the two 'basic theorems of classical welfare economics' (Arrow, 1951). Accordingly, Section 2 begins by reviewing very briefly the first of these two theorems. This is the remarkably robust result telling us that complete perfectly competitive markets produce Pareto efficient allocations. Yet efficiency does not preclude extreme injustice or poverty. From an ethical viewpoint, therefore, the second theorem set out in Section 3 is actually more interesting. It says that any Pareto efficient allocation, including any that is also distributively just, can be achieved through complete perfectly competitive markets. Unfortunately this theorem is much less robust, so it is important to understand something of the conditions under which it is not true, and when the invisible hand of a market system may need a more visible helping hand.

Complete perfectly competitive markets are likely to remain forever as an unattainable theoretical ideal. Liberalizing policies are intended to make the market system less incomplete and less imperfectly competitive by removing some restrictions on free trade and competition. The desirability of such policies is the topic of the third theorem of neoclassical welfare economics, concerning the gains from trade and other forms of liberalization. This is the subject of Section 4. The theorem claims that liberalization makes Pareto improvements possible, but they cannot be guaranteed unless those directly harmed by liberalization are suitably compensated.

The most serious problems in applying the three theorems arise when there is private information, as discussed in Section 5. In particular it is noted how workers' private information regarding their true skill levels makes it almost impossible to achieve fully optimal allocations, or to ensure classical 'lump sum' compensation for those who lose from a liberalizing reform. The reason is that private information creates 'incentive constraints' limiting what allocations are truly feasible. Moreover Section 5 argues that expanding markets, as in a liberalizing reform, can tighten these incentive constraints and so lead to inferior allocations.

Even though private information does create severe incentive constraints, there is still a remarkably general case to be made for having production arranged efficiently. For, as Diamond and Mirrlees (1971) observed, there are circumstances allowing production gains to be converted into gains for everybody, even if lump sum compensation of losers is incentive-incompatible, or impracticable for other reasons. Their argument is reviewed and somewhat extended in Section 6. It creates a 'second best' case for liberalization, but only a weak case, since it rests on an extremely judicious and implausible choice of other policy instruments in order to ensure that the losers from liberalization are compensated.

So it is hard to arrange that everybody gains from liberalization, despite the claims of the third theorem. Nor is it necessarily desirable that all should gain, even if that were possible. Many economic systems are bedevilled by greedy and powerful people who have consumed excessively in the past and retain undue wealth to this day. A reform that makes them worse off in order that others who have suffered past deprivation should experience moderate gains seems preferable to a reform bringing small benefits to all, whether they are deserving or not. So the case for liberalization depends on being able to find accompanying reforms in which individual gains outweigh individual losses, taking into account what the different gainers and losers each deserve. This is the topic of Section 7, which argues that, for economic liberalization to remain credible as a desirable reform strategy, careful consideration must be given to any adverse effects and to what should be done in order to mitigate them.

2   THE FIRST THEOREM: EFFICIENCY OF THE INVISIBLE HAND

As remarked in the introduction, the first theorem says that equilibrium allocations are Pareto efficient provided that markets are complete and perfectly competitive. Actually this is only true under the additional mild assumption that consumers' preferences are locally non-satiated – otherwise equilibrium allocations are only *weakly* Pareto efficient in the sense that it is impossible to make *all* consumers better off. In addition the first theorem is generally false in certain 'overlapping generations economies' having an infinite number of individuals and an infinite number of goods, as Samuelson (1958) pointed out.

Many advocates of free markets appear to understand this first theorem, and invoke it as justification for liberalizing economic systems. Yet it is important to understand what the theorem does *not* say, as well as what it does. It does not say that markets will produce ethically acceptable allocations. One obvious reason is that what consumers prefer is not always ethically desirable, as in the case of teenage drug or alcohol abuse, or the desire to buy firearms for personal misuse. Another reason is that the Pareto efficiency criterion says nothing about distributive justice or the avoidance of poverty. It can be Pareto efficient for a cruel dictator to run the whole economy for his own personal benefit, with all other individuals functioning as slaves and only allowed to survive as long as the dictator benefits more from their work than is lost from providing for their basic needs. This dictatorship would be Pareto inefficient only if: (a) the dictator could be made even better off; or (b) some slave's lot could be made less miserable without making the dictator worse off. And such a dictatorial allocation would result from a perfectly competitive market system in which all wealth is owned by the dictator, provided such a system admits an equilibrium.[2]

Gross inequality and extreme poverty are, I presume, not ethically acceptable to most of us. Yet they abound in present-day market economies, as they did in the past. Pareto efficiency on its own is not an adequate ethical criterion. It is also quite wrong to try to separate efficiency from distributional issues. Once the latter are recognized as important, what role should we give to market systems, and what value should we attach to liberalization?

3   THE SECOND THEOREM: OPTIMAL ALLOCATIONS

The first theorem concerns allocations that emerge from markets where no explicit attention is paid to distribution, and shows that they are Pareto efficient. The second theorem concerns the converse: that any Pareto efficient allocation can be brought about through perfect markets. In particular, under conditions to be discussed below, this will be true of any allocation which distributes goods justly, as long as it also meets the test of Pareto efficiency.

That is the claim. Yet some very significant assumptions have to be met before this second theorem is valid, either in its first general modern version due to Arrow (1951), or in one of its many later refinements such as Hildenbrand (1974), Coles and Hammond (1991) or Hammond (1992, 1993). For example, consumers must have preferences which are not only locally non-satiated, as assumed in Section 2, but are also continuous. There also has to be enough convexity, either because consumers and producers are both small and very numerous, or because they have convex preferences and feasible sets anyway. Finally, Arrow's (1951) 'exceptional case' needs to be ruled out. Even when all these extra assumptions are satisfied, however, there still remains one more extremely important qualification. Obviously markets are only compatible with distributive justice if there is an appropriate distribution of purchasing power in the market economy. Such a distribution typically requires transfers from those who are going to do well in the market economy to those who would be excessively poor if they had no additional source of wealth provided for them. These transfers should be *lump sum* in the sense of being independent of market transactions. This is important because transfers that depend on transactions are like commodity subsidies (or taxes) that face traders with distorted price ratios and so destroy Pareto efficiency, in most cases at least. Lump sum redistribution plays a large role in the ensuing theoretical discussion. And the second theorem only has practical or ethical significance to the extent that one can rely upon lump sum redistribution to bring about distributive justice.

In the end it may seem ironic that, as Barone (1908) first pointed out, an optimally functioning planned economy would produce the same allocations as a perfect market economy. Yet obviously both optimal planning and perfect markets, with ideal redistribution, are unattainable ideals. Is there really no better case for economic liberalization?

4 THE THIRD THEOREM: GAINS FROM LIBERALIZATION

The first theorem shows that perfect markets generate Pareto efficient allocations. Under several important qualifications, the second theorem shows that any particular Pareto efficient allocation can be achieved through perfect and complete competitive markets with appropriate lump sum redistribution of wealth. Yet in practice it appears that, rather than strive for unattainable full Pareto efficiency, we would do better by being content with Pareto improvements. By definition, these make every consumer better off. But they do not necessarily reach the Pareto (efficiency) 'frontier'. If we can find such Pareto improvements, then should we not all be willing to agree to what benefits us all?

There are in fact some serious ethical problems with Pareto improvements.[3] For suppose that the status quo is distributively unjust, with some relatively needy individuals who should ideally be given more, even if this can only be done at the expense of some other prosperous individuals who should ideally be given less. Now suppose that a Pareto improvement is put into effect which greatly benefits those who are already prosperous, but benefits the needy only a little. Such a reform would seem to create even more distributive injustice. If all further reforms also have to be Pareto improvements, then the economy will be committed to that even more unjust distribution of resources, which further Pareto improvements may only be able to correct very slowly over time. So it is important to allow some reforms that are not Pareto improvements, provided that those who lose are less needy than those who gain, on the whole.

Nevertheless the generally accepted rationale for liberalizing reforms appears to be that they allow Pareto improvements, which is what the third theorem is all about. Suppose that the economic system initially generates some feasible allocation of resources. Of course, if the allocation is already Pareto efficient, then no Pareto improvement is possible. But if it is Pareto inefficient, then the third theorem claims that it is possible to reform the original economic system by having more extensive perfectly competitive markets, and to do so in a way which generates an equilibrium allocation that is Pareto superior to the original allocation. As stated above, the third theorem is almost an easy corollary of the second. For if there is one Pareto superior allocation, then there is typically also another Pareto superior allocation that is on the Pareto frontier and so Pareto efficient. In order to move to this efficient and superior allocation, simply institute the perfect market system that produces it, assuming that the conditions of the second theorem are all met so that such a system does exist. The only thing that has to be shown is that there really is a Pareto efficient allocation which is Pareto superior to the original allocation.

One problem with this version of the third theorem is its unrealistic presumption that liberalization will result in the economy being steered to some Pareto efficient allocation. This is the same presumption that was criticized above in connection with the second theorem. A partial remedy is suggested by Grandmont and McFadden's (1972) discussion of the gains from international trade. They provide an ingenious sufficient condition which ensures that, no matter what equilibrium emerges from free trade, the result is an allocation which, even if not a Pareto improvement, at least leaves no consumer worse off. For this they require that the wealth distribution be adjusted as prices move towards equilibrium so that all consumers can always afford whatever goods and services they enjoyed individually in the original economic system, provided that they each supply the same labour services and so on. Of course, at the prices which rule in the liberalized market economy, consumers may well exercise their option to change their allocation by moving within the budget set of allocations that they can afford. Grandmont and McFadden gave sufficient conditions for the existence of a market equilibrium in such a liberalized system. And the system of redistribution that they devised at least gives all consumers the option to stay where they were before the reform, so that nobody is forced to become worse off. With any slack in the original system, moreover, it is typically possible to arrange a strict Pareto improvement.

Though Grandmont and McFadden considered specifically the gains from international trade, in Hammond and Sempere (1992) we show how similar arguments apply to rather general liberalizing reforms. At first, therefore, the case for liberalization may appear strong, but in fact formidable difficulties remain. The usual convexity and continuity assumptions must be met to ensure that the liberalized market economy has a general equilibrium – indeed it is also necessary, but entirely reasonable to assume that there are enough bounds on what allocations are possible so that there are no unbounded Pareto improvements. Otherwise, if equilibrium does not exist, the third theorem is invalid and, more seriously, our theoretical model of liberalized markets is unable to make any prediction of what will happen. Of course liberalization could still bring benefits even if economic theory is unable to explain why, but then the theory needs to be improved.

A more serious practical problem, however, concerns the ingenious redistribution mechanism that Grandmont and McFadden devised. It requires knowing, in principle, what allocations would have gone to each consumer in the unreformed economic system, so that any losers from liberalization can be duly compensated. In particular, the original lifetime career plans of displaced workers must be known, since their appropriate amount of compensation depends upon what they would have earned for as long as they were going to remain in their existing jobs, and in any jobs they were planning to move on to next, and so on. Also relevant are their original lifetime plans to buy food, drink, clothing and shelter, to receive health care, to send their children to school, and so on. Of course nobody knows even their own lifetime plans completely, thus making it practically impossible to determine what compensation is appropriate to consumers who are forced to change their plans.[4]

5   PRIVATE INFORMATION AND INCENTIVES

The three theorems set out above are significant intellectual accomplishments. In various simplified versions, they have been widely taught to economics students – especially in nations with free enterprise economic systems, for obvious reasons – and they underlie a great deal of contemporary economic policy analysis. Yet they are also widely misinterpreted and thought to be more widely applicable than is true in practice.

It has been seen that the first theorem by itself pays no attention to extremes of poverty or inequality; and that the second and third theorems rely on suitable mechanisms for lump sum redistribution of wealth: either (a) to achieve a desirable Pareto allocation, as in the second theorem; or (b) to have the gainers from a liberalization policy compensate the losers, as in the third theorem. Yet can such redistribution be put into practice? And is liberalization desirable if compensation is not paid to the losers (whether it can be or not)? Mainstream economists have paid far too little attention to these fundamental questions in my view.

In the case of the second theorem it is effectively presumed that limitless redistribution is possible, should it be desirable. So, in order to reach a Pareto efficient allocation without poverty, the economic system is required to pay lump sum subsidies to those who would be unduly poor without them, and to finance those subsidies by means of lump sum taxes on those who can most afford to pay them. The problem, however, comes in identifying those who would inevitably be poor in the absence of subsidies. Many of the poor are disadvantaged in various ways beyond their control and so clearly deserve support. Yet it is a fact of human nature that at least a few among the poor will exploit whatever scheme of support they may be eligible for in order to avoid work they find unpleasant, to become or remain alcoholics or drug addicts, or to be irresponsible in other ways. What is worse, as more adequate schemes of support are provided for the truly disadvantaged, this strengthens the temptation which others face to appear disadvantaged so that they can also receive support. It turns out that, apart from the most obvious unfortunate cases where people are physically unable to work, the status of being truly disadvantaged is not easy to observe. It is an instance of *private information*. So is the inherent ability to pay tax of those who are better off. Moreover the more obvious methods of unmasking such private information are all too likely to involve unwarranted intrusions into personal life, together with violations of civil rights.

For these reasons, if one tries to institute lump sum redistribution from those who appear able to pay taxes to those who appear in real need of subsidies, the economic system will become distorted. The taxes on the rich will not be truly lump sum, but will become taxes on labour income and on the acquisition of useful skills. The subsidies to the needy will also discourage work effort and skill acquisition, since they will be reduced if earned income starts to rise. Incentives inevitably become blunted. In fact truly feasible economic systems must be *incentive-compatible* in a more technical sense – they can only make use of private information like true ability if they do not make individuals who reveal such information think that they are worse off than they would be by concealing that information. The unfortunate characteristic of progressive redistribution from the well endowed to the poorly endowed is precisely that the quality of a person's endowment is typically private information. Too much redistribution will damage people's incentives to use their endowments fully. The Marxian prescription, 'From each according to their ability, to each according to their need', cannot be carried out in practice because both ability and need depend on private information.

Many economists appear to understand the essence of this incentive argument, yet manage to draw entirely the wrong conclusion from it. For it is too often claimed that there should be no redistribution at all. This does not follow. Incentives certainly make most redistribution costly, but not so costly that all attempts to redistribute are futile, or even inefficient, in the relevant sense. Of course incentive problems do restrict the instruments that can be used to redistribute. Lump sum taxes and subsidies are generally not possible. But progressive income taxes which finance income subsidies for those below a certain poverty line clearly are possible, since we see them in most economically advanced countries. Such taxes create mild disincentives for the rich – or incentives to work unduly hard for individuals whose labour supply curves are backward bending, perhaps because they have already committed a large fraction of their earned income to fixed expenditures like mortgage repayments. It is true that poorly devised schemes of income support create 'poverty traps', making it hard for the able poor to earn more income without excessive reductions in their combined income from both earnings and welfare payments. Better schemes could help avoid such traps, however. And anybody who views poverty as a valid ethical concern will surely think it right for society to incur some costs so that the most deserving can be helped.

A somewhat ironic feature of markets is the way they can limit the scope of redistribution through progressive income tax, or through commodity taxes on goods mostly consumed by the well off which are used to subsidize goods that the poor really need. To see this, note that in markets buyers and sellers come together in order to arrange mutually beneficial trades. One obvious way of increasing the mutual benefit, at the expense of the tax authorities, is to evade the tax system. Thus many casual workers are willing to receive a lower payment in cash, with no records kept. Street traders can afford to sell their wares at lower prices to the extent that they avoid taxes, not to mention the cost of maintaining a shop, etc. An undesirable extreme is one in which the tax base disappears entirely in a complete black market system.[5] In any case, an important extra cost of any taxation scheme is the need to maintain clerks or bureaucrats to administer it, as well as tax collectors, police, lawyers and even prisons to enforce it. In devising taxation schemes it is important to keep such costs as low as possible.

6   THE 'SECOND BEST' CASE FOR LIBERALIZATION

The third welfare theorem discussed in Section 4 makes the 'first best' case for liberalization. That case is weak because of the problems in arranging the appropriate lump sum compensation which is typically needed to achieve Pareto superiority. Beyond the third theorem, however, is a much more interesting 'second best' case for liberalization. This is based on ideas originally due to Diamond and Mirrlees (1971) on optimal taxation, as well as work by Little and Mirrlees (1968, 1974) on cost–benefit analysis, and by Mirrlees (1969) on measuring national income. The argument relies on being able to use liberalization in order to generate Pareto gains, or other welfare improvements, even in the absence of lump sum compensation. In the context of international trade, these theoretical possibilities have been discussed by Dixit and Norman (1980, 1986) and Dixit (1987) in particular. For the most general 'second best' version of the third theorem that I know, see Hammond and Sempere (1992). Jaime Sempere has also worked on further extensions for his PhD thesis at the European University Institute.

Diamond and Mirrlees argued as follows for the desirability of any reform which would achieve production efficiency: if the economy is inside its aggregate production frontier, then there must be a reform which allows the economy to produce more of every output using less of every input. In other words, the *net output* of each good can be increased. Then the issue is whether these extra net outputs of each good make possible Pareto or other welfare improvements. The claim was that they sometimes would, in an economy permitting unrestricted commodity taxation. For suppose that commodity tax rates are first varied in order to hold consumer prices constant even while producer prices vary. Suppose too that, secondly, the tax rate on some good which every consumer buys is not held fixed, but allowed to decrease slightly. Then every consumer would be slightly better off, since the only consumer price change is a small decrease in the price of a good which everybody buys. Assuming that aggregate demand is continuous, it would change only slightly too. So, for a small enough change in that consumer price, the extra net outputs of every good would be enough to meet the slightly changed demands, and any surpluses could be thrown away. Alternatively, if there is some good such as labour which every consumer sells, then the tax rate on it could be slightly decreased, and the same argument would work. Or, perhaps better, all consumer prices could be frozen, and a small poll subsidy or allowance paid out to each consumer.

This claim of Diamond and Mirrlees sparked some immediate controversy. In fact Mirrlees (1972) himself produced an early interesting counter-example in which achieving production efficiency would entail a change in the distribution of dividend income, with owners of a less efficient firm losing while owners of a more efficient firm gain. In that example, attempts to compensate the owners of the inefficient firm through commodity tax changes alone could not work because they had similar tastes to the owners of the efficient firm, and there were insufficient overall gains to permit all to benefit. To avoid this kind of example, Sempere and I have considered the implications of supplementing a freeze on consumer prices and after-tax wages with an additional freeze on after-tax dividends, before any further adjustments are made in order to allow a Pareto improvement.

Another problem with the Diamond–Mirrlees argument is its reliance on free disposal. This is clearly an untenable assumption when we start to include some kinds of public good or environmental variables in the commodity space, as we need to do when discussing externalities, for instance.[6] It is also problematic even if only desirable goods need to be thrown away, since that is itself a costly activity, in general. Also, allowing surpluses to leak on to markets instead has side-effects which may not always be desirable. Think, for example, of the way in which selling off European Community (EC) stocks of excess food appears to be hurting some farmers in many other countries. In fact my paper with Sempere shows how to avoid the assumption of free disposal. Lowering producer prices for EC agriculture while subsidizing farmers' after tax incomes directly, if carried far enough, would eliminate surplus production. Indeed this is the direction that overdue reform of the EC's contentious Common Agricultural Policy is currently planned to take, roughly speaking.

So, for the moment, there is a *prima facie* case for production efficiency. Can this be translated into a case for liberalization? The answer is a highly qualified 'Yes'. Suppose that a liberalizing reform takes an economy towards its aggregate production frontier by making the allocation of production activity more efficient. Then a Pareto improvement can be brought about, even in the absence of lump sum compensation for those who would otherwise lose from liberalization. Instead, it is enough to freeze consumers' after-tax prices, wages and dividends, and to use the efficiency gains to pay out a uniform poll subsidy to all consumers. All consumers will clearly benefit if this change can be made feasible. In fact feasibility can be assured by allowing producer prices to vary freely so as to clear (perfectly competitive) markets in the usual way. Then there will actually be efficiency gains in production which can finance such a poll subsidy, provided that firms in the aggregate earn more profit than they would have done, at the new producer prices, by ignoring producer price changes and remaining with their prior production plans and resulting net output vectors. This is the general result that we prove under rather standard 'neoclassical' assumptions, such as continuity of demands and supplies, overall convexity and so on. Gains from international trade or market integration are one special case, in which trade serves to improve efficiency in the international distribution of production activities through exploitation of comparative advantage. Another special case is when a project passes a cost–benefit test at post-project producer prices. For traded goods in a small country unable to affect its terms of trade, these producer prices will be equal to border prices.

Our argument works only for liberalizations of the 'supply side' of the economy, however: that is, only for reforms which increase production efficiency without directly affecting consumption. Many economists have argued for other liberalization policies such as abolishing food or wage subsidies, or harmonizing or reducing consumption taxes. The argument is that distortions are lowered by aligning consumer prices closer to producer prices. This has some theoretical merit in a 'first best' world where lump sum compensation is possible: for example, for those who would otherwise starve if they had to pay the full market price for their food. Such liberalization may also have merit in a 'second best' world, but *only* if other forms of compensation for deserving losers are arranged: for example, an adequate universal basic income paid to *all*, regardless of economic or social situation, and financed by taxes on those whom the fiscal authorities can identify as truly able to pay.

Recently liberalization in many national economies has included privatization of some enterprises that were previously wholly or partly owned by the state. The obvious change of ownership has many effects that depend on factors such as whether the firm was originally profitable, the terms under which shares are created and then sold, the rates at which profits are either paid out as dividends or reinvested, both the corporate and individual income tax systems, regulatory policies and so on. There is no reason to believe that merely changing ownership will produce a Pareto or even a welfare improvement, however. Of course, to the extent that privatization also brings in new managers who really do make the enterprises work more efficiently, we have a supply-side or efficiency-enhancing liberalization of the kind discussed already in this section. But some instances of privatization merely replace one inefficient monopolist that happened to be publicly owned with a new one that happens to have become privately owned. Then there is no efficiency gain whatsoever. Moreover the chance to arrange a much better reform may even have been lost for an extended period, until the next major crisis provokes a reconsideration.[7]

7   CREDIBLE LIBERALIZATION

Those economists whose advice is most sought nowadays generally seem to be in favour of liberalizing policies. Their recommendations are affecting not only the reform process in what were the command economies, but also international trade negotiations, and the terms under which international organizations offer loans or aid to national governments. These economic advisers are probably quite right in claiming that considerable efficiency gains can be realized from the policies they advocate. In some cases they may even be right to discuss *only* those efficiency gains, at the present time, for a little while, so that the message they convey is more effective because of its simplicity.

Yet there are enormous risks in focusing only on efficiency gains, without apparent concern for distribution. In the short run, there is a danger of causing too much unnecessary suffering if no systematic thought is given to the problem of how to compensate those who are least able to protect themselves from liberalization's adverse effects: the pensioners, the sick, those workers with only very specific skills who have devoted themselves to careers in industries that the reform makes uncompetitive, as well as public employees in hospitals, schools and other services who rely on government funding in order to carry out the essential jobs they are asked to perform. In practice these groups too often lose out from liberalization, it seems. And when they do they will naturally blame the liberalizing reform process for making their lives miserable. Those reforms then become harder to implement in the fact of threats of revolt, riot or strikes affecting essential public services. The general population may also sympathize with those who choose to protest, and if military leaders see their positions as unduly threatened, there is even risk of a *coup d'état*. At best there will be a sullen group of people who, even if liberalizing reforms are mutely accepted, come to distrust the promises of the politicians who advocate them. Some potential benefits of liberalization get thrown away as people lose patience and demand that the process be slowed or even reversed.

Thus can the credibility of market economics become easily tarnished. So can that of economists. Bungled liberalization may lead voters to choose different political leaders, and new leaders may well be less receptive to the standard advice on offer by most contemporary economists. International organizations may still be able to dictate policy to the desperate, but should not expect to be admired for doing so. In fact there has been some recent work on important issues in making reforms credible. Calvo and Frankel (1991, p. 143) tell us that 'a credible transformation program is likely to result in short-term hardships'. But then (p. 147) they write: 'if political support is insufficient to provide credibility for a first-best reform program, it may not be desirable to undertake it, since the lack of credibility amounts to a distortion' (see also Calvo, 1989). Rodrik (1989, p. 2) writes: 'It is not trade liberalization *per se* but *credible* trade liberalization that is the source of efficiency benefits.' Their work largely neglects distributional questions, however. Rodrik (1989, pp. 7–8) does mention redistributive effects of trade liberalization, but under the title 'Anticipated Political Costs Due to Redistribution'. Later Rodrik (1992, p. 91) writes of the possibility that 'workers and students riot in the streets of the capital'. So, while much of these writers' analysis is surely correct, it is also seriously incomplete, for there is no discussion whatsoever of how judiciously adding policies to alleviate hardship can make such a transformation more credible and increase political support for it, even if this forces us to contemplate a 'second-best' reform.

Looking once more towards the future, the 1990s could even be the decade that determines whether we make an almost irreversible move to an appropriately liberalized and much more integrated world economy, or towards some other system that would almost surely be much less desirable. That is how much appears to be at stake. The liberalizers will need a lot of help if they are to prevail peacefully, without too many disasters on the way. What they do not need are outdated doctrines based on the classical theorems of welfare economics. That is how they have been misled into neglecting the distributional questions associated with economic reform. The theorems are elegant. The liberalizing policies they suggest may even raise gross domestic product in many cases. But often they also cause needless suffering, and not just because of protest action by those who are the first to become clearly worse off. Of course it does not help if world lay opinion feels entitled to regard such protests as not only excusable, but an entirely proper reaction to needlessly harsh and unjust policies.

Advocates of liberalization also do not need the 'second best' case which I discussed in Section 6. That depends on impractical policies like freezing the intertemporal path of consumer prices, take-home pay and after tax dividends at levels which they would have had in the absence of the liberalizing reform. What economist could even tell us with confidence what this path would have been? An alternative would be to have faith in governments' ability and political will to set optimally differential tax rates on all commodities, types of labour and dividend income, but clearly this is not viable, at least for the foreseeable future.

It is very proper to object that my theoretical discussion omits many factors of great practical relevance. Time, externalities, public goods, private information and imperfect competition have been mentioned only very peripherally, risk and uncertainty not at all. More systematic work is needed to understand how these affect the arguments for and against liberalization. I do not believe, however, that such complications will make the case for liberalisation much stronger – indeed they typically bring new reasons for other forms of government intervention to accompany any liberalizing reforms.

Ultimately, therefore, liberalization by itself is a blunt policy instrument. In some forms it can be useful, especially when it concentrates on enhancing the aggregate efficiency of production. However that usefulness depends on there being accompanying policy measures designed to protect the economically weak. And some liberalizing reforms definitely seem harmful, especially those seeking to remove so-called distortions involving consumers, such as subsidies on goods which are consumed proportionally more by the deserving poor. As for privatizing state-owned enterprises, the only reason for doing so is if it really will lead to aggregate efficiency gains in production. Private ownership by itself confers no particular benefits.

Where does this leave an economic theorist like myself? Unable to draw general theoretical conclusions that are practically relevant, of course. Once impractical 'first best' theory confronts reality, especially in the form of private information and the consequent need to respect incentive constraints, the wonderful and elegant generality of the three classical theorems almost entirely disappears. Yet a theorist can still suggest where to look for desirable policy changes, as I have done here by discussing when liberalization is most likely to be beneficial. In the end, however, identifying good policy changes requires careful empirical study of whom they benefit, whom they harm and by how much. At this stage the theorist can suggest what should be measured and perhaps even how to make the measurements, but then has to remain silent – or become an empirical economist.

Notes

1. I am especially grateful to Amartya Sen for his kind invitation to present a paper to the session on 'Welfare Economics and Ethics' at the conference. Sections 4 and 6 summarize some results of collaboration with Jaime Sempere of El Colegio de México, undertaken while we were both at the European University Institute. Helpful suggestions from the discussant Alan Kirman, the editor Dieter Bös, as well as from Jean Drèze and Michael Smart, are also gratefully acknowledged.
2. Bergstrom (1971) shows how perfect market allocations exist and are Pareto efficient in a slave-owning economy. Coles and Hammond (1991) prove similar results when it is not required that all individuals survive, even in equilibrium.
3. Starrett (1988, p. 10), for instance, has an interesting discussion of the ethical issues surrounding the use of the Pareto criterion.
4. See Feenstra and Lewis (1991) for other work on the difficulty of arranging lump sum compensation for those who lose from trade liberalization.
5. Some theoretical results along these lines are presented in Hammond (1987) and in Blackorby and Donaldson (1988).
6. See Hammond (1993) for just one of many discussions of the first two efficiency theorems with externalities and public goods. The third theorem with externalities and public goods remains to be covered in future work.
7. Inevitably this one-paragraph discussion of privatization remains very superficial. For a much more thorough analysis, see especially Bös (1988, 1991) and Vickers and Yarrow (1988), as well as the other works reviewed by Sawkins (1992).

References

Arrow, K.J. (1951) 'An Extension of the Basic Theorems of Classical Welfare Economics', in Neyman, J. (ed.) *Proceedings of the Second Berkeley Symposium on Mathematical Statistics and Probability* (Berkeley: University of California Press) pp. 507–32; reprinted in 1983 in *Collected Papers of Kenneth J. Arrow, Vol. 2: General Equilibrium* (Cambridge, Mass.: Belknap Press of Harvard University Press).

Barone, E. (1908) 'Il ministero della produzione nello stato colletivista', *Giornale degli Economisti*, vol. 37, pp. 267–93, 391–414; translated as 'The Ministry of Production in the Collectivist State', in Hayek, F.A. (ed.) (1935), *Collectivist Economic Planning* (London: Routledge & Kegan Paul) pp. 245–90, and reprinted in Newman, P. (ed.) (1968), *Readings in Mathematical Economics, Vol. I: Value Theory* (Baltimore, Md.: Johns Hopkins Press) pp. 319–64.

Bergstrom, T.C. (1971) 'On the Existence and Optimality of Competitive Equilibrium for a Slave Economy', *Review of Economic Studies*, vol. 38, pp. 23–36.

Blackorby, C. and Donaldson, D. (1988) 'Cash versus Kind, Self-Selection, and Efficient Transfers', *American Economic Review*, vol. 78, pp. 691–700.

Bös, D. (1988) 'Welfare Effects of Privatizing Public Enterprises', in Bös, D., Rose, M. and Seidl, C. (eds) *Welfare and Efficiency in Public Economics* (Berlin: Springer Verlag) pp. 339–62.

Bös, D. (1991) *Privatization: A Theoretical Treatment* (Oxford: Clarendon Press).

Calvo, G.A. (1989) 'Incredible Reforms', in Calvo, G.A., Findlay, R., Kouri, P. and de Macedo, J.B. (eds) *Debt, Stabilization and Development: Essays in Memory of Carlos Díaz-Alejandro* (Oxford: Basil Blackwell; Helsinki: WIDER) pp. 217–34.

Calvo, G.A. and Frankel, J.A. (1991) 'Credit Markets, Credibility, and Economic Transformation', *Journal of Economic Perspectives*, vol. 5, no. 4, pp. 139–48.

Coles, J.L. and Hammond, P.J. (1991) 'Walrasian Equilibrium Without Survival: Equilibrium, Efficiency, and Remedial Policy', Working Paper ECO No. 91/50, European University Institute, Florence.

Diamond, P. and Mirrlees, J. (1971) 'Optimal Taxation and Public Production, I and II', *American Economic Review*, vol. 61, pp. 8–27, 261–78.

Dixit, A. (1987) 'Tax Policy in Open Economies', in Auerbach, A. and Feldstein, M. (eds), *Handbook of Public Economics, Vol. I* (Amsterdam: North Holland).

Dixit, A. and Norman, V. (1980) *Theory of International Trade* (Welwyn, Herts.: James Nisbet).

Dixit, A. and Norman, V. (1986) 'Gains from Trade without Lump-Sum Compensation', *Journal of International Economics*, vol. 21, pp. 99–110.

Feenstra, R. and Lewis, T. (1991) 'Distributing the Gains from Trade with Incomplete Information', *Economics and Politics*, vol. 3, pp. 21–40.

Grandmont, J.-M. and McFadden, D. (1972) 'A Technical Note on Classical Gains from Trade', *Journal of International Economics*, vol. 2, pp. 109–25.

Hammond, P.J. (1987) 'Markets as Constraints: Multilateral Incentive Compatibility in Continuum Economies', *Review of Economic Studies*, vol. 54, pp. 399–412.

Hammond, P.J. (1992) 'Irreducibility, Resource Relatedness, and Survival in Equilibrium with Individual Non-Convexities', Working Paper 89/427 European University Institute Florence; revised version in Becker, R., Boldrin, M. Jones, R. and Thomson, W. (eds) (1993) *General Equilibrium, Growth and Trade, II: The Legacy of Lionel W. McKenzie* (New York: Academic Press).

Hammond, P.J. (1993) 'Efficiency and Market Failure', in Kirman, A.P. (ed.), *Elements of General Equilibrium Analysis* (Oxford: Basil Blackwell).

Hammond, P.J. and Sempere, J. (1992) 'Limits to the Benefits from Market Integration and Other Supply-Side Policies', Working Paper ECO No. 92/79, European University Institute, Florence.

Hildenbrand, W. (1974) *Core and Equilibria of a Large Economy* (Princeton: Princeton University Press).

Little, I.M.D. and Mirrlees, J.A. (1968) *Manual of Industrial Project Analysis in Developing Countries, Vol II: Social Cost Benefit Analysis* (Paris: OECD); revised, 1974, as *Project Appraisal and Planning for Developing Countries* (London: Heinemann).

Mirrlees, J.A. (1969) 'The Evaluation of National Income in an Imperfect Economy', *Pakistan Development Review*, vol. 9, pp. 1–13.

Mirrlees, J.A. (1972) 'On Producer Taxation', *Review of Economic Studies*, vol. 39, pp. 105–11.

Rodrik, D. (1989) 'Credibility of Trade Reform – A Policy Maker's Guide', *The World Economy*, vol. 12, pp. 1–16.

Rodrik, D. (1992) 'The Limits of Trade Policy Reform in Development Countries', *Journal of Economic Perspectives*, vol. 6, no. 1, pp. 87–105.

Samuelson, P.A. (1958) 'An Exact Consumption Loan Model with or without the Social Contrivance of Money', *Journal of Political Economy*, vol. 66, pp. 467–82.

Sawkins, J. (1992) 'Privatisation', *Journal of Economic Surveys*, vol. 6, pp. 271–85.

Starrett, D.A. (1988) *Foundations of Public Economics* (Cambridge: Cambridge University Press).

Vickers, J. and Yarrow, G. (1988) *Privatization: An Economic Analysis* (Cambridge, Mass.: MIT Press).

Part II

Economic Organization in Transition

3 Capitalism, Socialism and Democracy after Fifty Years

Arnold Heertje[1]
UNIVERSITY OF AMSTERDAM

1 SCHUMPETER'S 1942 BOOK

Schumpeter dealt with five topics in his famous and much debated book *Capitalism, Socialism and Democracy* (CSD) published in 1942. He started with a thorough discussion of the Marxian doctrine, which is a brilliant analysis of Marx the prophet, the sociologist, the economist and the teacher. Then follows part two, which has attracted most attention, on the development or rather the decay of capitalism. Part three deals with the question 'Can socialism work?' and part four is a treatment of socialism and democracy. In the closing part five, Schumpeter presents a historical sketch of socialist parties.

Schumpeter motivates his discussion of Marx by referring to his message as one of vitality. In 1942, Schumpeter was able to speak of a Marxian revival, even in the United States. Many of us have experienced a revival of Marx's ideas in the 1960s and 1970s and some of our readers have even taken part in it. There is nothing to be ashamed of. Marx may seem dead for good now, but there is reason to believe that one day economists and others will turn back to a study of his views on the development of capitalism, the role of technical change in society, the degree of monopolization and the relationship between the economic structure of production and social and institutional changes at large. The Congress being in Moscow, one might even put forward the thought that what has happened in recent years in this area of the world can be better explained by the analysis in *Das Kapital*, published in 1867, than what has happened in and after 1917. For this very reason Schumpeter's brilliant analysis of Marx's thinking remains relevant and up-to-date.

The decay of capitalism may almost be reduced to the bureaucratization of the entrepreneurial function, which is to reform from

43

within the economic structure by exploiting an untried technical possibility for producing a new commodity or producing an old one in a new way, in short by being innovative. While in his earlier work (Schumpeter, 1912, p. 159) the most typical case of an innovation was the formation of a new enterprise, it is of the utmost importance to note that Schumpeter in CSD no longer refers to the establishment of new firms or to the entry of new entrepreneurs; innovative activity, if it exists at all, is concentrated in large monopolistic firms that block potential competition. The people who carry out this function of introducing new combinations financed by banks, and who are able to get things done, are called entrepreneurs. They operate in an uncertain world, have the courage to start new ventures and they must be strong to swim against the tide of the society in which they are living.

The process of destroying the old economic structure and creating a new economic picture is called by Schumpeter 'creative destruction' and is in his view the essential fact about capitalism. The evolutionary character of capitalism is *discontinuous*, owing to the qualitative changes that are brought about by the new products, the new methods of production and transportation, the new markets and the new industrial organization. These changes are the product of Schumpeterian entrepreneurial activity, so that almost by definition the decay of capitalism is the decay of the entrepreneurial function. In Schumpeter's view economic performance is measured by total output during a year, so that the entrepreneurial function is directed towards a permanent increase of total output. He is fully aware of the limited significance of output as a measure of economic welfare, as he acknowledges that the satisfaction of wants not only depends on the quantity but also on the quality of production (1942, pp. 66, 190). In fact, as an Austrian, he is an adherent of the broad concept of economic welfare, which relates the satisfaction of wants to the allocation of scarce resources and which is formal and subjective. In CSD, Schumpeter nevertheless has founded both the analysis and the prediction on a material interpretation of welfare.

According to Schumpeter, innovation will be more and more reduced to routine and the personality and willpower of entrepreneurs will be less relevant as people become accustomed to change. The reduction of the entrepreneurial function, especially in the big monopolistic firms, is an essential and necessary building-block in Schumpeter's pessimism about the future of capitalism, but it is not sufficient to lead to any definite conclusions. The disappearance of small and medium-sized firms and traders helps to weaken the political structure of capitalism and makes the prospect of the system even more dependent on the vanishing role of the Schumpeterian entrepreneur in big business. The institutions of private property and free contracting are pushed into the background and even more so because in big companies ownership by a single individual is rare and is replaced by other types of property rights. An atmosphere of universal hostility develops, linked to the success of capitalism in terms of profits and material production and fed by the feeling of the have-nots that they will receive something from the haves by pleading for a redistribution of income. A special role is played in this respect by the intellectuals, of which the educational process produces such a large number that extensive unemployment is unavoidable. Their writings, which are often of a journalistic nature, help to mobilize public opinion and to demotivate entrepreneurial activity. The incentive to carry out the entrepreneurial function and to make profits is also threatened by the disintegration of the bourgeois family and the tendency of men and women in society to depart from traditional arrangements and to calculate in terms of individual advantages and disadvantages. In sum, the already deteriorating position of the entrepreneurs is surrounded by growing hostility, so that in the end they will cease to function. The system disintegrates and declines gradually into socialism.

Socialism, in the sense of an institutional pattern in which control over the means of production and production itself is vested in a central authority, can work, according to Schumpeter. His affirmative answer has to be understood against the background of capitalism having used up its potential and being transformed from a competitive into a monopolistic system. Socialism is a workable and even a more efficient alternative to mature capitalism, which is characterized by a few big companies managed by bureaucratic individuals. Against L. von Mises he puts forward the claim that there is nothing wrong with the logic of socialism and refers to E. Barone for a formal proof of the possibility of an efficient allocation of resources without the introduction of markets. Innovation, now being mechanized and a matter of routine within the walls of a small number of giants, can be made part of the socialist set-up in Schumpeter's view. Explicitly Schumpeter reduces economic efficiency to efficiency of production of consumer goods. Comparing socialism with mature capitalism, taking into account the absence of business cycles and unemployment, he argues that the socialist system produces in the long run the larger stream of consumer goods. Schumpeter points out that socialist management may be superior to big business capitalism, that rational bureaucrats can replace the former managers of fettered capitalism and that the complexity of a modern economy can be taken care of by a huge and all-embracing bureaucracy. In Schumpeter's view the bureaucracy is not an obstacle but a complement to democracy under socialism.

In the fourth part, on socialism and democracy, Schumpeter introduces his now famous definition of democracy as an institutional arrangement for decision making in the public sphere, where individuals try to get power by means of a competitive struggle for the people's vote (1942, p. 269). This insight can be looked at as an application of methodological individualism (Heertje, 1991) and has been the starting-point for Downs's economic theory of democracy (Downs, 1957) and in a wider perspective for public choice theory.

Now, fifty years later, there is at first sight strong evidence that Schumpeter did miss the mark with his vision of the evolution of capitalism. The entrepreneurial function in many economies seems to be more lively than ever. The conclusion that a capitalistic sector still plays an important role seems to be unavoidable. However this does not imply necessarily that Schumpeter was wrong. It may still be that there is a large public sector, taking many regulating measures, so that Schumpeter would be at least partly right. Of course, not only these questions have to be addressed, but also the transition from socialism to capitalism in Eastern Europe and in particular, the former USSR. But let us first go back to the beginning of the 1980s.

2 CAPITALISM, SOCIALISM AND DEMOCRACY AFTER FIFTY YEARS

Scitovsky addressed the American Economic Association at their 1979 Christmas meeting with the question, 'Can Capitalism Survive?' (Scitovsky, 1980). He more or less took Schumpeter's side by pointing out that capitalism is becoming less flexible and less adaptable. He also emphasized that the Keynesian stabilization policies of the 1960s and 1970s were becoming more and more ineffective and unacceptable in a rigid, fragmented and heterogeneous economy. Scitovsky spoke roughly ten years after the turmoil at the universities of Berkeley, Harvard, Paris, Amsterdam and Berlin, a turmoil that fitted in with Schumpeter's picture of the evolution of capitalism and that went along with a negative attitude to entrepreneurs, the making of profits and the existing income distribution for the public at large. In general there was a demand for a stronger role for the government in economic life; and not only the civil servants behaved as bureaucrats, but even many of those working in the private sector acted as if certainty was the rule and the taking of risks irresponsible.

In 1981 the book which started the Schumpeter revival appeared (Heertje, 1981). In this book Paul Samuelson, Tom Bottomore, William Fellner, Gottfried Haberler, Robert Heilbroner, Henk Lambers, Arthur Smithies, Peter Wiles and Herbert Zassenhaus all addressed the same question as to whether Schumpeter's expectations had proved to be correct or not. It is interesting to note that the former Dutch Central Banker, Dr J. Zijlstra, in his introduction to the book rephrased Schumpeter's questions in the following way: 'Can dictatorship survive? No, it cannot. Can democracy survive? Of course, it can.' Zijlstra clearly did foresee the destruction of the institutional framework of the socialist societies. The authors from different countries, sometimes for different and sometimes for the same reasons, all came to the conclusion that they disagreed with Schumpeter's main thesis. In view of the recession in the world economy around 1980 and the general pessimism about the future of the capitalist society, the rejection of Schumpeter's vision was a remarkable outcome. What played an overwhelming part was that socialism seemed to display an increasing lack of attraction as an alternative. This factor outweighed the recognition that Schumpeter was right in pointing out that capitalism would produce an army of critical and frustrated intellectuals, who would help to establish an atmosphere in which private property and bourgeois values are daily under attack by journalists and public opinion, and that he was right in foreseeing the growth of the public sector, the increase in the tax burden and the interventions of the government.

3 THE VIABILITY OF CAPITALISM

Since the beginning of the 1980s we have seen a remarkable comeback of several capitalistic features in the Western world. Many new firms have been established, partly in the services sector of the economy and almost always based on the application of the diffusion of new technology. We have seen a further development of multinationals, mergers and takeovers in the sphere of big business on the one hand and the emergence of many small firms on the other. The driving force behind this scene is the availability of an ever-increasing stock of new technical possibilities, which may lead to the application of new methods of production and new products. There is room for actual economic growth both in the quantitative and qualitative sense on the basis of a huge potential. A new army of entrepreneurs, even in the Schumpeterian sense, is stimulated to get things done, if the prospects for often impressive profits are there. The overall picture, on the basis of divergent and heterogeneous microeconomic actions and initiatives, is not a smooth pattern, but rather a dynamic melting pot of conflicting tendencies, ups and downs, major risks and minor certainties. Economic life is full of sudden jumps and unforeseen calamities, but also of unforeseen breakthroughs, which enhance welfare in the broad sense. Information technology is a case in point; it did really change life in a discontinuous way and has left a mark imprinted on everybody's mind that knowledge and information is power.

The market as an institution is no longer under these circumstances a mechanism for the allocation of resources, but a device for the discovery of new methods of production and new products which satisfy new wants. Entrepreneurs are chasing each other in the market in this dynamic sense, trying to use, to develop and to apply bits of local and particular information and knowledge, in order to win the race for a monopoly position, which in most cases is at best temporary.

Technical change, the market as a mechanism for discovery, globalization of markets and institutions, and the emergence of new firms and entrepreneurs are factors whose joint effect has produced an astonishing vitality in the private sector of the economy on the basis of capitalistic values. Together with the co-ordinated restrictive monetary policy of the major central banks, which kept inflation under control, it may explain the high level of growth in most countries for most of the 1980s. But there is more. In almost all countries the role of the public sector has been restricted. Public deficits have been reduced and regulation diminished. Decentralization of decision-making and privatization have been aims of the policy of many governments. Serious attempts to reduce the tax burden have been made in Western Europe and the USA. Apart from these developments, it seems appropriate to draw attention to the fact that the public sector itself is changing. Instead of the traditional bureaucracy, which consists typically of civil servants not used to taking risks, more and more an entrepreneurial attitude has to be adopted in view of the changing environment, the influence of technology and globalization. Governments compete to attract economic activity by lowering taxes and by restricting regulation. This causes civil servants and politicians, although they are not entrepreneurs, at least partly to absorb an entrepreneurial attitude. In short, Schumpeter's entrepreneurial function is in full swing in the private as well as the public sector fifty years after his prediction to the contrary.

On top of these already amazing facts, the world is confronted with the collapse of socialism in Eastern Europe. Without technical change, I am convinced that nothing would have changed behind the Iron Curtain. Indeed a centrally planned economy can act as a stand-in for a market economy, if technology and preferences are given. It may work very inefficiently and with a certain degree of dictatorship and secret policing, but it works. However, as soon as technology changes in the rest of the world, so that new methods of production and new products become available, which are held to raise the welfare of the people, central planning is no longer effective in imitating a market economy that accounts for the increase in welfare. The problem came to light in a negative way through the nuclear disaster at Chernobyl. Those who had the knowledge to take measures and to take initiatives were not allowed to do so, and those who had the authority and power at the top to take decisions suffered from a complete lack of knowledge and information. Since Chernobyl, I have been convinced that the USSR would collapse. Freedom of religion, speech and travel, in particular for the Jews, were allowed as a natural consequence of the economic necessity of decentralizing decision making in order to develop and to exploit technical knowledge. In this sense the collapse of the USSR is a purely Marxian event. As only bits of information and knowledge are embodied in individuals, their transformation into technical applications can only be carried out by individuals; no authority being capable of knowing everything, the system has to invent the entrepreneur and to create the conditions for the entrepreneurial function. It is interesting to note in this respect that, in the USSR, the entrepreneurial function never completely disappeared from the scene, having been hidden in the informal and black economy. I agree with Rosser and Rosser (1992) that information technology played a part in bringing about the collapse, but I am still inclined to regard technical change in general as the driving force which led to understanding of the reality that the only institution capable of exploiting the potential of technology is the market as a discovery mechanism for individuals, who are in a competitive environment on the look-out for new profitable technical possibilities and applications. In short, socialism collapsed because central decision making and the production, development and use of knowledge at lower levels became completely separated.

4 WHERE SCHUMPETER WENT WRONG

We are faced with the paradoxical situation that, in order to illustrate where Schumpeter went wrong, we have only to consider the typical Schumpeterian features, which together make up his dynamic view of capitalism. Both in the economic literature and amongst the wider public, Schumpeter's name is linked to technical change, the foundation and entry of new firms, the role of creativity in entrepreneurship, the dynamic significance of monopoly, bureaucracy and methodological individualism and an Austrian view of welfare. These features, dealt with separately or taken together, are appropriate to constructing a theory of a lasting capitalistic system. Instead Schumpeter managed to come up with a theory according to which capitalism evolved into socialism, despite the fact that all these ingredients must have been in the back of his mind. Can we solve this apparent paradox?

Let us start with technical change. Prior to CSD, he discusses growth, development, economic development, economic evolution and business cycles primarily as a result of innovations, but in his 1942 book he also deals with the effects of innovation on the evolution of capitalism. It is interesting to note that in Schumpeter's view new technical methods tend to become increasingly capital-saving and that almost any new process that is economically viable economizes on both labour and capital (1942, pp. 119–20). There is reason to contrast Schumpeter's concept of innovation with technical change. The process of technical change consists of the development and diffusion of new technical possibilities, the application of new methods of production and products and the diffusion of those applications. Schumpeter's innovations belong to the category of application, but not all of them have the character of a technical innovation. For example, the opening up of a new market may, but need not, imply a product innovation. An existing product may be introduced in another market, so that a commercial but not a technical innovation is at issue. Some of the technical innovations mentioned by Schumpeter are nowadays called process innovations, and others are known as product innovations. In Schumpeter's scheme, the process innovations, which are fundamental, belong to the category of technical change embodied in capital. New capital goods are needed to implement new technology. Originally Schumpeter conceived of innovations as independent of inventions, and he treated invention as an exogenous factor without any economic implications. In his discussion of oligopolistic capitalism in CSD, he presented a slightly more integrated view of invention and innovation, both being products of giant firms with strong market positions, and invention, moreover, being the product of investment in research and development. In CSD the entrepreneur is, in particular, a manager of an already existing and established firm, usually large, with a department for research and development, so that invention and innovation are linked to one another. Within this context, the innovative role of the entrepreneur is less prominent. There is no theory of the diffusion of technical change in Schumpeter's writings. However the role of imitations of the original innovations in the cyclical process of economic evolution may be considered a vehicle for diffusion of applications of new methods of production and of product innovation. The imitations are governed by the profit motive, just like the innovations, but there is no theoretical analysis of the speed of diffusion or of the time patterns.

Schumpeter's discussion of the role of innovation in capitalism explains why his name is often mentioned in connection with the economic analysis of technical change. His treatment of innovation as an endogenous process, triggered by entrepreneurs who implement new combinations in order to make profits, justifies this practice. On the other hand, technical change in the sense of the development of new knowledge and possibilities and the diffusion of knowledge is almost wholly absent from his exposition. The mutual relationship between development and application of new technology is outside the sphere of his analysis. The circular character of invention, diffusion, innovation and imitation does escape Schumpeter's attention. Although he introduced the idea of creative destruction to describe the evolution of capitalism, he does not deal with the factors that might influence the creativity of investors and entrepreneurs in a positive way. So we are left with the paradoxical conclusion that Schumpeter did not reflect enough on the factors that lie behind innovation, to understand and foresee the inclination of people, both as individuals and in organizations, to remain creative and to produce new technical insights, even if others tend to prefer the status quo and become victims of routine and a bureaucratic attitude.

In his book on economic development (Schumpeter, 1912) the most typical case of a new combination, which encompasses all possibilities and represents the new organizational, commercial and technical aspects, is the formation of a new enterprise. In that book, Schumpeter has, in general, the creation of a new firm in mind when writing about new combinations. In his book on business cycles (Schumpeter, 1939, pp. 94–6), written just a few years before CSD, Schumpeter is even more outspoken about the role of new firms: 'Most new firms are founded with an idea and for a definite purpose. The life goes out of them when that idea or purpose has been fulfilled or has become obsolete or even if, without having become obsolete, it has ceased to be new. That is the fundamental reason why firms do not exist forever.' New production functions are introduced into the system through new firms and as long as there are new ideas new firms will be founded. In CSD, Schumpeter no longer refers to the establishment of new firms or to the entry of new entrepreneurs. He seems to have lost sight of the relative importance of new, often small, firms as the sources of minor and sometimes major innovations, not to speak of their role in the process of invention. His slightly more integrated view of invention and innovation in CSD goes along, more or less, with a change in view about the entrepreneurial function. The entrepreneur is no longer an outsider who sets up a new firm with a new product and new capital equipment. It is again paradoxical to conclude that one of the reasons for Schumpeter's prediction of the decay of capitalism lies in his overlooking the fact, which we have experienced again since the beginning of the 1980s, that, notwithstanding the existence and emergence of large, monopolistic and often multinational firms, technical change provides the opportunity to establish many new firms operating on a small scale, both in the industrial and service sectors and in the formal and informal sectors of the economy. If Schumpeter had been faithful to his original idea of considering the setting up of new firms as the important vehicle for innovations, he would on balance not have lost his confidence in the dynamics of capitalism as he would have been less strong in his pessimism about the other reasons for the decay of capitalism.

The proposition that a monopolistic market structure with a considerable degree of market power is the price society has to pay for technical change has come to be called the Schumpeterian hypothesis (Nelson and Winter, 1982, p. 279). Oakley (1990, p. 208) pointed out that this idea was never incorporated in Schumpeter's theory of motion, but it is present in CSD (pp. 87 ff). Here monopolistic firms are more innovative than competitive firms and large firms contribute more to innovations than small companies. The paradox is that the explanation of the decay of capitalism partly rests on the opinion that in the mature phase of capitalism the economy consists of a small number of giant firms, whose innovations are carried out internally, in an efficient but mechanical manner (Swedberg, 1991, p. 159). The transition to socialism will be easy and peaceful. But even without the setting up of new firms, in Schumpeter's own view the 'monopoly position is in general no cushion to sleep on' (CSD, p. 102). It is only possible to make these divergent views of monopoly compatible by taking into account the differing role of potential entry in both cases and, in fact, the globalization of production through multinational firms is a new phenomenon that fits in a Schumpeterian framework.

Schumpeter did not foresee the recent declining role of the government in economic life, the tendency to privatization and the attempts to lower the tax burden. He could not foresee that in our day politicians and civil servants tend to behave to some extent like entrepreneurs under the pressure of technical change and globalization. The prediction of the decay of capitalism went astray, not only if one restricts Schumpeter's forecast to the capitalistic sector but also if it is understood to apply in the broader sense to the economy at large, including the public sector.

Schumpeter's positive opinion of the working of a bureaucracy under socialism is not easy to understand against the background of his writings on the evolution of capitalism. It is even more difficult to grasp in view of his chapter on methodological individualism in his first book (Schumpeter, 1908, pp. 88–98). He points out that for the description of economic phenomena individual behaviour is the starting-point. It would have been natural to apply this insight to his discussion of bureaucracy and democracy. Such an analysis along the lines of modern public choice theory would probably have made Schumpeter less optimistic about the actual outcome of bureaucratic procedures and the possibility of combining socialism with democracy (Frey, 1981, p. 133). Schumpeter, in the footsteps of Menger, the founder of methodological individualism, did not adhere to his own understanding of the working of the economic process, and was not aware of this inconsistency (Heertje, 1991).

Fifty years after the publication of CSD, the world is confronted with the Schumpeterian paradox of a transition of socialism into capitalism. According to Allen (1991) Schumpeter wrote paradoxical books, a statement that refers undoubtedly to CSD. The question arises how the transition can take shape. At stake is the establishment of the market as a discovery mechanism in the Hayekian sense, within the framework of a completely new set of institutions and communication networks. The decentralization of decision making must go along with the acceptance of entrepreneurs, who introduce and develop new methods of production and new products, and who try to satisfy new wants. Exit and entry of firms and product differentiation have to become visible in the daily life of the economic system. The development and application of new technology must become the driving force behind social change.

Our market economy reflects Schumpeter's picture of capitalism more than the neoclassical scheme (Murrell, 1991). The former socialist economies have to be attracted by a Schumpeterian and not a Walrasian perspective. This does not imply that the market as an allocation mechanism is not a building-block in the reform of the economies of Eastern Europe. The opposite is nearer to the truth. The existence of the market in the traditional sense is an essential source of information on scarcity, prices and costs. The market structure and the day-to-day activities of firms are the basis and background for risky experiments centred upon new technology with an uncertain and unpredictable commercial outcome. Society has to be aware of the profit motive of firms and to accept the making of profits and the inequality of incomes that may result from the market process. A certain level of unemployment also seems to be a natural consequence of the transition from socialism to capitalism. There is no change without continuity, no disturbance without rest, no innovation without tradition or even stagnation, no chaos without order, no evolution without equilibrium. Markets and firms as established institutions are the backbone of the process of discovery of new technology and methods of organization.

Loasby (1991) recently argued that in order to co-ordinate the growth of knowledge a certain balance is needed between structures that embody equilibrium and continuity and an informal framework of assumptions, conventions and procedures that enable people to depart from the status quo, to introduce changes, to innovate and to provoke evolution. A major and time-consuming learning process is involved. It may take a long time before Schumpeterian entrepreneurs are produced from within, although the informal economy did prepare individuals for a managerial role in the official economy.

It would be a serious mistake to neglect the role of the government in the process of transition to a market economy. Not only has the government to implement new rules to provide law and order and the infrastructure and public investment to complement private investment, but also an active role by government is needed for the preservation of nature and the quality of the environment. In view of unavoidable unemployment, the government has also to make sure that the unemployed receive payments as a form of social security. In a modern complex economy, with networks of knowledge and technical change, even civil servants behave like entrepreneurs. They take risks, compete with the bureaucracy in other countries and are sensitive to innovation. In sum, after fifty years we are witness to the impressive spectacle of a move from socialism to capitalism, guided by creative destruction, the interesting paradox being that the former USSR and its allies are trying to merge with economies in the West, reflecting dynamic aspects *à la* Schumpeter: new firms, technical change and entrepreneurial activity in the private and public sectors.

My last observation on the paradoxes in Schumpeter is about the broad concept of welfare. A subjective and formal interpretation of welfare would have made Schumpeter less oriented to industrial production as the sole yardstick of economic performance. Starting from the perspective of the consumer would have made him more sensitive to the role of services and to environmental factors in economic life. I suppose also that the significance of job satisfaction would have come more to the fore in his picture of capitalism. The discussion of these topics would have made socialism as an alternative to capitalism less appealing. The paradox is that his restriction to material welfare is at odds with his Austrian background. In sum, Schumpeter went wrong in his prediction of the decay of capitalism, because his reasoning in CSD does not build on his earlier analysis and is even in striking conflict with the vision he stands for; at least in his scientific work he appears to be a man of contradiction and conflict.

5 SCHUMPETER AND DISCONTINUITY

From a theoretical point of view Schumpeter is the economist of discontinuity. His emphasis on major innovations by way of jumps and fundamental qualitative changes in economic life does distinguish him from mainstream economics. Here also lies his striking difference from Keynes, who was able to prove the existence of equilibrium at low levels of unemployment. At the time, the mathematical apparatus could take care of continuity both in micro- and macroeconomics. But the mathematical technique was not able to crack Schumpeter's vision.

One of Schumpeter's outstanding pupils, R.M. Goodwin (1990) has made major contributions in relating chaos theory to Schumpeter's work. The combination of non-linear equation systems and changes in initial conditions does produce, from within a deterministic set-up, irregular and unpredictable movements of economic time series. This is exactly what Schumpeter had in mind when he did not accept the reference to exogenous shocks as the explanation for unforeseen qualitative changes. Ursprung (1984) describes Schumpeterian discontinuity in terms of catastrophe theory. According to Barkley Rosser (1991) who has written the first, and in my view a brilliant, book on the theory of economic discontinuities, chaos and catastrophe are part of the idea of bifurcation. In case of non-linearity of functional relationships, bifurcation refers to the splitting of equilibria at critical points. Catastrophe theory deals with discontinuity in the large and chaos theory with discontinuity in the small. In his book Schumpeter's approach is described by means of Rosser's concept of technique clusters, which refer to pages of the book of blueprints more closely related than they are to any other. Allowing for the possibility that the book of blueprints is not known in advance, Schumpeter's discontinuity evolutionary framework may be described by way of mathematical formulation of a switch from one kind of technique to a very different kind of technology.

Following Schumpeter, the economic process is more and more looked at as an unpredictable combination of a self-organizing system and a self-disturbing mechanism, where minor changes in initial conditions cause major unforeseen developments after some time. This picture of reality becomes even more confusing if we try to describe it in mathematical terms by assuming that the changes in the initial conditions have a permanent character, so that the system starts every day anew. Against this background prediction and policy making can at best be carried out in a spirit of the greatest modesty.

There remains the fundamental problem of how the dynamics of the macroeconomic system can be related to the behaviour of consumers, producers and owners of the factors of production at the micro level. (Weidlich and Braun, 1992). It seems that in this respect the so-called master equation can be applied. This equation is capable of describing physical and social phenomena. Roughly the equation describes how the probability over time of the emergence of a set of macroeconomic variables changes with the behaviour and movements of the economic actors at the micro level. The master equation may be the tool to present Schumpeter's vision of economic evolution in a rigorous way.

6 CONCLUSION

It is paradoxical to conclude on the one hand that Schumpeter's prediction of the decay of capitalism did not come true for reasons he himself had put forward, and on the other hand that his vision of the discontinuous character of economic evolution may give rise in the coming years to a new paradigm in economic theory, structured by recently developed mathematical tools. We face not only paradoxes with respect to Schumpeter's work, but also with regard to his person- ality. Research carried out by R.L. Allen (1991) and R. Swedberg (1991) in the Harvard archives has brought to light negative aspects of Schumpeter's personality. It appears that during the Second World War he had an admiration for Hitler, Nazi Germany and Japan. He thought that the British and the Jews had won the war with the help of the USA. The whole thing was in his eyes a Jewish victory. We are confronted with what I would like to call the Schumpeter Problem. How can we explain that a man of his stature, with deep knowledge of historical events and social movements and a sense of tolerance and wisdom as expressed in his writings, displays not only such hatred of the Jews and a hardly concealed regret that Hitler had lost the war, but also a complete misunderstanding of the political picture? This Schumpeter Problem is even more puzzling in view of his well-balanced chapter added to the second edition of CSD on the consequences of the Second World War.

On balance, Schumpeter is a man of conflict both in his writings, his life and his character. Most of us are, as conflict appears to be the essence of life. But Schumpeter's tragedy is that he was never able to solve the conflicts and contradictions his brilliant mind was able to produce in such a feverish way.

Note

1. I would like to express my gratitude to Professor Dr Piëter Hennipman
who for more than forty years has been my source of inspiration and
encouragement and who is still willing to be instrumental in improving my
writings.

References

Allen, R.L. (1991) *Opening Doors, The Life and Work of Joseph Schumpeter, Volume I* (New Brunswick and London: Transaction).
Downs, A. (1957) *An Economic Theory of Democracy* (New York: Harper & Row).
Frey, B. (1981) 'Schumpeter, Political Economist' in Frisch, H. (ed.) *Schumpeterian Economics* (Eastbourne: Praeger Publishers).
Goodwin, R.M. (1990) *Chaotic Economic Dynamics* (Oxford: Clarendon Press).
Heertje, A. (ed.) (1981) *Schumpeter's Vision, Capitalism, Socialism and Democracy after 40 years* (Eastbourne: Praeger Publishers).
Heertje, A. (1991) 'Methodologischer Individualismus bei Schumpeter', in Hanusch, H., Heertje, A. and Shinoja, Y., *Schumpeter der Ökonom des 20 Jahrhunderts*, (Düsseldorf: Verlag Wirtschaft und Finanzen).
Loasby, B.J. (1991) *Equilibrium and Evolution* (Manchester: Manchester University Press).
Murrell P. (1991) 'Can Neoclassical Economics Underpin the Reform of Centrally Planned Economies?', *Journal of Economic Perspectives*, vol. 5, no. 4, pp. 59–77.
Nelson, R.R. and Winter, S.G. (1982) *An Evolutionary Theory of Economic Change* (Cambridge, Mass.: Belknap Press of Harvard University Press).
Oakley, A. (1990) *Schumpeter's Theory of Capitalistic Motion; A Critical Exposition and Reassessment* (Aldershot: Edward Elgar) p. 208.
Rosser, B.J. (1991) *From Catastrophe to Chaos: A General Theory of Economic Discontinuities* (Boston: Kluwer Academic).
Rosser, B.J. and Rosser, M.V. (1992) 'Schumpeterian Cycles and the Transition from Socialism to Capitalism', paper for the Tenth World Congress of the International Economic Association, Moscow, August 1992.
Schumpeter, J.A. (1908) *Das Wesen und der Hauptinhalt der theoretischen Nationalökonomie* (Leipzig: Verlag von Duncker and Humblot).
Schumpeter, J.A. (1912) *Theorie der wirtschaftlichen Entwicklung* (Leipzig: Verlag von Duncker and Humblot); 2nd edn, 1926; translated into English by Opie, R. (1961) *The Theory of Economic Development* (Oxford: Oxford University Press).
Schumpeter, J.A. (1939) *Business Cycles* (New York and London: McGraw-Hill) pp. 94–6.
Schumpeter, J.A. (1942) *Capitalism, Socialism and Democracy* (New York and London: Harper and Brothers); 2nd edn 1947, with an additional chapter on the consequences of the Second World War as part of a historical sketch of

socialist parties; 3rd edn 1950, with a new preface and the text of his address
before the American Economic Association in New York on 30 December
1949 on The March into Socialism.

Scitovsky T. (1980), 'Can Capitalism Survive? An Old Question in a New
Setting, *American Economic Review*, vol. 70, pp. 1–9; and in Scitovsky, T.
(1986) *Human Desire and Economic Satisfaction* (Brighton: Wheatsheaf) pp.
83–94.

Swedberg, R. (1991) *J.A. Schumpeter, His Life and Work* (Cambridge:
Polity Press).

Ursprung, H.W. (1984) 'Schumpeterian Entrepreneurs and Catastrophe
Theory or A New Chapter of the Foundations of Economic Analysis',
Journal of Economics, vol. 4, pp. 39–70.

Weidlich, W. and Braun, M. (1992) 'The Master Equation Approach to
Nonlinear Economics,' *Journal of Evolutionary Economics*, vol. 2, no. 3,
pp. 233–65.

4 Public Finance, Unemployment and Economies in Transition

John S. Flemming

EUROPEAN BANK FOR RECONSTRUCTION AND DEVELOPMENT

1 INTRODUCTION: THE PROBLEM

Price reform, the dismantling of subsidies and opening to trade do nothing to impair the productive potential of an economy: indeed the removal of distortions should facilitate the more efficient use of its resources and thus contribute to higher production, consumption and welfare. Yet what we see in formerly centrally planned economies adopting such policies is a substantial fall in measured output – typically 25 per cent over about three years.

This paper is not an attempt to explain the actual course of output in reforming economies. History does not offer pure experiments. External conditions changed, exports to the USSR became more difficult and imports of oil and gas from it more expensive. Stabilization policies involved restrictive fiscal and credit policies; the change of system involved both a short-run speculative inventory cycle and a major one-time adjustment to the higher carrying cost and the lower inventory requirements of a market-clearing context (Winiecki and Winiecki, 1992). These factors, rather than the mechanism highlighted in this paper, might account for the remarkably uniform reduction of output across many industrial sectors of the Polish economy, for example (Berg and Sachs, 1992).

Though theoretical, this paper may be very relevant to policy decisions. Among its less plausible assumptions is that it relates to an economy with well functioning competitive markets; but if it can be shown that the elimination of long-standing distortions in such an economy cannot be relied upon alone to raise welfare in the short to medium term, should we not at least pause in recommending such programmes in formerly planned economies? Moreover it will be shown that the 'safety net' measures beloved of those anxious to limit the cost of rapid macrostabilization may aggravate the undesirable consequences of trade and price liberalization. The remedy proposed, a *temporary* shift in the burden of taxation away from the costs of employment, is similar to one I recommended for the UK in the mid-1970s when OPEC's first oil price shock created relative price changes but, as Britain was, in a present value sense, broadly self-sufficient in oil, did not change permanent real national income (Flemming, 1976). I then proposed a reduction in employers' national insurance contributions, in effect switching taxation from human capital to the new or prospective resource rents and allowing industry to pay unchanged real wages despite the squeeze higher energy prices applied to their margins. In a lecture in 1990 (Flemming, 1990) I proposed a similar temporary shift in taxation for countries in transition to the market, involving additional taxation of the quasi-rents of those benefiting from unexpected changes in relative prices at the enterprise level and subsidies, or tax reduction for those experiencing negative quasi-rents. This paper represents a further development of that idea.

Before developing any model in greater detail, the objective of any possible policy intervention should be spelt out. In fact there are several possible welfare bases for intervention in the face of radical relative price changes:

1. Even if markets are perfect and clear, there may be a case for intervention to make the effects of reform more nearly Paretian. This case would be strengthened by capital market imperfection.
2. Even if markets are perfect and clear, it is possible that a temporarily low wage would depress labour supply, reducing output and investment in the restructuring of the economy. Those impatient for change might choose to intervene.
3. Labour market distortion, for instance by a minimum wage and unemployment insurance (which probably reflects capital market imperfection) may convert relative price shocks into reduced employment, output, consumption and investment. An intervention raising all of these would be beneficial on many criteria. Consumption would be likely to be more sensitive to employment and output the less perfect the capital market.

We thus have three possible criteria:
(a) Pareto improvement;
(b) more investment, to speed structural change; and

(c) conventional welfare enhancement with its emphasis on consumption (and its distribution).

Though different, these criteria do not typically conflict directly, the exception being in case (2) above where conventional welfare (c) would be sacrificed to stimulate investment and change (b). This case depends on all markets being perfect. Observed labour markets differ only in the degree of their imperfection, typically being more imperfect in Europe than in North America. Under these circumstances, and especially if consumers do not have access to perfect capital markets, interventions may exist which improve the situation by all of the criteria, (a), (b) and (c). That is what this paper aims to demonstrate in a model in which, for reasons to be explained, a minimum wage and unemployment compensation (possibly at the same level) are in force.

Suppose that, in a two-sector economy, one sector has for many years been subsidized and the other taxed to finance the subsidy. Both capital and labour are employed disproportionately in the subsidized sector whose production also increases and accounts for an inflated proportion of consumption. The distorting tax and subsidy, which are both related to value added, are then abolished. Resources should then move from the previously subsidized (S) to the previously taxed (T) sector, both of which are assumed to be competitively organized. Capital however is specific, and while homogeneous labour is unspecific, the marginal product of labour falls away rapidly in both sectors beyond a point corresponding to the design level of employment on the installed equipment. Thus the (post-tax) value added margin falls in the previously subsidized sector, lowering the value marginal product of labour, and while the margin widens in the previously taxed sector only a small transfer of labour can occur before its physical marginal product falls sharply.

In the limiting case of zero *ex post* factor substitution the wage in the formerly subsidized sector falls at least as low as the value added per man while the formerly taxed sector need pay no higher wage as labour is readily available from the other sector at that level. In this case, output is unchanged but income is redistributed from wages, in both sectors, to profits in the T sector. These profits are a signal to expand that sector and are also available for that purpose, though if the government, which owns both, chose to make transfer payments to households (or to cut their net tax payments) it would be free to do so, in the process making the reform package more nearly Paretian (criterion (a)). The temporary reduction in the real wage might reduce labour supply, output and the speed of change in the economy. Though not necessarily welfare enhancing, a wage subsidy could actually accelerate the process of change (criterion (b)); if it raised output more than consumption it would boost investment in the expanding sector. It might also meet criterion (c). Thus even with market clearing a case could possibly be made for intervention under any of the criteria (a), (b) or (c).

Moreover this case is strengthened if value added by the previously subsidized sector is negative at the new prices – and negative value added at world prices is widely reported in Eastern Europe (see Hughes and Hare, 1992). In this case it is unclear what prevents the wage falling to zero. Among the candidates are:

- the disutility of work and the ability to maintain adequate consumption by dissaving;
- subsistence requirements or efficiency wages;
- a statutory minimum wage;
- unemployment compensation or social security benefits.

The second and third of these call for supplementation by the fourth if the unemployed do not have good access to capital markets and are not to starve.

Removal of a sizeable tax/subsidy distortion could reduce the market-clearing wage below the statutory minimum wage (as is inevitable if the subsidized sector was value subtracting at world prices) with several consequences:

1. The wage falls to the minimum.
2. Unemployment rises as jobs in the formerly subsidized sector are lost.
3. Unemployment compensation absorbs part, presumably much, of the additional profit earned by the formerly taxed sector.
4. Output of the formerly subsidized product falls.
5. The surplus of total production over consumption probably falls – it certainly does if the subsidized sector has positive value added while all labour income and transfers are consumed and only net profits are invested.

2 THE MODEL CASE FOR SUBSIDIES

The limiting case of a full static equilibrium with zero *ex post* substitutability and zero excess capacity is not very interesting. In fact, even in a putty-clay world, cohorts and vintages of capital will generally differ either by virtue of their age or of the technology ruling at the time of their construction. Technical progress implies obsolescense and a decision as to when to scrap equipment no longer used or only infrequently used. Uncertainty about possible relative price (or wage) changes would typically lead to some deferral of scrapping and the retention of some flexibility in the available capacity. This situation is depicted in Figure 4.1, where the technology is identical in the two sectors and the distortion such as to ensure they are the same size ($AD = BD$). Equilibrium (E) is represented by the equality of marginal value products (at the distorted prices) in the two sectors. The distance DC represents the scope for additional employment in the taxed sector on old vintages of equipment not profitable at initial prices and the market clearing wage W_0. Given a similar margin of unused capital in the subsidized sector small fluctuations in relative prices, represented by relative vertical displacements of the two functions, have little or no effect on the market clearing real wage. But as Figure 4.2 illustrates, large shocks will have a downward bias, as the market-clearing wage falls from W_0 to W_1, although the switch in employment from S to T raises world price gross domestic product (GDP). The switch in employment CD from the S sector to the T sector, made possible by the initial margin of less than fully utilized capacity, raises world price GDP by $FLG'F'$. For reform to bring about the Pareto improvement that this makes possible employment has to be subsidized so that the real wage is unchanged at the initial level W_0 (which involves some assumption about the relevant numeraire). If, as we assume, wage income is consumed while profits are invested, a wage subsidy ($W_0 - W_1$) maintaining real wages would lead to all of the extra output being invested. Alternatively the extra output could be divided between additional investment and consumption by an even larger employment subsidy.

Figure 4.3 shows that a big enough shock would generate partial unemployment even in the absence of a minimum wage, or dole, or reservation wage, if the least productive vintages in the formerly subsidized sector are so inefficient in the use of materials as to be incapable of positive value added at world prices. Introducing a minimum wage W and dole d into the situation illustrated in Figure 4.2 has the effects shown in Figure 4.4, where some of the workers in the previously subsidized sector become unemployed. Their consumption falls from W_1 to d, while that of workers in the T sector rises from W_1 to W, and investment in the T sector (consisting of the surpluses of both sectors) is reduced by the fiscal transfer necessary to

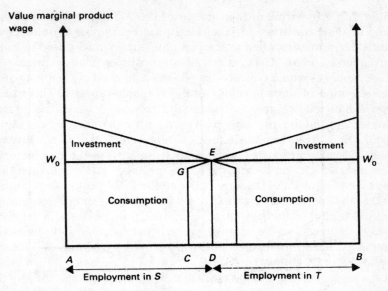

Figure 4.1 Initial equilibrium with distorted prices

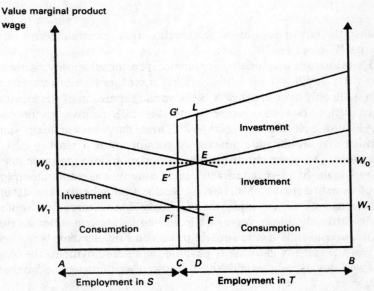

Figure 4.2 Market-clearing outcome with free prices (i): low but positive real wage

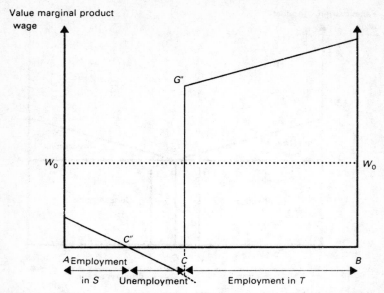

Figure 4.3 Market-clearing outcome with free prices (ii): some negative value added, unemployment even at a zero wage

finance the payment of the dole as well as by the extra labour cost of paying W instead of W_1.

This situation is clearly suboptimal. Even those whose criterion is the most rapid possible shift of resources between sectors can rationally only measure this by the *absolute* expansion of the formerly taxed sector, and we have seen that this falls relative to the market-clearing outcome of Figure 4.2. There must exist a lump sump transfer that would raise welfare of consumers at a smaller cost to investment (all of which can be relied upon to go into the profitable T sector) than that associated with the minimum wage and unemployment benefit scheme. Moreover, even if that scheme is a datum, there may well be an employment subsidy that restores full employment, at the minimum wage, while adding less to consumption than to output and thus increasing net profits and investment. Note that, even if the subsidy is formally payable on all employment, the wage in T will not rise above W if the subsidy raises the wage in S only to that level.

An employment subsidy $E = W - W_1$ would, in this case, restore full employment, as in Figure 4.5, adding $JCF'K$ to output and

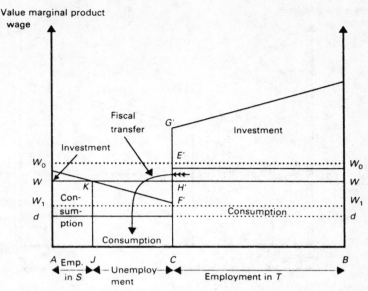

Value marginal product wage

Figure 4.4 Equilibrium with minimum wage above market-clearing level and transfer-financed unemployment compensation

reducing the dole by $JCdd$ so that welfare and investment both rise as long as $JCdd > F'KH'$ or, in the linear case illustrated, if $d > (W - W_1)/2$. This is very likely if the new market-clearing wage (W_1) is positive, as the dole (d) commonly exceeds half of the minimum wage $(W/2)$.

Figure 4.6 depicts the case in which full employment could only be achieved by indulging in some value subtraction but there is also some scope for adding value in the S sector (in the case illustrated the subsidy equals $(W - d)$). What subsidy should be paid in this case? A subsidy at least equal to the dole d. Consider raising the subsidy from $d - \varepsilon$ to d. The additional employment, say, δN contributes $(W - d) \times \delta N$ to output and saves $d (\delta N)$ on the dole while the consumption of the newly employed also rises from d to W and the subsidy bill rises by $d(\delta N)$, the additional subsidy payable to those already employed (in either sector) being offset by reduced pre-tax wages. Thus raising the subsidy from $d - \varepsilon$ to d is fiscally neutral, neutral with respect to investment, and raises output and consumption by $(W - d) \times \delta N$. It thus meets criteria (a) and (c) and is unobjectionable on (b). Criteria (a) and (c) would indeed require a higher level of subsidy.

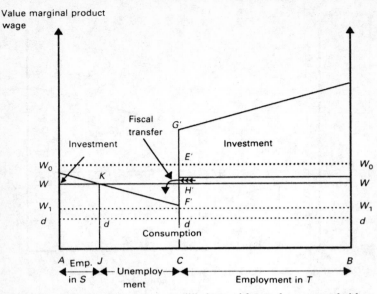

Figure 4.5 Full employment equilibrium with employment subsidy financed by fiscal transfer

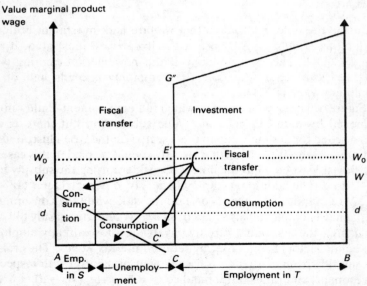

Figure 4.6 Unemployment equilibrium with investment-maximizing employment subsidy

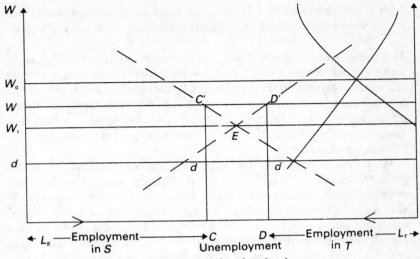

Figure 4.7 A more conventional technology

How sensitive is this argument to the assumption of fixed coefficients in production? Nothing much changes if GC, $G'C$ and $G''C$ are not strictly vertical but remain significantly steeper than the slope of the function when employment in T is less than BC. Figure 4.7 corresponds to a more conventional technology and, although a sharp fall in the market-clearing real wage is much less likely in this case, it shows that a subsidy equal to $W - W_1$ would be beneficial as long as the triangle $C'D'E$, representing that part of the cost of employing the additional labour not covered by the value of its output, is smaller than the area $CDdd$ representing the saving on the dole. Again $d > W - W_1$ is amply sufficient and $d > (W - W_1)/2$ probably sufficient.

3 THE DISTINCTIVENESS OF THE CASE

The proposition that it might be better to use dole monies to subsidize employment is, of course, an old one for which little if any preference has been revealed. What is peculiar about the case made here? It has three distinguishing features:

1. It is developed in the context of a binding minimum wage (although this is not true of the Paretian argument).
2. The subsidy proposed is temporary.

3. It is not proposed as a remedy for Keynesian unemployment but for sectorally classical unemployment arising from large shocks.

The present case relates strictly to a *temporary* subsidy. The argument is that the subsidy increases investment in the expanding sector, allowing labour also to be transferred to that sector. As output in the S sector falls, so the market clearing wage (W_1) rises through relative price effects and, if there is any, factor substitutability, as labour's marginal product there rises. As W_1 rises so the subsidy necessary for full employment falls.

What would happen if the subsidy were not actually cut at this point? Competition would ensure that the wage actually paid did not exceed W so that the excess subsidy would simply depress the presubsidy wage. Eventually, of course, investment in the T sector would raise the market-clearing wage above W. The subsidy might also persist into this period without distorting a deterministic economy with homogeneous labour – at least if the value added tax (VAT) was of consumption type and there were no administrative costs of collecting it and distributing the proceeds as the employment subsidy. It is well known that in the long run a proportional consumption tax and wage tax are equivalent. Thus a VAT and wage subsidy are offsetting and although the employment subsidy might not be *ad valorem* but *ad* (full-time equivalent) *hominem* there is no difference as long as labour is homogeneous. Of course in reality labour is not homogeneous and, were a per capita employment subsidy to be retained for an unnecessarily long period, it would increase the progressiveness of the tax system, taxing value added proportionately and subsidizing employment. High value added per man hour activity would be discouraged relative to that with lower value added per man hour. Thus a permanent employment subsidy would be somewhat distortionary but not, I suggest, very seriously so. Moreover in practice it might be easier to implement a payroll subsidy than an employment subsidy. This shows that a transitional employment subsidy differs from a phasing out of the original sectorally distorting tax/subsidy scheme. As the speed of phasing out declines, the distortion of the sectoral tax subsidy is undiminished, while the effects of the employment subsidy, for both good and ill, would tend to diminish with the passage of time. The case that is made here does not relate to Keynesian unemployment, the introduction of which would require a different model and is beyond the scope of the present paper.

4 LINKS TO SPECIFIC MARKET IMPERFECTIONS

In the story above, not only was factor substitutability initially set equal to zero but consumers simply spent their income without undertaking any intertemporal optimization. More formal dynamics would also enable one to optimize the trajectory of the subsidy along the economy's adjustment path. Nevertheless this course is not pursued here, for two reasons: one is simplicity but, at least as importantly, if one were to assume a perfect capital market the newly unemployed would probably not reduce their consumption significantly. Indeed I have argued elsewhere (Flemming, 1978) that observed unemployment income replacement rates can only be rationalized by extreme capital market imperfection. Moreover, were the capital market perfect, the employment subsidy would not significantly raise the consumption of the otherwise unemployed – intertemporal optimization by households, if feasible, would thus tend to strengthen the case on some criteria (for example, (b) above) for an employment subsidy simply to raise output, investment and the speed of adjustment.

Here the argument is only that a temporary employment subsidy at a rate declining over time is an appropriate response to abnormal relative price shocks which leave potential national output unaffected (or increased). The case may be clearest in the presence of minimum wages and unemployment compensation but they reflect a concern with income distribution which may suffice on its own to warrant a transfer from profits to wages.

There thus emerge four possible cases for a temporary employment subsidy in response to a shock that takes us into a region in which *ex post* factor substitutabilities at the market clearing real wage are markedly asymmetrical:

1. Capital market imperfect, labour market clears, price shock temporarily lowers the market clearing real wage; an employment, or wage, subsidy raises welfare by improving intertemporal consumption distribution (and political support for reform); that is, subsidy meets criteria (a) and (c) but not (b).
2. Capital market imperfect, labour market distorted by W and d; price shock temporarily reduces output, employment and consumption – the last less than the first, so that a subsidy may raise both consumption and investment; that is, meeting criteria (a), (b) and (c).

3. Capital market perfect, labour market distorted by W, so that a price shock temporarily reduces employment, output and investment – which would be boosted by an employment subsidy; that is, meeting criteria (a), (b) and (c).

4. Both markets perfect – labour reservation wage high, so a wage subsidy increases output and employment and investment, but not welfare; that is, only criterion (b) is met.

5 A CONTINUUM OF PROCESSES

A related argument, applicable to a continuum of technological processes, is that a radical price reform raises the dispersion of value added and profits at the prices enterprises face. This means it may be hard to reconcile a reasonably small proportion of non-viable enterprises with a reasonably low average profit rate simply by varying the real wage (for example, in the short run, by devaluation). An employment subsidy financed by profit or value added taxation, in particular, should reduce the dispersion allowing a reasonable average real wage to co-exist with a reasonably small proportion of enterprises appearing unviable.

One might represent a centrally planned and distorted economy as one in which implicit (credit) subsidies make all enterprises equally profitable (at the distorted prices). Thus the distribution of the ratio of enterprise value added to their average wage would be very concentrated – if capital intensity were uniform all the density might be at a ratio of about $1\frac{1}{2}$ (that is, labour's share is 2/3) as in Figure 4.8.

Now shock the structure of relative prices by eliminating all domestic distortions and opening to trade. If the resulting shocks were normally distributed and wages unchanged, the situation would be as in Figure 4.9, with the mean still at 1 1/2, if any change in the unique real wage matched any change in real GDP. Enterprises to the left of the origin are those that subtract value at free (world) prices. All those to the left of the unit VA/W ratio are absolutely unprofitable, making no contribution to capital costs.

Few people would oppose the closure of all negative value added enterprises, though McKinnon (1991) has advanced the contrary view. Should all the unprofitable ones be closed? This is not economically or socially appropriate if it implies a very high level of unemployment, as it would if the variance of the distribution in

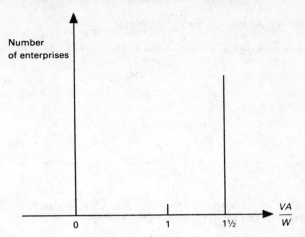

Figure 4.8 The degenerate distribution of the ratio of value added to wages under central planning

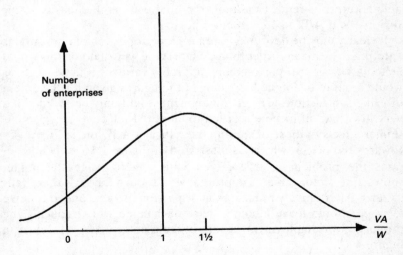

Figure 4.9 The exceptional dispersion of the ratio of value added to wages on liberalization

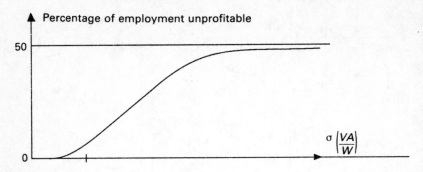

Figure 4.10 The relationship between the incidence of unprofitability and the dispersion of the ratio of value added to wages

Figure 4.9 were very large. As illustrated in Figure 4.10, as the variance approaches infinity so the share of employment in unprofitable enterprises tends to a limit of 50 per cent as the density in the region $1 < VA/W < 1\frac{1}{2}$ becomes negligible.

It clearly may be desirable to reduce the proportion of unprofitable enterprises by means other than closure. One way of doing this would be to vary wages proportionately, but if the variance is at all large, as would seem to be implied by many of the figures given for the extent of value subtraction, high unemployment would only be avoided if a very low share of income accrued to labour. Reducing the wage has similar effects to those of shifting the critical VA/W line in Figure 4.9 towards the origin, which, as illustrated in Figure 4.11, only ameliorates the problem a little. Even with a zero wage the value-subtracting sector remains unprofitable, although labour's share falls to zero. Alternatively reducing the dispersion of value added relative to wages would leave labour's share unchanged while reducing the proportion of employment in unprofitable enterprises, as shown in Figure 4.10.

If closing all unprofitable enterprises caused excessive unemployment, there would their be a very strong case for considering measures that reduce the dispersion of VA/W. A proportional tax on profits or value added, paid out as a per capita employment subsidy, clearly has this effect and, in disequilibrium, one paid as a payroll subsidy should do so too. Another approach would be to drive a wedge between the distributions at world and domestic prices with a suitable tariff struc-

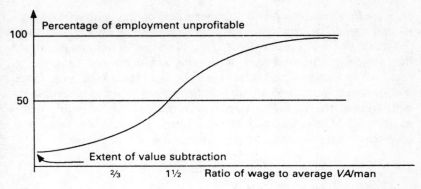

Figure 4.11 The relationship between the incidence of unprofitability and the ratio of the wage to average value added per man

ture (as recommended by McKinnon), provided that the initial distortions represented commodity-specific, rather than enterprise-specific, taxes and subsidies.

6 THE ALTERNATIVES TO SUBSIDY OR PROTECTION SUBVERT FINANCIAL DISCIPLINE

The failure to reconcile free prices with acceptable and efficient employment levels by an explicit subsidy while extending credit to enterprises trading unprofitably jeopardizes any attempt to harden budget constraints. Hard budget constraints imply a real threat of bankruptcy. The machinery of bankruptcy must be triggered whenever creditors think it best protects their interest. Its application cannot be tempered by considerations such as that to bankrupt all insolvent enterprises would lead to excessive unemployment. Such tempering would imply extending continuing credit flows to some insolvent enterprises and the further accumulation of bad debts, with damaging effects on the prospects for once-for-all balance sheet cleansing and the privatization of financial enterprises, or others extending such bad credit, as well as its takers. Indeed it would be subversive of all financial discipline, as loss makers expecting to be bailed out would see no need to minimize losses, and their lenders no need to discriminate between good and bad credit prospects.

Even if no subsidy were paid it would be possible to use the magnitude of an enterprises loss per man, or the ratio of losses to payroll, as a ranking criterion for closures. Depending on one's judgment of the regenerative capacity of the economy one could say that state-owned enterprises accounting for say 5 per cent of the sector's (or total) employment would be liquidated each year (over and above privatization) in order of the ratio of losses to payroll. This would make the liquidation criterion objective, as is required for hardened budget constraints, even though it would not solve the problems arising from the continued accrual of bad debts.

7   PRACTICAL CONCLUSIONS

So far I have abstracted from all practical considerations; and I have written almost indifferently throughout of employment (or wage, or payroll) subsidies. What are their respective merits? How large should they be? Might a subsidy *vis-à-vis* the status quo ante be achieved by reducing existing taxes on employment/wages/payroll and making up the difference from a profits tax or VAT?

Given the low initial level of unemployment, artificial though it was, a Paretian argument would involve a very low target level or a very high level of compensation. More realistically the disequilibrium adjustment being experienced in Eastern Europe means that their nascent market institutions are unlikely to be able to deliver a better unemployment performance than the 10 per cent achieved in Western Europe in the 1980s. There are also serious questions about the policing of the payment of unemployment compensation in countries in which having two jobs has become a way of life (see Burda, 1993). As argued above, in an imperfect world, a restrictive criterion for the scope of any subsidy scheme would be its effect on the quantity of resources going into the expanding sectors (criterion (b)).

How would the level of subsidy or payroll tax adjustment be set? In the two sector cases considered it would ideally be equal to the gap between the market-clearing and minimum wages – indeed in the fixed coefficient case anything less is pointless. We have also seen that one would be unlikely to want to pay an employment subsidy greater than the dole. A fairly extreme reduction in the market clearing wage would be 50 per cent while the minimum wage might be 2/3 to 3/4 and the dole 1/2 of the average, suggesting a subsidy in the range of 15–25 per cent of the average wage – but in general we have seen that any transitional reduction in the dispersion of post-tax value added per man is likely to be helpful.

The case for a subsidy, in whichever form, is strongest immediately after price and trade liberalization, while satisfactory VATs are unlikely to be in place, except in Hungary, for several years. Is there any other revenue source? Or could the tariff system be used to protect employment and labour's share while generating revenue? What structure of tariffs would this support and should countries invoking this procedure exempt (totally or partially) trade between each other? The distributional case for an employment subsidy points to a per capita rather than *ad valorem* basis; if financed by a VAT it transfers from high to low value-added-per-man enterprises rather than from those in which capital accounts for a large share of value added. If paid as an explicit subsidy, however, a per capita one may be more open to abuse by adding false names to the register of employees without needing to adjust audited financial flows. We also saw above, as indeed the present argument implies, that an inappropriate employment subsidy could be more distorting than the corresponding wage subsidy.

The final argument would not apply if there were a per capita element in the pre-existing social security tax arrangements which could be scaled back as the VAT was raised. This would be my first preference, followed by a payroll subsidy which could, in almost every case, take the form of reduced payroll taxation (which averages 50 per cent in Central Europe). If deemed appropriate to enhance tax compliance, the payment of the subsidy, or remission of payroll tax, could be made contingent on profit tax authorities being satisfied that they had received their due.

Thus the key issue is whether anything approximating enhanced VAT revenue is practicable in the short term. If the answer is negative, we have to consider the scope for using temporary trade tariffs either to generate the revenue or to protect employment. Clearly in a case like that of Russia a transitional export tax on (previously underpriced) energy and a tax on imports competing with low-quality domestic manufactures would provide qualitatively appropriate protection as well as generating revenue enabling the payroll (or employment) tax to be lower than it otherwise would have been (for a given net fiscal position). One criterion for designing the initial protective structure might be to approximate as closely as possible the originally distorted price situation. This might, however, require effective protection in excess of 100 per cent to keep value-subtracting activities in business: it might be better to set a limit on effective protection at 100 per cent. Note that, if the main distortion was the underpricing of a domestically produced input, such as energy, the distribution in Figure 4.9 might be bimodal with a cluster of world-price-negative-value-added energy-intensive sectors and another of high value added energy-producing ones. This would change situations considerably.

Whether a temporary employment subsidy or a temporary protective structure, the credibility of the phasing out of the measures suggested in this paper is crucial to their success. Such credibility could be enhanced by international commitments, for example to the IMF, the EC, the General Agreement on Tariffs and Trade (GATT) or indeed other countries in transition. The ratio of benefits to costs of the type of protection considered here is very sensitive to the size of the economy concerned. If several formerly centrally planned economies (CPEs) had suffered similar distortions in the past, and embarked on reform at the same time, they might be amenable to a common temporary external tariff which would not distort trade between them.

If the relevant international bodies would agree, the logic would point to the following type of schemes (for details see Aghion *et al.*, 1992). A CPE just implementing a big bang reform might have a highest protective duty 50 percentage points higher than its projected long-run level. It might also hope to enjoy a 50 per cent abatement of OECD tariffs under the General System of Preferences (GSP). Both of these might be planned to be phased out over ten years. Another country whose big bang had been a year earlier would have a maximum 45 percentage point tariff premium and would enjoy only a 45 per cent GSP abatement from OECD countries and would itself extend a 5 per cent GSP abatement of its tariffs to the country following one year behind it. It is debatable whether such a scheme should be rigidly time-related, as just presented, or should involve measuring each country's position on the spectrum between CPE and market with those closer to CPE imposing import duty premia on those closer to the market at rates reflecting the difference between them. The advantage of the rigid time-based procedure, as long as the dates of respective national big bangs are well defined, is that it does not establish any protectionist incentive to delay progress to the market.

References

Aghion, P., Burgess, R. and Fitoussi, J.P. (1992) 'Towards the Establishment of a Continental European Customs Union', in Flemming, J.S. and Rollo, J.M. (eds) *Trade, Payments and Adjustment in Central and Eastern Europe* (London: Royal Institute of International Affairs) pp. 157–80.

Berg, A. and Sachs, J. (1992) 'Structural Adjustment and International Trade in Eastern Europe – The Case of Poland', *Economic Policy* (14), April.

Burda, M. (1993) 'Unemployment, Labour Markets and Structural Change in Eastern Europe', *Economic Policy*, 16, April, pp. 101–27.

Flemming, J.S. (1976) 'Adjusting the Real Elements in a Changing Economy', *Catch 76*, Occasional paper 47, Institute of Economic Affairs, pp. 9–16.

Flemming, J.S. (1978) 'Aspects of Optimal Unemployment Insurance', *Journal of Public Economics*, vol. 10, pp. 403–25.

Flemming, J.S. (1990) 'Gradualism and Shock Treatment in Tax and Structural Reforms', *Fiscal Studies*, vol. 2, no. 3, pp. 12–26.

Flemming, J.S. and Rollo, J.M. (eds) (1992) *Trade, Payments and Adjustment in Central and Eastern Europe* (London: Royal Institute of International Affairs).

Hughes, G. and Hare, P. (1992) 'Industrial Policy and Restructuring in Eastern Europe', *Oxford Review of Economic Policy*, vol. 8, no.1, pp. 82–134.

McKinnon, R.I. (1991) *The Order of Economic Liberalisation*, (Baltimore, Md.: Johns Hopkins University Press) ch. 12.

Winiecki, E. and Winiecki, J. (1992) *The Structural Legacy of the Soviet-Type Economy* (London: Centre for Research into Communist Economies).

5 The Economics of Workers' Enterprises

Paul R. Kleindorfer
UNIVERSITY OF PENNSYLVANIA

and

Murat R. Sertel
BOĞAZIÇI UNIVERSITY

1 INTRODUCTION

The economics of labour management and producer cooperatives began in earnest with Ward's celebrated paper in 1958 (Ward, 1958). The Wardian theory of the labour-managed firm (LMF) was extended in the early contributions of Domar (1966), Vanek (1970) and Meade (1972) to a general theory of labour-managed industries and economies. A basic characteristic of this literature was the maintained assumption that workers in the LMF would maximize dividend per worker-member, defined as the value added per worker. Thus, the LMF chooses inputs in the long and short run so as to maximize

$$v = \frac{V}{L} = \frac{pY - rK}{L} = \frac{pF(K, L) - rK}{L} \tag{1}$$

where V is value added, L is labour, K is capital and p is the market price for the firm's output $Y = F(K, L)$, r is the rental price of capital, and F is the firm's production function which is assumed to exhibit positive and decreasing marginal products of capital ($\partial F/\partial K$) and labour ($\partial F/\partial L$).

A very robust consequence of the Wardian assumption of dividend maximization is the perverse response of these firms to autonomous upward shifts in price or, in imperfect competition, inverse demand: their employment and output falls in response to such shifts. Moreover the dividend-maximizing LMF exhibits fundamental inefficiencies in that the marginal value product of labour of the LMF exceeds the reservation wage level in the economy and marginal value products are not equalized across firms and industries. In spite of such perverse behaviour, the LMF continued to be an object of keen research interest as economists variously studied the possible advantages of better monitoring, incentive and X-efficiency properties which might arguably result from more closely identifying worker interests with enterprise results.[1] The resulting theory of LMFs and their variants has been summarized in several surveys of the past decade, including those of Ireland and Law (1982), Sertel (1982), Weitzman (1984), Meade (1986), Bonin and Putterman (1987), Drèze (1989) and Bonin *et al.* (1992). A basic feature of this theory is the continuing presence of perverse adjustment to price changes in both input and output markets and resulting inefficiency of the LMF as a form of economic organization.

Results at the industry level have been no more promising. A particularly troubling theoretical result was that of Laffont and Moreaux (1983) who demonstrated that, with firms behaving in the Wardian perverse fashion, the industry may be denied a free entry equilibrium. Hill and Waterson (1983) and Neary (1984) compare the long-run equilibrium numbers of firms for profit-maximizing and labour-managed (that is, Wardian) oligopolies, where no product differentiation is present. Okuguchi (1992a, 1992b) extends these results to a Cournot oligopoly with product differentiation and characterizes the conditions required for such an oligopoly to have a stable equilibrium. When this equilibrium is stable, the traditional perversity and inefficiency of the Wardian LMF carries through to the industry equilibrium.

Taken together, the theory of the Ward–Domar–Vanek LMF yields consistent and robust evidence that this form of enterprise design is fundamentally flawed. However the growing shadow of persistent inefficiency and non-viability of LMFs began to lift when it was demonstrated that certain norms of the LMF were efficient. The key institutional design factor influencing efficiency, as developed in Sertel (1982, 1987a), is that the firm's shares and capital structure be valued and sold to both present and potential future employees competitively. This requirement essentially capped a period of debate begun by Joan Robinson (1967) who questioned whether the perverse short-run behaviour of the Ward–Domar LMF was not, in fact, due simply to the perverse assumption of the Wardian analysis that the LMF could contract and expand at will, possibly laying off or hiring new members even if some of these existing or new members were disadvantaged in the process. This suggestion was taken up positively by Meade (1972) and again by Steinherr and Thisse (1979) who showed that some (but not all) of the perversity of the Ward–Domar–Vanek LMF would disappear if workers were required to agree unanimously *ex ante* on the process by which changes in their membership would be accomplished in response to market conditions. In the Sertel framework, this unanimous agreement is required also to hold *ex post*. Thus, in the Sertel framework, any expansion of the membership roster requires the approval of both the new candidates for worker partnership and the current members, just as contraction of the list necessitates the mutual consent of those who are to leave and those who are to stay. Such consent is open to the usual bargaining with side payments that might be expected in an economic organization, and the resulting price for membership rights may be thought of as equilibrating in a deed market the supply and demand for membership in the LMF. Surprisingly the simple requirement of a competitive market in the deeds or ownership rights for partnership membership translates otherwise inefficient LMFs into efficient workers' enterprises (WEs). Indeed, from the standpoint of the physical input and output of such enterprises, they are in every way equivalent to their profit-maximizing 'twin' (that is, a profit-maximizing firm with the same access to factor markets and the same production technology). In the language of Sertel (1987a), a competitive deed market for membership 'tames' the perverse LMF into an efficient WE. More recent research, reviewed below, has shown that this taming characteristic of the competitive deed market is rather robust and carries over to a multi-period setting and a variety of market imperfections.

In the next section we provide a brief theoretical overview of WEs, contrasting them with LMFs of the Ward–Domar–Vanek type and reviewing the fundamental proposition of their tameness when membership is determined competitively. We note their viability in a mixed economy composed of such WEs, together with similarly endowed profit-maximizing entrepreneurial firms (EFs) of the traditional neoclassical variety. We also review recent theoretical work extending and delimiting these results for a multi-period setting and various market imperfections. In Section 3, we briefly inquire, as in Dow (1993), as to why so few WEs are to be found in practice. We provide several hypotheses in two general areas: (a) internal incentive and transactions cost problems of organizations with strong participatory decision making; and (b) the difficulty of ensuring a competitive membership deed market. In our concluding remarks in Section 4, we mention several open areas of research on WEs, including the issue of how worker-ownership structures of various types might serve as an appropriate vehicle for privatizing businesses in Eastern Europe.

2 WORKERS' ENTERPRISES *v.* 'LABOUR-MANAGED FIRMS'

To grasp the important distinction between a WE and a so-called LMF, it is critical to understand the definition of a WE: *a workers' enterprise (WE) is a firm whose workers and partners coincide.* Normally a firm is managed in the interests of its partners, who have ordinary property rights as owners of the firm. In the 'usual' theory of the LMF, however, this intuitive principle is not applied, so we theorize about a 'firm' whose managers are its workers, so that management is in their interests, but it is unclear who are its owners. Could we interpret this theory as having left this ownership issue flexible and, so, as a general theory which affords of many special cases, one of which is that where the owners are the workers themselves? Unfortunately not, for this theory takes as the *defining* characteristic of a LM 'firm' its maximization of the function v in (1), the per capita (of worker) amount of value added by labour. It is clear that this is inconsistent with the workers being owners of the 'firm', since changing business conditions may very well render a maximum of v at a lower number L of workers today than yesterday, requiring some to be dismissed, which would be impossible if these workers were actually owners. Thus the LMF of the usual theory *cannot* be interpreted as a workers' firm, belonging to its workers. In fact whether there could even be conceived economic agents who could be owners of the LMF has to be answered in the negative, for the maximization of v could only be understood as sensible if the recipients of v were the owners, but we have just seen that this interpretation is also logically blocked. Thus the LMF is an entity which admits of no owners. Having no owners, that is partners, it is somewhat surreal to conceive of the LMF as a 'firm'. Returning to the WE, its defining characteristic unambiguously identifies its roster of owners with that of workers, thus placing it in utter contrast with the unowned LM 'firm'.

Of course, v is the income of the typical worker–partner of a WE, so the firm will not be averse to maximizing v as a function of variables *other than* L, the number of worker–partners. Thus the maximization of $v(K, L)$ as a function of K calls for the first order condition $\partial V/\partial K = 0$, which is the same as the first order condition, $\partial \Pi/\partial K = 0$, for the maximization of profit $\Pi = V - wL$ in an 'entrepreneurial' firm (EF) where labour is hired at a wage w. Hence the WE and its twin EF (equipped with the same production function F and facing the same markets) which we could contemplate in its place would exhibit identical behaviour in adjusting K. In this matter, the behavioural equations of the LMF are no different, and neither is this where the problems with LMFs lie. To illustrate, let us reconsider the well-known perversity of the LMF in the labour market.

In the labour market the ordinary EF adjusts L so as to maximize profit Π, obeying the first order condition $\partial \Pi/\partial L = 0$, that is the equation

$$(p + p'Y)\frac{\partial F}{\partial L} = w \tag{2}$$

where p' stands for $\partial p/\partial Y$ and $Y = F(K, L)$. This dictates behaviour generally disagreeing with that of a LMF maximizing v as a function of L, for the latter requires setting $\partial v/\partial L = 0$; that is,

$$(p + p'Y)\frac{\partial F}{\partial L} = v \tag{3}$$

From equations (2) and (3) and $\Pi = V - wL$, it follows that the marginal value product of labour will exceed the reservation wage w whenever the LMF is profitable. As a result the LMF produces less output with fewer workers than its EF twin.

How does the twin WE behave in the labour market? In fact, the WE does not *hire* labour, so it does not deal in the labour market directly. Instead it procures workers in the form of worker–partners, and this happens in the worker-partnership market (WPM), which serves both as labour market and in a role parallel to that of the stock market for stock companies, in the sense that shares are bought and sold, and the partnership expands and contracts here. So how is it that L is adjusted in a WE? A typical outsider who sells his labour in the ordinary labour market for a wage w facing a WE with L worker–partners where the typical member receives $v(L)$, is willing to pay up to a *demand price* of

$$d(L) = v(L) - w \tag{4}$$

to enter the WE as a member. But the entry of a marginal worker will change the income v of each of the L incumbent members by an amount $\partial v/\partial L$, so the minimal compensation required to obtain the consent of the L incumbents will be

$$s(L) = -L\left(\frac{\partial v}{\partial L}\right) \tag{5}$$

which we term the *supply price* of a share in this WE with L members. So long as $d(L)$ exceeds $s(L)$, we may expect an influx of members, since outsiders will be willing to pay enough to obtain the consent of insiders to their entry, new partnerships being issued and sold to newcomers by the incumbents, and L growing. So long as $s(L)$ exceeds $d(L)$, we may expect an exodus of members, some members' shares being withdrawn by the group of the remaining fellow members, and L shrinking. The *equilibrium* of the WPM is where

$$d(L) = s(L) \tag{6}$$

and this is nothing but the equation $v - w = -L(\partial v/\partial L)$, which we compute by way of

$$\frac{\partial v}{\partial L} = \frac{(p + p'Y)\dfrac{\partial F}{\partial L} - v}{L} \tag{7}$$

to have a right-hand side of

$$-L\left(\frac{\partial v}{\partial L}\right) = v - \left[(p + p'Y)\frac{\partial F}{\partial L}\right] \tag{8}$$

Thus the WPM equilibrium condition that $v - w = -L(\partial v/\partial L)$ turns out to be nothing but, once again, the equilibrium condition (2) of the EF in the labour market.

We see the *equivalence principle* that the WE exhibits exactly the same behaviour in adjusting K and L, and so Y, as its twin EF, so no new microeconomic theory is required to analyze the *physical* economics of an economy with the WEs instead of some or all of the customary EFs. The distribution of welfare will, of course, differ in a WE, for the per worker profit, Π/L, of an EF goes to the typical worker–partner (worker cum entrepreneur, if you wish) in the twin WE, where the typical member earns $v = w + (\Pi/L)$. The equivalence principle established above (by mimicking Sertel, 1982, 1987 and 1991) for a competitive WPM applies whether the firm is a price-taker, in which case set $p' = 0$, or a Cournot competitor. Thus Cournot equilibrium as in a conventional model, along with its existence and other physical properties, is copied intact in an economy with WEs. This goes also for a free entry Cournot equilibrium (Sertel, 1991), in contrast to the non-existence of such equilibria in the case of an industry populated by LMFs (Laffont and Moreaux, 1983). A similar analysis by Sertel (1990) in a price-setting model establishes parallel results for Bertrand equilibrium.

It is interesting to represent the dynamic adjustment of the WE toward the equilibrium (6) through a bargaining-theoretic framework for out-of-equilibrium adjustment. We sketch the basic idea here for the case where profits are positive ($v > w$) and where the current workforce level is L_0 with $d(L_0) > s(L_0)$, so that L_0 is lower than the efficient level. A similar logic applies for the case where profits are negative or where the current workforce level is higher than is efficient.

In the present case (where $d(L_0) > s(L_0)$), we may imagine a group of potential worker partners of size $\Delta > 0$ requesting membership rights in the WE. Before they join the WE, every worker–partner in the workforce of size L_0 is earning an income v_0, and after they join every worker–partner in the workforce of size $L_1 = L_0 + \Delta$ is earning v_1, with v_0 and v_1 given by

$$v_i = \frac{pF_i - rK_i}{L_i} \qquad i = 0, 1 \tag{9}$$

We can imagine representatives of the Δ potential new partners bargaining with the current L_0 partners over the price/payment for membership rights. One representation of the outcome of this bargaining process would be the Nash bargaining solution with side payments, which would be the solution to the following generalized Nash product:

$$\underset{d \,\geqslant\, 0}{\text{Maximize}} \left[\left(v_1 + \frac{d\Delta}{L_0} - v_0 \right)^{L_0} (v_1 - d - w)^{\Delta} \right] \tag{10}$$

where d is the deed price paid by each of the Δ new members to the existing L_0 worker–partners.

The interpretation of (10) is the following. If agreement is reached and the Δ new members join at deed price d, then each of the current L_0 members will enjoy an income per period of $v_1 + d\Delta/L_0$, since the total income from new deeds will be $d\Delta$, which must be split among the L_0 initial partners. If they do not come to agreement, then the default option has value of v_0 for the original membership. In similar fashion, the income per period of a new member is clearly just $v_1 - d$, and the default payment for the new members is just the going wage rate w.

Now, using the assumption that $v_0 > w$, it is straightforward to show that the Nash bargaining solution to (10) involves co-operation when $d(L_0) > s(L_0)$; that is, there are gains to trade from having the Δ new partners join the WE. Indeed the noted gains to trade do not all go to the current partners, but are split at the solution to (10) according to the following:

$$d^*(\Delta) = \frac{L_0}{L_1}(v_0 - w) = \frac{L_0}{L_0 + \Delta}(v_0 - w) \tag{11}$$

Note finally from (10) that the surplus generated at the Nash bargaining solution for each of the L_0 initial partners is just

$$\Gamma(\Delta) = v_1(\Delta) + \frac{d^*(\Delta)\,\Delta}{L_0} - v_0 \tag{12}$$

where $v_1(\Delta)$ is given in (9) with $L_1 = L_0 + \Delta$ and $d^*(\Delta)$ is given in (11). It is straightforward to show that $\Gamma(\Delta)$ is positive precisely until the equilibrium point (6) is attained, so that there will be a continuing incentive for the current partners to hire new partners until (6) is achieved.

We have illustrated the bargaining adjustment process for the case where the initial workforce is too small. A similar logic would apply in the case where the initial workforce was too large (that is, $d(L_0) < s(L_0)$), except here the initial workforce would find it desirable to pay some of its membership to take jobs in the external labour market, with gains to trade continuing until the equilibrium condition (6) was obtained.

Clearly the above bargaining model of the dynamics of WPM

adjustment is but one interpretation of the way the incentive and behavioural aspects of adjustment in the WPM might occur. In particular, the same general characteristics of movement towards the efficient equilibrium (6) would result with other bargaining solution concepts than Nash.[2] All that would change would be the division of the gains to trade between present and future worker–partners. We leave the further study of these matters to future research.

All of the above analysis is based on the assumption that the WPM is resolved competitively, in the sense that a constant reservation wage is given. An interesting alternative is where the alternative wage rate is specified by a $w(L)$ schedule which rises as a function of the size L of the WE. In this case the analysis depends on the exact charter of the WE. In particular, as shown in Fehr and Sertel (1991) and Fehr (1993a, 1993b), it matters whether new members are admitted sequentially and the incumbents can act as a discriminatory monopoly in selling new membership shares, or only a simple monopoly position is enjoyed by the WE in its WPM. The first of these cases is called a (sequentially) discriminating WE (DWE) and is to be compared with the twin EF which is in a discriminatory monopsony position in its labour market. In the (sequentially) non-discriminating WE (NDWE), on the other hand, members are admitted *en bloc* at a uniform deed price, the highest deed price which the last to be admitted is willing to pay. All the proceeds from the sale of the deeds go to the initial incumbents, the newcomers receiving only their share in the firm's value added by labour. The NDWE, enjoying a simple monopoly position in the WPM is interesting to compare with its twin EF which enjoys a monopsony position in the labour market. While they are both inefficient, employing too little labour, the NDWE is less inefficient, employing more labour that its EF twin. Fehr and Sertel (1991) show a further interesting feature of the NDWE to be that it iterates toward the same efficient size as the DWE. The logic of this iterative process is similar to that embodied in the bargaining solution convergence noted in (10)–(12) above, with newcomers continuing to pay a lower deed price (which is then shared among the growing current membership) until efficient membership size is attained, that is until (6) is satisfiied.

Fehr and Sertel's conclusions can be summarized as follows:

Membership deed market

Perfect competition
Flat supply curve for labour

Imperfect competition
Upward-sloping supply curve for labour

DWE	WE employs the same efficient amount of labour as its EF twin	WE employs the same efficient amount of labour as its EF twin
NDWE	WE employs the same efficient amount of labour as its EF twin	WE employs more labour and is less inefficient than its EF twin, and the WE iterates toward the efficient DWE size

The above results have also been examined for cases in which membership deeds are provided at different prices to workers of different qualifications (see Kleindorfer and Sertel, 1982; Fehr, 1993b). The basic equivalence principle of Sertel (1982, 1987a), as sketched above, is robust to this extension.

A further important extension of the Sertel work on membership deed markets concerns optimal investment and growth of WEs. A good summary of recent work is Fehr (1993a). He notes that when new members are not required to pay a membership fee upon joining the WE, there will be under-investment by the WE. If new members pay nothing to join a profitable firm, this is tantamount to expropriation of initial members by new members which gives rise to a disincentive to invest. This is in addition to the underinvestment effect traditionally attributed to the LMF through the anticipated finiteness of tenure of members who cannot fully appropriate the cash flow results of internal investment (see Furubotn, 1976; Jensen and Meckling, 1979).

A fundamental question suggested by this result is whether a properly functioning deed market will enable the WE to achieve efficient dynamic investment. This was answered in the affirmative by Dow (1986, 1993), for a special form of WE. In the Dow framework, WEs or EFs operate over an infinite horizon and use the same fixed-proportions (that is, Leontief) production technology. In each (discrete) period, both firms determine operating and output decisions, taking capital as given. Both firms must make labour hiring decisions in each period before observing a random shock. Because the EF is obliged to pay a fixed wage to each employee, whatever random shock obtains, while the WE can absorb shocks by reducing *ex post* payments to worker–members, the EF chooses an inefficiently low static output level and labour force in each period, while the WE's labour input choices are first best. The choice behaviour of either EF or WE firms gives rise to stochastic dividends π_t per unit of capital in each period t and these have higher expected value for the WE than for the EF, for the reason just noted. The choice of capital stock K_t in each period is determined for both EFs and WEs from the solution to a problem of the following general form:

$$\text{Maximize}_{\{g_0,\, g_1 \ldots\}} \quad E \left\{ \sum_{t=0}^{\infty} \rho^t [\pi_t - I(g_t)] K_t \right\} \tag{13}$$

subject to

$$K_{t+1} = g_t K_t, \; \forall t \tag{14}$$

where the initial capital stock K_0 is given and ρ is the discount factor, which is assumed to be determined accurately from the market interest rate r. In (13), $I(g_t)$ is investment expenditure in period t. Assuming stationarity of demand, cost and exogenous random shocks, the π_t are independently and identically distributed random variables which are the result of operating and output choices of the firm in period t. Denoting their expected values for the WE and EF firm respectively by π_L and π_K. we have noted above that $\pi_K < \pi_L = \pi^*$, where π^* is the socially optimal per unit return to capital. The choice variable g_t is called the growth policy of the firm in period t. In Dow it is assumed that $I(g)$ is of the quadratic form $I(g) = a(g - \gamma)^2$, where $a > 0$ and $0 < \gamma < 1$, the latter condition ensuring that if $I(g) = 0$ then K_t converges to zero.

The central issue raised by Dow is whether EFs, whose partners are rewarded by the discounted stream of dividend payments π_t, are relatively more efficient in their choice of growth policy than their WE twins. In the comparison, the following are the determining factors. The EF discounts future returns correctly (that is, determines the returns from investments $I(g)$ according to the prevailing market interest rate), but makes inefficient static output choices (because it must pay a fixed wage to its labour force and absorb the consequences of random shocks); that is, $\pi_K < \pi^*$. A traditional LMF, on the other hand, makes efficient static output choices ($\pi_L = \pi^*$) but, because its members are assumed to have finite tenure with the firm, they adopt a higher effective discount rate and underinvest. If these same LMFs are converted to WEs with a properly functioning deed market, so that departing members are fully compensated for the value of the firm their past efforts have helped to determine, then the first-best growth policy is adopted by the WE. Members of the WE are able to appropriate fully the benefits of their investments upon departure. Based on this logic, Dow shows the dominance of WEs over traditional EFs. The logic of this demonstration points to a number of caveats about the robustness of this result. First, Dow's model assumes risk-neutrality by workers and capitalists alike. Second, Dow assumes equal access to the capital market by both EFs and WEs, so that differential credit rationing as in Gintis (1989) is not present. Most importantly it is assumed that all information (on firm technologies and profit possibilities) and available market returns are commonly held by all participants, so that the membership deed market functions under complete information. Economic policy could have an important role in making some of these assumptions credible, but they clearly delimit when one might expect WEs to provide a larger welfare cake than EFs. They may also provide some hints on why so few WE-like organizations are seen in practice, a point to which we return.

In the Dow approach, the deed market for the WE is assumed to equilibrate at the beginning of each period, with new members being attracted or retired as needed. Chiarella (1989) takes a similar approach in a deterministic setting. Okuguchi (1992c), on the other hand, provides a dynamic adjustment model for the deed market which allows for the deed market to be out of equilibrium. The Okuguchi (1992c) model considers an oligopoly with n WEs, with and without product differentiation, and derives sufficient conditions for the resulting Cournot equilibrium to be globally stable. Okuguchi's dynamic adjustment model describes the size of the labour force $L_i(t)$ in the ith firm in the oligopoly at time t through the differential equation:

$$\frac{dL_i}{dt} = \alpha_i[d_i(L) - s_i(L)] = \alpha_i\left[\frac{\partial V_i}{\partial L_i} - w\right] \tag{15}$$

where d_i and s_i correspond to the demand and supply price for membership deeds, as developed in equations (4) and (5), and where the α_i are positive constants.[3] The sufficient conditions derived by Okuguchi for stability (essentially resulting from the stability of the Jacobian of the dynamic system (15)), of the WE oligopoly are similar, but not identical, to those required for stability in the usual EF oligopoly. While they do not appear to be more or less onerous for the WE oligopoly than for the EF oligopoly, it is not known whether there is a relationship between the two sets of stability conditions. Note in any case that the equivalence principle implies that the resulting equilibrium, whether or not it is stable, is precisely the same as would result if some or all of the firms in the oligopoly were EFs and not WEs.

As observed above, constraining the deed price to zero (or to anything less than $s(L) = -L(\partial v/\partial L)$, the aggregate decremental value of the firm per worker resulting from an additional worker) robs incumbent members for future ones, and hence gives the incumbents deficient incentives to invest in the future of the firm. One might conjecture that WEs with functioning WPMs which set deed prices properly would achieve efficiency in an overlapping generations (OLG) economy. The Dow (1993) results, noted above, support this conjecture, but Dow's model of worker tenure is rather simple, and assumes that a fixed proportion (β) of workers in the WE leave in each period, with β determined exogenously to the modelling framework. More complex OLG models have been developed by Chiarella (1989) and Tutuncu (1992a, 1992b) who provide preliminary results also supporting the noted efficiency conjecture, but no general proof has yet emerged on this question.

3   ARE WORKERS' ENTERPRISES VIABLE IN A MIXED WE–EF ECONOMY?

The above review of theory raises a very basic question concerning the viability of WEs and EFs in an economy where both enterprise governance structures are possible. On the one hand, there is mounting empirical and theoretical evidence (Defourney *et al.*, 1985; Estrin *et al.*, 1987; Fitzroy and Kraft, 1987 and 1991; and Blinder, 1990) that profit sharing and participatory management of the sort envisaged in WEs have beneficial efficiency consequences. On the other hand, there is the continuing paradox of pure WEs being so rare in practice. We attempt here to summarize the current state of the debate on this point. First, we review a number of problems of WEs, based on the assumptions required for the efficiency arguments traced above. Second, we consider appropriate policy which would promote the development and entry of WEs in markets and industries where the WE form is efficient.

The problems facing a WE governance structure which might help explain the relative paucity of WEs in practice can be classified into two major areas:

(a) problems relating to the production and transactions cost efficiency of co-operative decision making;

(b) problems relating to the functioning of the deed market and access to capital markets.

Concerning (a), informed co-operation is not costless, especially in larger organizations (see Bös and Peters, 1991; Kleindorfer *et al.*, 1993, ch. 7). If the personnel of an enterprise could costlessly act co-operatively, it is easy to demonstrate that their collective behaviour would dominate, in both output and welfare terms, the corresponding behaviour of a non-co-operative organization.[4] However, there may be significant transactions costs in achieving cooperative and informed behaviour by all enterprise participants. Moreover these costs will tend to increase quickly as the size and technological complexity of the organizations increase. Thus, while employee ownership and profit sharing have been found to contribute to a firm's productivity and quality,[5] larger and more complex organizations tend to be managed hierarchically. And once hierarchical management is adopted, firms have tended to develop in the EF form and not the WE form of ownership. If we adopt a 'survival of the fittest' hypothesis (for example, Williamson, 1985) the prevalence of the EF form of organization in practice is consistent with the hypothesis of high transactions costs of achieving informed consensus and co-operation, especially in large and complex organizations.

Concerning (b), Fehr (1993a) and Gintis (1989) summarize the arguments as to why membership markets tend to be imperfect and/or difficult to establish. The most important of these reasons is that the deed market may be illiquid and informationally inefficient. Related to these issues, doubts of potential members as to whether the deed price reflects true expected returns to membership may make them reluctant to trade in the deed market. For reasons of moral hazard and informational complexity, suitable insurance to protect risk-averse workers from negative outcomes in their WEs is not likely to be available.[6] Normally protection against industry-specific shocks would be provided by diversification through the capital market, but this is clearly diluted if a worker has substantial holdings in a WE.[7] A problem specific to the transition phase of emerging market economies is the absence of a competitive capital market to determine the price of capital, an important determinant of the equilibrium deed price.

Returning to the question announced in the title of this section, the answer in theory is certainly 'Yes'. As reviewed in Section 2, WEs exhibit identical physical and market behaviour to EFs. Only internal income distribution is different. Thus WEs (but not LMFs) can and should compete as alternative governance structures with EFs. When they are more efficient than their EF counterparts, they will dominate. In view of the above discussion on the problems facing WEs, it is perhaps not surprising that most existing WEs have tended to be concentrated in small to medium-sized firms, where the incentive effects of ownership are strong and the returns to co-operative behaviour relatively large. This may be the result of the transactions cost and informational issues raised above. In any case a very central feature required to promote competitive viability and efficiency of the WE governance structure is a functioning membership deed market. For such a market to exist several policy measures are critical. Foremost are accounting and banking standards to ensure that prospective worker–partners can assess the value of ownership of a WE (defined in the usual growth and cash flow terms), assisting a prospective member to evaluate the reasonableness of a given deed price and departing members to evaluate the value of their deed. Furthermore worker–partners must have a clear understanding of how and when they can redeem their shares should they wish to leave the WE for employment elsewhere. While these problems are no different in principle from those of equity trading in developed capital markets or in employee stock option plans, they take on special importance in the context of WEs, as they are the driving force for the efficiency of such enterprises.

4 CONCLUSIONS

There seem to be two competing trends now emerging in organizational design and worker remuneration worldwide. On the one side are attempts to imbue in employees a stronger sense of co-operative, team behaviour and alignment with enterprise objectives. On the other side are the ever-present transactions costs of promoting co-operative discourse and consensus. In the evolving resolution of the tension between these two trends, worker ownership, either partial or whole, together with continuing professional management, is emerging as a useful middle ground to promoting incentive alignment and efficient organizational decision making.

In this regard, WEs are at one end of the spectrum of employee ownership, where every worker in a firm is a complete partner. On the other end of the spectrum are EFs in which only external capital providers are owners. In the middle of this spectrum are various forms of profit sharing, employee stock option plans and employee ownership. We have noted for WEs the essential ingredients to ensure efficient operation. These are, unsurprisingly, that worker–partners must be true owners in that their property rights to the usufruct of their productive activity should be appropriable and tradeable by these same worker–partners. This requirement is reminiscent of the celebrated Coase Theorem in indicating that it is less important for efficiency who is assigned property rights to the resources of an economy. What is critical is that all resources be assigned to someone and that all property rights be tradeable. The fact that WEs in which worker–partners own the property rights rather than external capital holders are just as efficient as EFs should therefore not be very surprising to today's economists. An interesting open question is the extent to which various other forms of ownership along the spectrum just indicated will also turn out to be efficient, both theoretically and in practice. A second and related open question is the theory of mergers and acquisition by and of WEs, EFs and other mixed forms of worker–entrepreneurial ownership. These issues of mixed ownership structure are likely to be especially important in the transition by way of privatization now occurring in Eastern Europe. There one can expect smaller firms to be at least partially privatized into the hands of current workers. Larger firms will require additional capital from the outside (either from the government or from external investors). In either case both pure and mixed forms of WEs will probably evolve in some sectors. Given the theory reviewed in this paper, it will be of considerable interest to trace the formation, evolution and viability of these WEs in the transition economies of Eastern Europe.

Notes

1. In related work by Weitzman (1984) and Meade (1986), it was also argued that the problem of absorbing macroeconomic shocks could be ameliorated by having worker remuneration based more on profit sharing and less on fixed wages. If a fixed portion of profits is distributed to labour, and each worker shares (not necessarily equally) in this 'wage fund', then the typical worker's income would be proportional to the dividend v in (1). Of course, in a capitalist-run sharing firm, this would not imply the maximization of (1) as an enterprise objective, but (1) nonetheless

becomes an important constraint in attracting labour from the market. In consequence some of the problems of the Wardian LMF turn out to be inherited by the Weitzman–Meade theory of the 'share economy' (see Sertel, 1987b).

2. Note that bargaining solutions have the malady of being manipulable by pre-donations, as noted in Sertel (1992). However we conjecture that the basic conclusion drawn here will be unaffected by this 'malady' in that (we conjecture) bargaining solutions, manipulated by pre-donations or not, will continue to reflect attainable surpluses from movements toward the equilibrium solution (6).

3. Note that d_i and s_i depend on the entire vector of industry employment levels $L(t) = (L_1(t), \ldots, L_n(t))$ of the, say, n firms in the oligopoly, since prevailing price (and therefore each firm's dividend v_i) will depend on total industry output. Thus the differential equations (15) must be solved as a system to determine global stability of the equilibrium point where $d_i(L) = s_i(L)$ for all i.

4. Various forms of co-operative and non-co-operative WEs in competition with EFs are modelled explicitly in Sertel (1982). For an empirical discussion of incentive and transactions cost issues, see Fitzroy and Kraft (1987, 1991). For a related discussion, see Holmstrom (1982) and Kleindorfer *et al.* (1993, ch. 7) who demonstrate that non-co-operative enterprise design cannot guarantee in general a first-best outcome, whereas co-operative design, for example as modelled by the outcome of a complete information bargaining process, can guarantee first-best results.

5. Indeed considerable attention has been devoted in the recent management literature to the issue of worker empowerment in order to promote productivity and quality. The empirical evidence – see, for example, Blinder (1990), Fitzroy and Kraft (1991), Kleindorfer *et al.* (1993) – has been broadly supportive of the intuitive conjecture that profit sharing, for example, through employee stock option plans, is a strong motivator for workers to undertake the steps necessary to make empowerment and participation programmes work. Many global companies (for example, Pepsi Cola, Avis, United Parcel Service and Promon) have programmes of this sort, ranging from extensive stock option plans (as in Pepsi Cola) to complete employee ownership (as in Avis, Promon and United Parcel Service).

6. See, however, Sertel and Steinherr (1984) for a simple solution to some aspects of moral hazard in WEs related to bankruptcy.

7. However it should be noted that producer co-operatives such as WEs may have important risk-sharing features which make them better able to absorb economic shocks than traditional EFs. This point was asserted strongly by Weitzman (1984). The evidence is reviewed in Bonin *et al.*, (1992). See also Bradley and Gelb (1987) who describe the additional features present in the Mondragon WEs (employing about 20 000 workers at this point) where the entire Mondragon co-operative sector, which is quite a diverse group of business activities, acts with the assistance of the Mondragon Co-operative Bank to provide smoothing, retraining and general insurance against industry-specific shocks.

References

Blinder, A.S. (1990) *Paying for Productivity: A Look at the Evidence*, (Washington, DC: Brookings Institution).

Bonin, J.P., Jones, D.C. and Putterman, L. (1992) 'Theoretical and Empirical Studies of Producer Cooperatives: Will Ever the Twain Meet?', working paper, Wesleyan University, Middletown, Conn., July.

Bonin, J.P. and Putterman, L. (1987) *Economics of Cooperation and the Labour-Managed Economy*, Fundamentals of Pure and Applied Economics, No. 14 (London: Harwood Academic Publishers).

Bös, D. and Peters, W. (1991) 'When Employees Free Ride: A Theory of Inefficiency', Discussion Paper A–327, SFB 303, Rheinische Friedrich-Wilhelms-Universität, Bonn, May.

Bradley, K. and Gelb, A. (1987) 'Cooperative Labour Relations: Mondragon's Response to Recession', *British Journal of Industrial Relations*, vol. 25, no. 1, pp. 77–99.

Chiarella, C. (1989) 'The Dynamic Behavior of Workers' Enterprises', *European Journal of Political Economy*, vol. 5, pp. 317–31.

Defourney, J., Estrin, S. and Jones, D.C. (1985) 'The Effects of Workers' Participation on Enterprise Performance', *International Journal of Industrial Organization*, vol. 3, pp. 197–217.

Domar, E.D. (1966) 'The Soviet Collective Farm as a Producers' Cooperative', *American Economic Review*, vol. 56, no. 4, pp. 734–57.

Dow, G.K. (1986) 'Control Rights, Competitive Markets, and the Labor Management Debate', *Journal of Comparative Economics*, vol. 10, pp. 48–61.

Dow, G.K. (1993) 'Democracy versus Appropriability: Can Labour-Managed Firms Flourish in a Capitalist World?', in Bowles, S., Gintis, H. and Gustafsson, B. (eds) *Democracy and Markets – Problems of Participation, Accountability and Efficiency* (Cambridge: Cambridge University Press).

Drèze, J.H. (1989) *Labour Management, Contracts and Capital Markets – A General Equilibrium Approach* (Oxford: Basil Blackwell).

Estrin, S., Jones, D.C. and Svejnar, J. (1987) 'The Productivity Effects of Worker Participation: Producer Cooperatives in Western Economies', *Journal of Comparative Economics*, vol. 11, pp. 40–61.

Fehr, E. (1993a) 'Labour-Management', in Duelfer, E. (ed.) *International Handbook of Co-operative Organizations* (Goettingen: Vandenhoeck and Ruprecht).

Fehr, E.S. (1993b) 'The Simple Analytics of a Membership Market in a Labour-Managed Economy', in Bowles, S., Gintis, H. and Gustafsson, B. (eds) *Democracy and Markets – Problems of Participation, Accountability and Efficiency* (Cambridge: Cambridge University Press).

Fehr, E. and Sertel, M.R. (1991) 'Two Forms of Workers' Enterprises Facing Imperfect Labor Markets', working paper, Boğaziçi University, Istanbul and (1993) *Economics Letters*.

Fitzroy, F.R. and Kraft, K. (1987) 'Co-operation, Productivity and Profit Sharing', *Quarterly Journal of Economics*, vol. 102, pp. 23–36.

Fitzroy, F.R. and Kraft, K. (1991) 'On the Choice of Incentives in Firms', Discussion Paper No. 9106, Department of Economics, University of St Andrews, Scotland.

Furubotn, E.G. (1976) 'The Long-run Analysis of the Labor-Managed Firm: An Alternative Interpretation', *American Economic Review*, vol. 66, no. 1, pp. 104–24.

Gintis, H. (1989) 'Financial Markets and the Political Structure of the Enterprise', *Journal of Economic Behavior and Organization*, vol. 11, pp. 311–22.

Hill, M. and Waterson, M. (1983) 'Labor-Managed Cournot Oligopoly and Industry Output', *Journal of Comparative Economics*, vol. 7, pp. 43–51.

Holmstrom, B. (1982) 'Moral Hazard in Teams', *Bell Journal of Economics*, vol. 13, pp. 324–40.

Ireland, N.J. and Law, P.J. (1982) *The Economics of Labor-Managed Enterprises*, (New York: St Martin's Press).

Jensen, M. and Meckling, W. (1979) 'Rights and Production Functions: An Application to Labor-Managed Firms and Codetermination', *Journal of Business*, vol. 52, pp. 469–506.

Kleindorfer, P.R., Kunreuther, H.C. and Schoemaker, P.S. (1993) *Decision Sciences: An Integrative Perspective* (Cambridge: Cambridge University Press).

Kleindorfer, P.R. and Sertel, M.R. (1982) 'Value-Added Sharing Enterprises', in Sertel (1982), ch. 9.

Laffont, J.-J. and Moreaux, M. (1983) 'The Nonexistence of a Free Entry Cournot Equilibrium in Labor-Managed Economies', *Econometrica*, vol. 51, pp. 455–62.

Meade, J.E. (1972) 'The Theory of Labour-Managed Firms and of Profit Sharing', *Economic Journal*, vol. 82, March (Supplement), pp. 402–28.

Meade, J.E. (1986) *Alternative Systems of Business Organization and of Workers' Remuneration* (London: Allen & Unwin).

Neary, H.M. (1984) 'Labor-Managed Cournot Oligopoly and Industry Output: A Comment', *Journal of Comparative Economics*, vol. 8, pp. 322–7.

Okuguchi, K. (1992a) 'Labor-Managed Cournot Oligopoly with Product Differentiation', mimeo., Department of Economics, Tokyo Metropolitan University and *Journal of Economics*, vol. 56, pp. 197–210.

Okuguchi, K. (1992b) 'Comparative Statics for Profit-Maximizing and Labor-Managed Cournot Oligopolies', mimeo, Department of Economics, Tokyo Metropolitan University.

Okuguchi, K. (1992c) 'Oligopoly with Workers' Enterprises: A Dynamic Analysis', mimeo., Department of Economics, Tokyo Metropolitan University.

Robinson, J. (1967) 'The Soviet Collective Farm as a Producer Cooperative: Comment', *American Economic Review*, vol. 57, pp. 222–3.

Sertel, M.R. (1982) *Workers and Incentives* (Amsterdam: North-Holland).

Sertel, M.R. (1987a) 'Workers' Enterprises Are Not Perverse', *European Economic Review*, vol. 31, pp. 1619–25.

Sertel, M.R. (1987b) 'On Conquering Stagflation', *Economic Analysis and Workers' Management*, vol. 21, pp. 433–41.

Sertel, M.R. (1990) 'Workers' Enterprises in Price Competition', Working Paper ISS/EC 90–09, Boğaziçi University, *Managerial and Decision Economics*. Istanbul; and (1993).

Sertel, M.R. (1991) 'Workers' Enterprises in Imperfect Competition', *Journal of Comparative Economics*, vol. 15, pp. 698–710.

Sertel, M.R. (1992) 'The Nash Bargaining Solution Manipulated by Pre-Donation is Talmudic', *Economics Letters*, vol. 40, pp. 45–56.

Sertel, M.R. and Steinherr, A. (1984) 'Information, Incentives, and the Design of Efficient Institutions', *Zeitschrift für die gesamte Staatswissenschaft*, vol. 140, pp. 233–48.

Steinherr, A. and Thisse, J.-F. (1979) 'Are Labor-Managers Really Perverse?', *Economics Letters*, vol. 2, no. 2, pp. 137–42.

Tutuncu, M.M. (1992a) 'An Infinite-Horizon Workers' Enterprise with Finitely-Lived Members of Different Ages', working paper, Pitzer College, Claremont, CA.

Tutuncu, M.M. (1992b) 'An Overlapping Generations Economy with Workers' Enterprises', working paper, Pitzer College, Claremont, CA.

Vanek, J. (1970) *The General Theory of Labor-Managed Economies* (Ithaca, NY: Cornell University Press).

Ward, B.N. (1958) 'The Firm in Illyria: Market Syndicalism', *American Economic Review*, vol. 48, pp. 566–89.

Weitzman, M.L. (1984) *The Share Economy* (Cambridge, Mass.: Harvard University Press).

Williamson, O.E. (1985) *The Economic Institutions of Capitalism* (New York: Free Press).

6 Public Expenditure and Tax Policy for Economic Development

Christopher J. Heady
UNIVERSITY OF BATH

1 INTRODUCTION

The purpose of this paper is to provide a survey of some aspects of public finance for developing countries. This implies that the subject is somehow different from public finance as it is applied to developed capitalist economies or the emerging market economies of central and Eastern Europe. As somebody who has worked on public finance issues in developing countries and in both the United Kingdom and Czechoslovakia, my view is that the same basic methods of analysis are applicable to questions of public finance in all countries. The special features of public finance for developing countries arise from two factors: their recent economic history and their special institutional structures. This paper will concentrate on these special features, but that should not obscure the similarities in general approach.

It is important to realize that recent economic history and special institutional structures are not the same for all developing countries. The World Development Report (World Bank, 1991a) provides basic data on 99 low- and middle-income countries from four continents. These are the countries that are generally regarded as being 'developing countries'. The gross national product (GNP) per capita for these countries ranges from US$80 to US$5350 with per capita growth rates ranging from −3 per cent to +8.5 per cent, while life expectancy at birth ranges from 42 years to 77 years. The structures of these economies also vary widely, with the share of agriculture in GDP varying from 3 per cent to 67 per cent and the share of manufacturing varying from 3 per cent to 35 per cent. The characteristics of their public finances are similarly diverse: the share of central government expenditure in GNP varies from 5.3 per cent to 58.6 per cent, while the central government overall position ranges from a deficit of 14.9

per cent of GNP to a surplus of 27.1 per cent of GNP.

This diversity of experience and structure means that there can be no single 'public finance of developing countries': the special factors will be different in different countries. No survey can provide a definitive account of the field. Instead we must be content with the consideration of a number of public finance issues that can occur in developing countries, always remembering that there will be some countries to which they do not apply.

The issues that will be addressed in this paper are the size and composition of public expenditure and tax policy. These are issues that have been major policy concerns in a large number of developing countries over the last ten or fifteen years. Often, but not always, they have arisen in the context of 'structural adjustment' programmes that have been implemented with the encouragement of the International Monetary Fund (IMF) and the World Bank. Section 2 therefore discusses the nature of structural adjustment. Section 3 discusses public expenditure and Section 4 discusses tax policy. Throughout the paper will contain a mixture of descriptive material and relevant theory. However there have been few recent theoretical advances in the theory of public expenditure in developing countries, while there is a substantial theoretical literature on tax policy. This difference will be reflected in the way the different topics are presented.

2 STRUCTURAL ADJUSTMENT

Structural adjustment programmes have been so widespread over the last fifteen years that it is impossible to think of public finance issues of development without considering their impact. Cornia, Jolly and Stewart (1987, p. 49) provide data on the number of countries initiating IMF-supported programmes: 'During the 1970s this number averaged about 10 per year, increasing to 28 in 1980, 31 in 1981, 19 in 1982, 33 in 1983, 20 in 1984 and about 26 in 1985. On average, every year from 1980 to 1985 there were 47 countries with IMF programmes.'

For many countries the structural adjustment programmes have arisen out of economic crises, normally involving substantial government budget deficits and balance of payments difficulties. In these circumstances the government will approach the IMF and possibly the World Bank to request loans. The loans that are granted are subject to the government's following particular economic policies that are expected to correct the major imbalances in the economy. It is this set of economic policies that constitutes the structural adjustment programme.

Most programmes involve two distinct components. The first is the stabilization phase, in which the imbalances are dealt with by reductions in expenditure. This is usually achieved by reductions in government expenditure and controls on credit creation. The second is the structural adjustment phase, in which the basic structure of the economy is altered in an attempt to improve the long-term performance of the economy. This second phase, the real structural adjustment, can itself often be divided into two parts: (a) policies to increase the supply of tradeable goods (both exports and import substitutes) and (b) policies to reduce government intervention and improve efficiency in the economy as a whole.

No two countries have had exactly the same experience of structural adjustment and it is not appropriate to provide a complete catalogue of experiences. Instead I will attempt to provide some idea of what is involved in structural adjustment by taking the experience of one country, Côte d'Ivoire, as an example. A more detailed account of Côte d'Ivoire's experience is provided by Blundell, Heady and Medhora (1992). The origins of the economic crisis in Côte d'Ivoire can be traced to the coffee and cocoa boom of 1975–7. This boom generated substantial government revenue that was used to finance increases in public expenditure, particularly investment. After the boom ended, the expenditure was sustained by foreign borrowing. In some respects, this policy was a substantial success: industrial production rose markedly and real GDP increased by 40 per cent between 1975 and 1981. However the policy involved running a budget deficit and a current account deficit on the balance of payments. At the same time inflation in Côte d'Ivoire was more rapid than in its main trading partners. This had a serious effect on the balance of payments because Côte d'Ivoire is part of the franc zone and so is unable to devalue its currency unilaterally.

The situation became unsustainable in 1980 when the current account balance of payments deficit reached 17.4 per cent of GDP and the budget deficit had risen to 11.9 per cent of GDP. The government of Côte d'Ivoire sought World Bank assistance and received Structural Adjustment Loans in 1981, 1983 and 1986. The main condition on these loans was the introduction of a structural adjustment programme, which started in 1981. The stabilization phase took the form of reductions in public investment and credit availability, together with a freeze on public sector pay and minimum wages. The reduction in public investment was substantial: from 11.6 per cent of GDP in 1980 to 3.2 per cent in 1985. By 1985 the budget deficit and the current account balance of payments deficit had both been eliminated, but this improvement was bought at considerable cost: per capita GDP had fallen by 26.2 per cent.

The structural adjustment phase started in 1985. As mentioned above there are usually two components to this phase. The policy most often used to stimulate the production of tradeables is devaluation. This could not be used in Côte d'Ivoire because of its membership of the franc zone, and so a combination of import duties and export subsidies was used to mimic a devaluation. In addition there was an attempt to move resources into the production of (mainly tradeable) agricultural goods by holding down urban wages. Policies to improve the overall efficiency of the economy included a move towards a more uniform pattern of trade protection and a reduction of subsidies to the inefficient sectors of the economy, particularly state-owned enterprises.

The attempt to mimic devaluation was not a success, partly because of administrative and budgetary difficulties in paying the export subsidies and partly because the franc appreciated against the US dollar, offsetting the mimicked devaluation. However the attempt to move resources into agriculture met with some success: there is evidence that labour moved from urban areas to rural areas. The attempts to improve the overall efficiency of the economy were also partially successful: the losses of public enterprises were reduced and the move to a more uniform pattern of trade protection was accompanied by a transfer of resources away from those industries that had previously been most heavily protected. However there is also evidence that the restructuring of the economy was held back by the severe shortage of credit that had resulted from the stabilization policies.

It is difficult to evaluate the success of structural adjustment in Côte d'Ivoire, as in all other countries that have applied similar policies. The immediate impact has been to depress living standards, which has caused serious hardship for the poor, but there is some evidence of improved efficiency in the economy and there is always the point that the government could not have maintained its level of expenditure even if it had not needed to comply with World Bank conditionality, so not all of the reduction in living standards can be blamed on the programme. Nonetheless it was hoped that the improved efficiency would have translated into higher growth and that hope has not yet been realized, at least in part because of a collapse in world cocoa prices in the late 1980s.

The experience of Côte d'Ivoire illustrates the importance of public expenditure as a determinant of the level of economic activity in many developing countries. It also illustrates another aspect of economic policy that has dominated thinking recently in many developing countries: the attempt to reduce the role of the government and allow market forces to act properly. In the case of Côte d'Ivoire that involved making trade taxes more uniform, but in many countries it has extended to considering reforms of all aspects of taxation. Sections 3 and 4 therefore look more closely at public expenditure and tax policy.

3 PUBLIC EXPENDITURE

The previous section showed the key role that public expenditure, and particularly public investment, played in the performance of one developing economy. This section looks more closely at both the size and composition of public expenditure. World Bank (1988, pp. 105–20) presents some data on the size and composition of central government expenditure in a variety of countries. Some of those figures provide a useful background to the discussion and are reported in this section. Unfortunately figures on local government expenditures are not available.

The share of central government expenditure in GDP is generally slightly lower in developing countries than in industrial countries (defined as high income countries that are not primarily oil exporters), although there is considerable variation. In 1985 the average for developing countries was about 25 per cent and the average for industrial countries was about 30 per cent. The composition of central government expenditure is also different. In industrial countries, in 1980, 6 per cent was spent on investment, 27 per cent on direct current expenditures (wages and goods and services) and 60 per cent on subsidies and transfers. In middle income countries the equivalent figures were 23 per cent, 36 per cent and 34 per cent; while for low income countries they were 16 per cent, 33 per cent and 39 per cent. In each case the remainder of government expenditure was interest payments. The two major differences revealed by these figures are the much higher level of expenditure on subsidies and transfers by developed countries and the higher proportion spent on public investment in developing countries.

Structural adjustment programmes have led to changes in both the scale and pattern of public expenditure in developing countries. A sample of fifteen countries showed an average reduction in real government expenditure of 18.3 per cent during the early 1980s. The cut in public investment was 35.3 per cent, while current spending fell by 7.8 per cent. This means that the share of public investment in government expenditure has fallen in recent years, but it is still of major importance.

As the rationale for each category of public expenditure is different, we will look at three broad areas in turn: public investment, direct public expenditure and subsidies and transfers.

3.1 Public Investment

Not only is public investment in developing countries a substantial share of public expenditure, it is also a major component of total investment. World Bank (1988, p. 47) provides figures for the share of public investment in total investment for twelve developing countries: the range was from 24 per cent to 68 per cent and the average was 43 per cent. This compares with a figure of 30 per cent as the average for a group of thirteen industrial countries.

There are two major reasons for the importance of public investment in developing countries. First, countries in the early stages of industrialization require considerable investment in infrastructure, which frequently has the character of a public good and is therefore unlikely to be supplied adequately by the private sector. Second, the existence of widespread market failure means that the provision of socially desirable private goods cannot be left to the profit-oriented private sector.

The formal procedure for selecting and approving many infrastructure projects in developing countries is the same as in the industrialized world: social cost–benefit analysis. Indeed cost–benefit analysis is normally required for any project that is funded by foreign aid. There is nothing particularly special about the cost–benefit analysis of infrastructure projects in developing countries as compared to developed countries. What is special is the extension of such analysis to a large number of ordinary production projects, an extension that is justified by market failures and is often required by foreign donors.

The classic works on cost–benefit analysis in developing countries are Little and Mirrlees (1974) and UNIDO (1972), both of which provide methods of estimating social costs and benefits of projects in the face of market distortions, particularly those related to international trade, the labour market and the capital market. They both gave rise to a considerable literature, but the basic principles and practices that they laid down have not been superseded. In view of the serious financial situation of many governments of developing countries in recent times, and their tendency to cut public investment, it is worth noting that both Little and Mirrlees and UNIDO provide a method for dealing with severe shortages of public funds. They both make a distinction between the value of private consumption and the value of public funds, and provide methods of estimating the difference. This allows planners to select projects in a way that penalizes the use of public funds and encourages the production of financial surpluses. The application of these methods would provide a rational way to decide which public sector projects should be dropped in times of financial pressure. However I know of no evidence to suggest that such methods were actually used.

An alternative to the application of cost–benefit analysis to projects that produce private goods is the removal of the market failures that made it necessary in the first place. This is attractive because it would allow projects to be evaluated simply in terms of profitability and would let the private sector compete on even terms with public enterprises. It is also argued that, in many countries, the major market failures are government-induced: excessive protection from international trade, minimum wage legislation and subsidized credit. Thus a reduction in government interference in the economy would improve efficiency. It is this idea that lies behind many of the provisions of structural adjustment programmes.

There is a great deal to be said for reducing state intervention in many developing countries, but that does not mean that all state intervention can be abandoned without considerable social costs and it certainly would be wrong to think that the removal of state intervention would produce perfectly functioning markets in all developing countries. For example, there are several countries with poorly functioning labour markets (demonstrated by long term large-scale unemployment) where minimum wages or other forms of government intervention do not appear to be a problem. It seems that the practice of social cost–benefit analysis will continue to be important for some time to come.

3.2 Direct Public Expenditure

Direct public expenditure involves such activities as government administration, military expenditure, education and health. Many developing countries have been criticized for their high levels of military spending and World Bank (1988, pp. 106–7) shows the Middle East and North Africa as having military expenditures in the region of 12 per cent of GNP. However other regions have substantially lower levels of expenditure and there was a slight reduction in the proportion of military expenditure in GNP for developing countries as a whole to about 5 per cent in 1984, when the equivalent measure for industrial countries was about 4 per cent.

The categories of current expenditure that are most relevant to economic development are health and, more particularly, education. The provision of both of these services is far below that in the industrialized countries. As far as health is concerned, developing countries had in 1984 an average of one doctor to every 4990 people and one nurse to every 1880 people, according to World Bank (1991a, pp. 258–9). The equivalent numbers for the industrialized countries were one to 470 and one to 140. Primary school enrolment is reported as close to universal in developing countries, but tails off in secondary and tertiary education. According to World Bank (1991a, pp. 260–1) the average developing country enrolment in 1988 was 42 per cent in secondary school and 8 per cent in tertiary education. The equivalent figures in industrialized countries were 93 per cent and 40 per cent.

With a situation like this, it is clear why most developing country governments would like to increase expenditure on both health and education, for economic as well as broader social reasons. The problem is that they have difficulty in raising additional revenue, so the increase in one category of expenditure must be at the expense of another. A major issue, therefore, is how to determine the priorities of the different categories of government expenditure. Unfortunately economics does not yet seem to have much to offer in deciding these priorities. However this does not seem to be a failing of development economists alone: the same comment could probably apply with equal force to the situation in industrial countries. It is political argument, rather than economic calculation, that determines the allocation of funds.

3.3 Subsidies and Transfers

It is in the area of subsidies and transfers that the expenditure of developing countries falls furthest behind that of the industrialized world. This is because developing countries have not been able to afford the large-scale social security payments that form such a large part of public expenditure in the richer countries. Despite this comparatively low level of expenditure, there is considerable concern about the desirability of these expenditures and they are often the target of structural adjustment programmes.

Part of the criticism is based on the fact that a substantial proportion of these subsidies go to support loss-making enterprises. These enterprises are loss-making either because they are inefficient or because they are subject to price controls. A common form of inefficiency is the employment of an unnecessarily large number of workers. The subsidy to the enterprise can then be seen as an employment subsidy. Such employment subsidies can be justified on efficiency grounds when there are certain types of labour market distortion, as shown by Heady (1988). However they are not an efficient way of helping the poor because employees of state-owned enterprises are usually a comparatively rich group. The poor people are usually those working in agriculture or in the urban informal sector.

If the subsidy is to compensate the enterprise for price controls on its output it is essentially a consumer price subsidy and can be regarded as equivalent to the direct consumer price subsidies that are also used in many developing countries. Such subsidies are typically justified in terms of maintaining a minimum living standard for the poor. However it has been shown by Atkinson and Stiglitz (1976), Deaton and Stern (1986) and Ebrahimi and Heady (1988) that direct payments, possibly tailored to different demographic groups, are usually superior to consumer price subsidies. The intuition behind this result is that richer people will consume more of the subsidized goods and therefore benefit more from the subsidy than poorer people. The direct payment is better because it will at least give everybody the same benefit and can sometimes be tailored to target particularly vulnerable demographic groups (such as single parents).

The applicability of this result clearly depends on the government's ability to administer direct payments, and it can be argued that many countries lack the administrative capacity to identify the recipients and prevent fraud. Thus this is an example of a case where the specific circumstances of a developing country may prevent a standard public finance result from being directly applicable. This does not mean that the theoretical result has no significance for developing countries. Some countries may be able to administer direct payments and, for those that cannot, the result points to the need to target consumer subsidies as well as possible. Subsidies should be applied to goods with a low, or even negative, income elasticity of demand.

4 TAX POLICY

The pressure from the World Bank and IMF to reduce government intervention in the economy has already been mentioned. In the area of tax policy this has involved the application of the idea of tax neutrality, an idea that has also gained in popularity in industrial countries. The idea is to design a tax system that can raise the necessary revenue with the smallest effect on the market allocation of goods and services. The main aim of this section is to look at the way the idea of tax neutrality is applied to developing countries and to question whether it is consistent with the results from the theoretical literature on taxation in developing countries. It is useful to start with a brief overview of taxation in developing countries. The presentation of both background information and theoretical analysis in this paper is necessarily brief and selective. A much fuller introduction to the field is provided by Newbery and Stern (1987).

4.1 The Revenue Pattern

The composition of tax revenue in developing countries is substantially different from that of industrialized countries. According to World Bank (1988), the revenue pattern for low income countries in 1985 was 25 per cent from income taxes, 4 per cent from social security and other direct taxes, 32 per cent from domestic commodity taxes and 38 per cent from international trade taxes. For middle income countries the revenue pattern was 32 per cent from income taxes, 17 per cent from social security and other direct taxes, 30 per cent from domestic commodity taxes and 19 per cent from international trade taxes. For industrialized countries the pattern was 35 per cent from income taxes, 34 per cent from social security and other direct taxes, 29 per cent from domestic commodity taxes and 2 per cent from international trade taxes.

From these figures it is clear that the largest difference is in the much greater reliance placed on international trade taxes by developing countries. This is balanced mainly by the much larger reliance that industrialized countries place on social security taxes. The differences in total income taxes are relatively modest, but there is a considerable difference in composition: developing countries receive over half of their income tax revenue from companies, while industrial countries receive over three-quarters of their income tax revenue from individuals. Finally the significance of domestic commodity taxes is very similar, and this still holds when the revenue is broken down between basic sales taxes or Value Added Tax (VAT) and excise duties.

The difference in revenue patterns is easy to explain in terms of administrative convenience. The heavy reliance placed on personal income and social security taxes in industrialized countries requires a large amount of information about individuals and is facilitated by the high proportion of the workforce who are employed by well-established companies. In contrast the developing countries' reliance on international trade taxes reflects the relative ease of observing and valuing goods as they cross international frontiers. The relatively heavy reliance on company taxation in developing countries also reflects the advantages of dealing with a small number of taxpayers.

However there are other, non-administrative forces at work. The low revenue from personal income taxes also reflects the small proportion of people in many developing countries whose incomes are substantially above subsistence. Also the use of export taxes in addition to import duties by some developing countries reflects in part their export of agricultural products in which they have some monopoly power.

4.2 Directions of Tax Reform

World Bank (1991b) and World Bank (1988) both provide insights into the thinking behind recent tax reforms. The general idea is to move towards tax neutrality. As taxes on international trade are seen as having a major distortionary effect, countries are frequently advised to reduce the rates of import duties and to make them more uniform. There is also advice to reduce and often to eliminate export taxes because they discourage exports. The argument that export taxes can exploit monopoly power in primary exports is viewed with some suspicion because of the threat of new entrants into the market if world prices rise too high.

The lost revenue from reducing trade taxes must be balanced by increases in tax revenue elsewhere. A common recommendation is to increase the revenue from domestic commodity taxes, which are less distortionary than trade taxes. A good deal of additional revenue can be obtained by broadening the base of domestic sales taxes, which often have large numbers of special exemptions. This broadening of the sales tax base is, in itself, a move towards tax neutrality because it is subjecting a wider range of goods to the same rate of tax.

VAT is often recommended as a replacement for existing commodity taxes, for three reasons: it broadens the tax base by including services which have usually not been taxed before; it eliminates the cascading involved in turnover taxes and some manufacturer's sales tax systems; and its self-enforcing mechanism means that enforcement is easier. However VAT does have problems if introduced into some developing countries. It is a difficult tax to administer, for both the taxpayer and the tax authorities. This has ruled it out as a possibility in some countries, and a wish to reduce its administrative complexity has usually led to advice that only a single rate of VAT should be used, the only exception being zero rating for exports. The only non-uniformity in the domestic commodity taxes would then be the excises on alcohol, tobacco and petrol and the exemptions from VAT that are granted to some traders mainly for reasons of administrative convenience.

The traditional argument against such a single rate VAT is its regressivity. In some developed countries, such as the UK, this is offset by applying a lower rate or even a zero rate to such items as food and children's clothing. However this is typically not advised for developing countries because of administrative problems, especially if VAT refunds have to be made to a large number of traders. Instead an exemption of small-scale agriculture can be used to give favourable treatment to the food consumed mainly by the poor. This has the added benefit of eliminating the administrative costs of assessing large numbers of small farmers for VAT.

The reforms to direct taxes are usually less far-reaching. The lack of scope for a mass system of personal income taxes in many countries has already been mentioned, but in those countries at a sufficiently high level of development to operate a significant personal income tax system there is often scope for reducing exemptions (broadening the base and promoting neutrality again) and simplifying the rate structure in much the same way as has been happening in industrialized countries. Similar modifications, together with improvements in accounting practices, have also often been recommended for company taxation.

4.3   Tax Theory and Policy

In order to consider whether the general recommendations summarized above are consistent with tax theory, it is important to consider the type of theory that is appropriate. It is here that the special institutional structures mentioned in the introduction become important.

A large part of tax theory for developed countries rests on two fundamental assumptions: first, it is generally assumed that the economy would produce an efficient (Pareto optimal) allocation of resources in the absence of distortionary taxes; second, it is typically assumed that there is a large variety of tax instruments available to the government – specifically taxes on all transactions and direct payments to households (which can be combined to produce the equivalent of progressive income taxes). Under these assumptions the standard tax reform recommendations are straightforward to justify. The idea that the pre-tax economy is efficient leads naturally to the goal of tax neutrality. The avoidance of taxes on international trade follows from the desirability of production efficiency, demonstrated in Diamond and Mirrlees (1971). Also, as discussed above in connection with consumer subsidies, the assumed availability of direct payments to households means that one does not have to worry about the distributional consequences of uniform sales taxes.

Strictly speaking, even these assumptions do not lead automatically to the desirability of uniform commodity taxes. Differences in the degree of complementarity between individual goods and leisure lead to non-uniform optimal commodity taxes. However Ebrahimi and Heady (1988) used UK data to show that the welfare loss of neglecting such optimal non-uniformities is very small, provided that the direct payments are set at optimal levels.

The issue of whether the tax neutrality recommendations are appropriate to developing countries therefore depends crucially on whether the assumptions of developed country tax theory are appropriate to developing countries. In some respects they are clearly inappropriate. It has already been stated that some countries are unable to administer direct payments to households. Many countries have even greater restrictions on their tax powers: the nature of peasant agriculture frequently makes it impossible to tax many agricultural transactions. It is therefore necessary to use a theory of restricted taxation in evaluating tax policy for developing countries.

Tax restrictions are not the only special feature of developing countries. The prevalence of market failures has already been noted in connection with public investment. These market failures mean that the pre-tax economy is not efficient, that resources need to be reallocated and that tax neutrality is not necessarily a desirable aim. However the mere recital of false assumptions is not sufficient to discredit policy advice. The critics must show that altered assumptions lead to altered conclusions. We shall therefore look in turn at the consequences for policy of allowing for tax restrictions and of recognizing market failures.

The consequences of not being able to implement direct payments to households has already been discussed in connection with consumer price subsidies. Reduced rates of tax, or even subsidies, can be justified by concern for the poor when direct payments are unavailable. This is recognized to some extent by the common practice of exempting some foods from commodity taxation. However it is possible that better targeting could be achieved by special treatment of particular foods or other items consumed heavily by the poor. The possibilities will vary from country to country, depending on the differences in patterns of expenditure by income class.

The consequences of further restrictions on taxation have been the subject of considerable study. In the context of many developing countries the most important tax restriction is the difficulty in taxing trades within agriculture. Such a tax restriction destroys the logic behind the Diamond and Mirrlees (1971) production efficiency result, because producer prices can no longer be manipulated to ensure production efficiency without a direct effect on consumer prices and hence welfare. Stiglitz and Dasgupta (1971) and Heady and Mitra (1982) show that commodity tax restrictions result in a divergence between domestic market prices and shadow prices (the prices at which public sector activities should be valued). However the result of Diamond and Mirrlees (1976) implies that shadow prices should still equal international prices for traded goods in which the country has no monopoly power. These two results imply that domestic market prices and international prices should diverge: there should be trade taxes or subsidies on agricultural inputs and outputs. In other words, an inability to tax agricultural transactions directly leads to the desirability of taxing agriculture through its trades with the rest of the world.

The next question is whether these theoretically optimal trade taxes are of any significant size. Heady and Mitra (1986, 1987a, 1987b) have used numerical models based on data from Turkey to investigate this issue. It was found that modest but significant trade taxes were optimal for a range of plausible parameter values. However this did not mean that the high rates of trade taxes that are often observed can be justified by these arguments.

Turning to the recognition of market failures, the labour market has often been cited as a significantly distorted market in developing countries and its relevance to tax design is analysed by Heady (1987, 1988) and Heady and Mitra (1986, 1987b). There are two types of distortion that can be considered: (a) the fact that, in some countries, migrants from rural areas are unable to sell the land they occupied restricts the movement of labour from agriculture to industry; and (b) the fact that, in many countries, the urban wage in 'modern' manufacturing is set above market clearing levels produces an incentive for people to leave agriculture to seek urban jobs despite the existence of urban unemployment and underemployment. Some countries may be affected by both problems.

Although the two distortions have opposite effects on migration out of rural areas, they both lead to the conclusion that too few people are employed in the modern manufacturing sector. It is this analysis that leads to the argument for employment subsidies that was mentioned in the discussion of public expenditure. The problem for tax theory is to design taxes that will raise the money to finance the subsidies. In the case of distortion (a), the obvious target for taxation is agriculture because that will encourage the movement into manufacturing, but the difficulties of direct taxation of agriculture have already been discussed. It therefore has to be taxed indirectly, through taxes on its input and outputs, something that is not consistent with uniform taxation. In the case of distortion (b), agriculture should not be taxed because there are already too many people in urban areas. It is the people in the 'informal' urban sector who should be taxed in order to discourage further migration. The very nature of informal employment means that income taxes cannot be used. The only way of taxing the informal sector is by placing particularly heavy taxes on the sort of goods that are consumed by informal sector workers. This clearly rules out the use of uniform sales taxes. A policy of taxing informal sector workers may seem very inequitable, but Heady (1987) uses a numerical model to show that it can be desirable, even for a government that is concerned about inequality.

This discussion of tax theory provides rather little support for the policy of tax neutrality that is frequently recommended for developing countries. This is not to say that developing countries are following optimal policies, or even that they are following policies that are better than the recommended tax neutrality. What it does imply is that countries might be able to do better than the tax neutrality policy with a carefully designed policy that included non-uniform sales taxes and modest trade taxes. Such a carefully designed policy needs accurate and up-to-date data for its formulation, and this is always a problem for developing countries. It could be argued, therefore, that, with a lack of data, the sensible policy is to follow tax neutrality. The answer to this will clearly depend on the nature of data availability in each country.

A sensible policy also needs to be administratively feasible, and this point is often used as an argument for tax neutrality. For example, it would obviously be impractical to have a large number of different commodity tax rates, especially if VAT is being used. However, well-targeted non-uniformities in taxes could well be practicable. Also there is no administrative argument against trade taxes: their ease of administration is the main explanation for their current widespread use.

5 CONCLUSIONS

This paper has provided an overview of some of the key aspects of public expenditure and tax policy in developing countries, paying particular attention to some of the ideas connected with the structural adjustment programmes that many countries have implemented in the last fifteen years. One of the main themes that has emerged in discussing these programmes is the move towards a reduction in the role of governments in the economies of developing countries, and it is worthwhile to conclude by considering whether this is desirable. As in developed countries, there is considerable disagreement about the role of the state.

Most people will agree about the need for government to provide major infrastructure. Also, in countries with generally low income levels, most people will accept the idea that the government should be the main provider of health care and education, although there may sometimes be a case for some user charges. The disagreements arise over the extent to which governments should become involved in the production of ordinary private goods and the extent to which they should use taxes to influence resource allocation. The argument often used is that resource allocation should be left to the private sector, and that government intervention does more harm than good.

It is certainly easy to find examples of countries in which government intervention has been harmful for almost all citizens, but the economies of many developed countries and many successful developing countries, such as those in South-East Asia, have been helped at crucial times by government intervention of one sort or another. It has usually not involved large scale public enterprises, but has involved temporary protection of growing industries or direction of bank credit to particular activities. This is consistent with the argument in much of the paper: that the prevalence of market failures requires some government action to improve the allocation of resources.

Unfortunately this conclusion is hard to implement, given the tendency of governments to expand their activities beyond that which is desirable, often prompted by undeserving special interest groups. It is easy to understand why some people argue that reduced government participation in the economy is the best practical option. Nonetheless the fear remains that, without government action, developing countries will never be able to reach the level of economic well-being of which they are capable.

References

Atkinson, A.B. and Stiglitz, J.E. (1976) 'The design of tax structure: direct versus indirect taxation', *Journal of Public Economics*, vol. 6, pp. 55–75.

Blundell, R., Heady, C.J. and Medhora, R. (1992) 'Labor markets in an era of adjustment: The case of Côte d'Ivoire', in Horton, S., Kanbur R. and Mazumdar, D. (eds) *Labor Markets in an Era of Adjustment* (Washington, DC: Economic Development Institute, World Bank).

Cornia, G., Jolly, R. and Stewart, F. (1987) *Adjustment with a Human Face* (Oxford: Clarendon Press).

Deaton, A. and Stern, N. (1986) 'Optimally uniform commodity taxes, taste differences and lump-sum grants', *Economics Letters*, vol. 20, pp. 263–6.

Diamond, P.A. and Mirrlees, J.A. (1971) 'Optimal taxation and public production: I and II', *American Economic Review*, vol. 61, pp.8 –27, 261–78.

Diamond, P.A. and Mirrlees, J.A. (1976) 'Private constant returns and public shadow prices', *Review of Economic Studies*, vol. 43, pp. 41–7.

Ebrahimi, A. and Heady, C. (1988) 'Tax design and household composition', *Economic Journal*, vol. 98, pp. 83–96.

Heady, C.J. (1987) 'Designing taxes with migration', *Economic Journal*, vol. 97, pp. 87–98.

Heady, C.J. (1988) 'Optimal taxation with fixed wages and induced migration', *Oxford Economic Papers*, vol. 40, pp. 560–74.

Heady, C.J. and Mitra, P.K. (1982) 'Restricted redistributive taxation, shadow prices and trade policy', *Journal of Public Economics*, vol. 17, pp. 1–22.

Heady, C.J. and Mitra, P.K. (1986) 'Optimal taxation and public production in an open dual economy', *Journal of Public Economics*, vol. 30, pp. 293–316.

Heady, C.J. and Mitra, P.K. (1987a) 'Distributional and revenue raising arguments for tariffs', *Journal of Development Economics*, vol. 26, pp. 77–101.

Heady, C.J. and Mitra, P.K. (1987b) 'Optimal taxation and shadow pricing in a developing economy', in Newbery and Stern (1987).

Little, I.M.D. and Mirrlees, J.A. (1974) *Project Appraisal and Planning for Developing Countries* (London: Heinemann).

Newbery, D. and Stern, N. (eds) (1987) *The Theory of Taxation for Developing Countries* (Oxford: Oxford University Press).

Stiglitz, J.E. and Dasgupta, P.S. (1971) 'Differential taxation, public goods and economic efficiency', *Review of Economic Studies*, vol. 38, pp. 151–74.

United Nations Industrial Development Organization (UNIDO) (1972) *Guidelines for Project Evaluation* (New York: United Nations).

World Bank (1988) *World Development Report 1988* (Oxford: Oxford University Press).

World Bank (1991a) *World Development Report 1991* (Oxford: Oxford University Press).

World Bank (1991b) *Lessons of Tax Reform* (Washington, DC: World Bank).

Part III

Distributional Effects of Social Policy

7 The Western Experience with Social Safety Nets[1]

Anthony B. Atkinson
UNIVERSITY OF CAMBRIDGE

1 INTRODUCTION: INSECURITY AND THE NEED FOR A SAFETY NET

This Congress is taking place at a time of historic changes in Russia and Eastern Europe. These changes offer great prospects and there will be greater freedom and opportunities for individual action. There is a desire to learn from the Western experience, but in the West too changes are under way: we have just seen the signing of the North American Free Trade Agreement; in Western Europe, the European Community is about to complete the common internal market and is in the process of enlargement.

These changes offer great prospects but are also a source of insecurity. There will be losers as well as gainers from economic reform. Anxiety is understandably felt by the elderly, by the unskilled, by those with little education, and by those in peripheral areas. Uncertainty is greatest for those without family or friends to help in the event of adversity. These concerns are not confined to countries in transition to market economies. In the European Community, too, there are fears that greater internal competition will weaken the position of marginal regions and that the constraints on macroeconomic policy will lead to a continuation of high levels of unemployment. There has indeed been concern for a number of years about those left behind by rising prosperity. The Commission's estimates for 1985 identified some 50 million of the Community's 320 million population as being in poverty (Eurostat, 1990). This figure is, interestingly, much the same proportion of the population as the 40 million figure given by the former USSR government for poverty in 1989 in the Soviet Union (Atkinson and Micklewright, 1992, p. 178).

Such concern raises the question of the protection which can be offered against insecurity. How far can help be provided to those who are the losers from economic change? This is the topic of my

Presidential Address, which is concerned with the 'social safety net'.

The need for a social safety net is widely recognized in international discussion of economic problems. Michel Camdessus, the IMF Managing Director, has emphasized the need for a social policy accompanying economic change. To quote from his address to the UN Economic and Social Council:

> the essential missing element . . . is a sufficient regard for the short-term human costs involved during adjustment or transition to a market economy (1992, p. 255).

To avoid such costs he argues for the installation of social safety nets. The study of the Soviet economy by the IMF, World Bank, OECD and EBRD in 1991 noted that the move to a market economy and removal of existing government intervention

> will impose substantial hardship on many groups of the population during the transition (1991, p. 331)

and went on to say that

> to minimize this hardship and to assure political support for economic restructuring, it is necessary to design policies that cushion the less well-off from excessive burdens (ibid., p. 331).

The Stand-By Arrangement agreed between the IMF and the Russian Federation in August 1992 included the statement that

> The Russian authorities are committed to protecting the most vulnerable groups of the population during the economic transformation process, while ensuring that social safety net expenditures are consistent with macroeconomic stabilization (IMF, 1992, p. 267).

Here I take it as agreed that there *should be* a social safety net, and I shall not examine the justifications that may be given (see Atkinson, 1991, for discussion of the different motives that may lie behind support for a safety net). What I want to do here is to make three points about such a safety net, based on the experience of Western countries:

1. That a safety net can have very different meanings, and that major decisions have to be made about its form and mode of operation.
2. That it is not easy to set in place an effective safety net, and its effectiveness depends on the policy choices made.
3. The design of a safety net should be an integral part of economic policy making, which must recognize the limitations to the protection that can be provided.

The first two of these points are dealt with in the substance of the paper; the third is treated in the concluding section.

   In making these points, I refer to Western experience, notably that of Europe and of the United States. This means that I should enter two important qualifications. The first is that I am concerned with medium term assistance rather than emergency relief to meet imminent risk of starvation or the consequences of natural disasters. I am not addressing the problem of famine, our understanding of which my predecessor Amartya Sen (1981) has done so much to increase. Secondly I should make clear at the outset that I do not believe that the experience of Western economies can be carried over unmodified to other countries – indeed this is evident from the diversity of practice among Western countries themselves – but I do believe that the experience of these countries raises questions which have to be answered in the design of policy in the successor states of the USSR and other countries in the process of moving to a market economy.

2 WHAT IS THE MEANING OF A SAFETY NET?

The need for a safety net is widely recognized. What is less widely appreciated is that a safety net can take many different forms. The choice of the form that such a safety net should take is an important question: it is not just a detail which can be left to be settled by junior policy makers.

2.1 Mechanism

The first issue concerns the *mechanism* by which the safety net is provided. It may be conceived very broadly, covering not just the whole range of cash transfers, but non-cash provision, such as food, health care, education, retraining or public employment for the unemployed, subsidies for housing, fuel and other essentials.

Here, I am going to focus on cash transfers. It is evident, however, that the importance of cash transfers depends on the extent of non-cash provision and of subsidy programmes. The role of cash assistance is less in an economy where there is state-provided health care and education, where housing is provided at low rents, where food is heavily subsidized, and where children are fed free at school. (The significance of such non-cash provision is documented in Saunders *et al.*, 1993.)

I am concentrating on cash transfers because it is clear that there has been a trend towards the reduction in non-cash provision. In many countries, food subsidies are being reduced or eliminated, the rents of state-owned property are being increased, often in association with the privatization of the housing stock, charges are being introduced for health care and education, and private provision is *de facto* or *de jure* replacing state provision. These changes reflect the exigencies of macroeconomic and budgetary policy, as well as the shift in both East and West towards a market ideology. In this way the form of the social safety net depends on other decisions made about the economic system. The provision of cash assistance is acquiring greater significance as other forms of intervention are curtailed.

Within the category of cash assistance, too, there are important distinctions to be drawn. Some people regard all cash transfers as forming part of the safety net including retirement pensions, unemployment insurance, disability insurance and so on. These programmes, however, have much wider functions than that of poverty relief. For this reason, when people talk of a 'safety net' in the West they typically have in mind transfers that are 'targeted' to those with low incomes via a test of means. Such means-tested,[2] or social assistance, programmes are operated in the USA as Aid for Families with Dependent Children (AFDC) or as the Supplemental Security Income (SSI) for the aged, blind and disabled, in the United Kingdom as Income Support and Family Credit, and in France as the Revenu Minimum d'Insertion (RMI). Some of the key features of these social assistance schemes are summarized in Table 7.1. It is on this type of social assistance that attention is focused here.

2.2 Level

If a means-tested programme aims to bring people to a specified minimum level of resources, then the choice of that level is clearly

Table 7.1 Examples of Western means-tested cash safety net programmes[a]

Programme	Brief description	Number of recipients
United States		
Aid for Families with Dependent Children (AFDC)	Primarily for single-parent families with children. Income and assets tests. Participation required in Job Opportunities and Basic Skills (JOBS) programme.	12.4 million in 1991
Supplemental Security Income (SSI)	Aged, blind and disabled. Income and assets tests.	4.8 million in 1990
United Kingdom		
Income Support (IS) (previously Supplementary Benefit)	Those not in full-time work. Income and assets tests. Availability for work and job search requirements (not single parents).	4.8 million in 1991
Family Credit (previously Family Income Supplement)	Families with children, where at least one parent in full-time work. Income and assets tests.	0.4 million in 1991
France		
Revenu Minimum d'Insertion (RMI), introduced 1988	All aged 25 and over, or with family responsibilities. Income test. Associated with contract of 'insertion'.	0.6 million in December 1991

Note: [a] The above brief account of the different transfer programmes does not take into account all of their complex features.

crucial. The European Community poverty estimates quoted earlier were based on a poverty line set at 50 per cent of average disposable income for each country. Such a 50 per cent target was the result of a political judgment, and it can clearly be debated whether this is the right percentage. Should, for example, the percentage be higher or lower in countries with a lower level of average income? One can imagine arguments which go in different directions, but it is interesting to note that the poverty line (of 81 roubles) used in the former USSR in 1989 was almost exactly 50 per cent of average household per capita income (Atkinson and Micklewright, 1992, Statistical Appendix, Tables UI1 and UP2).

The appropriateness of a particular level depends on whether we are concerned with a *partial* safety net, which assumes that people can supplement the payment from other sources, or whether we are aiming for a *total* safety net, adequate for people to survive without additional sources. In assessing the adequacy of the safety net to achieve the latter goal, one approach is to ask what can be bought with a particular amount of income. We can seek a foundation for the level of the safety net in a minimum basket of goods, or what has come to be known in the development literature as 'basic needs'. This has of course a long history, including the work carried out in the early days of the Russian Republic in 1918, when minimum budgets were worked out by town departments of the Labour Department and by trade unions (Matthews, 1986, p. 15). More recently, under Khrushchev, calculations were made by Sarkisyan and Kuznetzova (1967) and colleagues of 'current', 'prospective', and 'rational' minima, the latter two providing a dynamic to the policy objective.

In the constitution of such budgets, the scope of the safety net is made concrete and it takes account of non-cash forms of support. The Khrushchev budgets for 1965 reflected, for example, the subsidies to rents, with housing accounting for only 5 per cent of the total (Matthews, 1986, p. 20), compared with a figure of 12 per cent for actual budgets at that time in the United Kingdom. Little provision was required in the Khrushchev budgets for education and medical care. In the work which is no doubt being done today, the composition of the minimum budget is likely to look rather different. If subsidies are being removed, and if provision in kind is being reduced, then the amount of cash provision has to be correspondingly higher.

2.3 Structure of Minimum Scale

The minimum budget must also reflect the composition of the spending unit. Suppose, for example, that a household consists of a couple, their son aged 14, their daughter aged 20, a friend of the daughter who is lodging with the family and the wife's mother. There are six people in the household and the simplest procedure is to take a safety net which is six times that for a single person: in other words, to apply a per capita scale. This has indeed been the standard way of presenting income distribution data in the former USSR or in Czechoslovakia, Hungary or Poland. On the other hand, it has been less common in the West. Such a distribution is not officially published for the United Kingdom and, indeed, the main long term series of income distribution data in the United Kingdom treats all families in the same way, making no allowance at all for differences in their size[3]

If one has to choose between these extreme ways of allowing for family size, then it seems to me that there is a lot to recommend a per capita calculation. There is little apparent justification for ignoring family size: the needs of the family of six *are* greater than those of a single person. It may be more attractive, however, to make an intermediate calculation, as has been the common practice in many countries which apply an 'equivalence scale'. According to such a scale, a couple are rated as more than one but less than two, children receive a weight less than adults, and so on. The derivation of such an equivalence scale raises many issues, and any choice must be governed by the ultimate objectives of the safety net. Here I want simply to emphasize that the decision regarding the equivalence scale can make a major difference as to which families qualify for the safety net. In Figure 7.1 are shown calculations made for the former USSR in 1989 for the population of worker families with children with income below 75 roubles a month. For this purpose I take a simple equivalence scale, where the needs of a family of size S are given by S to the power α where α is a constant. A value of $\alpha = 1$ corresponds to the per capita figure, treating a family of six as the same as six single people. This is shown at the right-hand end of the diagram. At the other extreme, at the left-hand end, is the value of $\alpha = 0$, which treats all families as having the same needs. In the middle are cases like S to the power of a half, where a family of six is equivalent to 2.45 single people. One can see how the composition of the low-income families changes with different values of α.[4] With no allowance for the differences in family size, families with one child account for over 40 per cent of the total number of low income families, and large families (four or more children) are only about 8 per cent. With $\alpha = 0.5$, one-child families are about twice as important as large families; and with $\alpha = 1$ they are about equally important. It is evident that the conclusions drawn with respect, for instance, to the structure of the safety net for families of different sizes may be quite different.

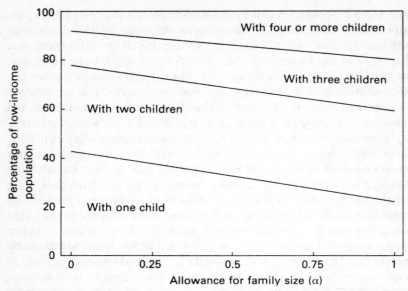

Figure 7.1 Composition of low-income families[a] in former USSR, 1989

Note: [a] Less than 75 roubles a month.

Sources: The figures are calculated from Table UI5 in Atkinson and Mickel-wright (1992), using the proportions in different family size groups taken from the report of the 310 000 March Household Survey (Goskomstat, 1990, p. 175): one child (49.9 per cent), two children (37.7 per cent), three children (8.1 per cent), four children (2.5 per cent), and five or more children (1.8 per cent). The figures relate to worker and employee families.

2.4 Conditionality

There are many more elements that enter the design of a safety net, but here I want to refer to only one other – the conditions, other than income, which have to be fulfilled in order to qualify. Economists tend to assume that a minimum income guarantee simply depends on income, but in reality it is rare to find safety net schemes that involve *only* a test of means; the typical scheme also involves categorical conditions. The claimant has to satisfy conditions other than lack of resources, as is illustrated in Table 7.1.

Categorical conditions are particularly relevant to the labour market. First, there is an important distinction between safety net schemes that cover the whole population and schemes that exclude people in work. The latter is the case in the United Kingdom, where

Income Support covers all families *except* those supported by a person in full-time work. (It is complemented by the Family Credit scheme which provides assistance to low earners, but this covers only people with dependent children.) A person in full-time work, and without children, is categorically excluded from assistance, irrespective of the level of earnings, which may be below the safety net level.

Second, categorical conditions may limit the coverage of those not in work: for those of working age, and capable of work, assistance may be conditional on labour market participation. This condition may require registration at a public employment agency; it may require evidence of job search; assistance may be terminated if the claimant refuses to accept suitable employment. The French Revenu Minimum d'Insertion, introduced in 1988, gives a central role to such conditions, payment beyond the first three months being linked to the condition that a contract for 'insertion' in the labour market has been negotiated with the recipient and that the terms of this contract are respected. In the United States, AFDC recipients may be required to take part in the Job Opportunities and Basic Skills (JOBS) training programme. Where these conditions are not satisfied, the safety net protection may be withdrawn.

It is important to stress these categorical elements of safety net schemes, since a *conditional* safety net cannot be guaranteed to be fully effective. There is always the possibility that a person is unable, or unwilling, to satisfy the conditions; if those in work do not qualify, then the scheme does not resolve the problem of the working poor. People will fall through the safety net, which brings me to the question of Western experience regarding its effectiveness.

3 HOW SUCCESSFUL HAVE SAFETY NETS BEEN IN WESTERN ECONOMIES?

In considering the role of means-tested safety net programmes in Western economies, one should first underline their quantitative importance. Whereas one might have expected their significance to decline with the development of modern forms of cash transfer programme, such as social insurance, this has not been the case. In the United Kingdom, for example, it was envisaged in the Beveridge Plan of 1942 that social insurance benefits, paid as of right on the basis of contribution and not subject to a means test, would progressively replace the traditional social assistance:

the scope of assistance will be narrowed from the beginning and will diminish . . . the scheme of social insurance is designed of itself when in full operation to guarantee the income needed for subsistence in all normal cases (Beveridge, 1942, p. 12).

This has not in fact happened. In 1948 the number of recipients of National Assistance was around 1 million; in 1991–2 Income Support was paid to 4.8 million. The growth in the role of the safety net is illustrated in Figure 7.2, which shows how the proportion of the population receiving cash assistance rose steadily over the postwar period and then jumped in the 1980s. Recipients may have others dependent on them, so that the total proportion of the population living in families in receipt of assistance (adding in those provided for by Family Credit) is about one in six of the population.

Indeed in quite a few OECD countries there has been a growth in the number receiving benefits under safety net programmes. In the USA, the number of recipients of AFDC rose from around 2 million in 1950 to 7 ½ million in 1970 and, despite the Reagan cuts, was 12 ½ million in 1991. The number receiving SSI (or earlier Old Age Assistance) grew from 3.1 million in 1970 to some 5 million in 1990 (Committee on Ways and Means, 1992, p. 813). While social insurance grew faster, social assistance did not die away (Burtless, 1992). In West Germany, the total receiving Sozialhilfe in 1964 was 1.4 million; by 1986 it had risen to 3.0 million (Hauser, 1990, p. 25).

The spending on safety net programmes is substantial. In the United Kingdom in 1990–91 spending included (£ million):

Income support	9 310
Family credit	494
Housing rebates	5 279
Total	15 083

(HM Treasury, 1992, Table 2.5.)

This amounted to 2.7 per cent of GDP. In the USA in 1990 the total spending of federal and state governments combined on the major means-tested programmes was as follows ($ billion):

Medicaid	72.5
Food stamps	17.7
Family support (AFDC)	21.2
SSI	16.6
Earned income tax credit	6.9

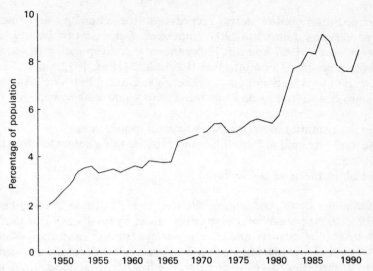

Figure 7.2   Receipt of social assistance in Great Britain, 1948–91

Sources: 1948–65 (National Assistance) from National Assistance Board, *Report for the Year Ended 31 December 1965*, p.54, figures for December of each year; 1966–87 (Supplementary Benefit) from Department of Health and Social Security, *Social Security Statistics 1980*, Table 34.30, and Department of Social Security, *Social Security Statistics 1989*, Table 34.29, figures for November or December; 1988–91 (Income Support) from Department of Social Security, *Social Security – The Government's Expenditure Plans 1992–93 to 1994–95*, p.41.

The population figures are the mid-year estimates from Central Statistical Office *Annual Abstract of Statistics 1992* (no. 128), Table 2.1 *1961* (no. 98), Table 6 *1938–1950* (no. 88), Table 6.

Federal housing assistance	15.7
Other	12.1
Total	162.7

(Committee on Ways and Means, 1992.)[5]

This is a slightly higher percentage of GDP (3.0 per cent) than in the United Kingdom. It may be noted that a relatively small part (0.7 per cent of GDP) was in the form of cash transfers (AFDC and SSI).

3.1   The Extent of Poverty

The expansion of these programmes, costing substantial sums, has however coincided with continuing concern about the extent of poverty. In the United States, according to the official poverty line, the poverty rate fell in the 1960s from over 20 per cent to around 12 per cent, but in 1990 was still 13.5 per cent – corresponding to some 34 million people (Committee on Ways and Means, 1992, pp. 1274–5). Despite the safety net programmes, a sizeable minority of Americans are considered to be in poverty. This could be because

- the programmes are not targeted on the poor, or
- the amounts paid are insufficient to raise people above the poverty line, or
- not all of the poor are covered.

As far as the first is concerned, Weinberg (1987, Table 2) identified for 1984 those people whose incomes, apart from all cash transfers, were below the poverty line (the 'pre-transfer poor') and shows that 86 per cent of all spending on income-conditioned programmes went to this group. In terms of *vertical target efficiency* (that is, accuracy in assisting only the poor), the US programmes appear relatively well targeted.[6] Nevertheless, a substantial proportion of the population remain below the official poverty line. The most obvious reason for this is that the income cut-offs for the safety net programmes are below the official poverty line. As a result, families may receive less than the amount required to reach the poverty line; or they may be in poverty but be disqualified on income grounds from AFDC or food stamps.[7] This is illustrated by Figure 7.3, which shows the maximum AFDC and food stamp benefit as a percentage of the poverty line by state in the USA. For only those states unshaded was the percentage 80 or more. The median state offered 72 per cent. For those states shown in black the percentage was below 60 per cent, the lowest being Mississippi, with 46 per cent.

That the government safety net level should be set below the official poverty line may appear like a lack of co-ordination; however it is perfectly consistent if the government is seen as pursuing this objective subject to constraints. These constraints may be those of budgetary cost, or they may be concerned with the possible effect of safety net provision on work or other incentives. If, in terms of the Tinbergen (1952) theory of economic policy, the poverty target is 'flexible', rather than 'fixed', then it may not be fully achieved. The operation of a safety net is then a compromise between aspirations, on the one hand, and constraints, or competing objectives, on the other.

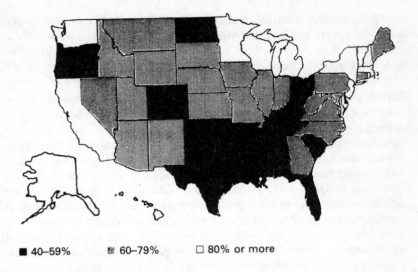

■ 40–59%   ▨ 60–79%   □ 80% or more

Figure 7.3   Maximum AFDC/Food stamp benefit[a] as a percentage of official poverty line, USA, 1992

Note: [a] For a one-parent family of three.

Source: Committee on Ways and Means (1992), p.635.

This is not however the only reason why safety net programmes fail to be fully effective, as is shown by evidence from those countries that judge effectiveness in relation to the standard set in the safety net programme itself. In the United Kingdom, the effectiveness of the safety net in meeting its own objectives was the subject of official reports on 'Low Income Families', which estimated the proportion of families (benefit units) with incomes below the level at which they would become entitled to Income Support (then called Supplementary Benefit). In 1985, 5.6 per cent of all families had incomes (net of housing costs) which were below the entitlement level, containing 4.5 per cent of the population (Department of Health and Social Security, 1988). The limited success of safety net programmes is reported in a variety of other countries. In the case of West Germany, the social assistance level has been used in a definition of 'combated poverty' (those in receipt of assistance) and 'concealed poverty' (those eligible on the basis of income, but not in receipt). The results of Hauser and Semrau (1990, p. 37) show that, in 1983, 2.6 per cent of the population were in receipt of social assistance, but that 1.3 per cent of the population were in concealed poverty. On this basis the safety net had left a third of the problem unsolved.

3.2 Failure of Safety Net Coverage

There are several reasons why coverage may be incomplete. First, there are the categorical conditions for entitlement. Where the programme excludes certain categories, or requires claimants to meet certain conditions, then it is by definition incomplete. Of those below the social assistance level in the United Kingdom, a sizeable fraction are not eligible for the safety net because they are in full-time work (full-time is defined as 24 hours or a more a week). Since there is no minimum wage, there is no guaranteed minimum income for those in work, and low-paid workers may fall below the safety net level.

Second, we have made no allowance so far for the problems of administration: there may be rejection of valid claims by administrative error. The application of the means test is a complicated basis. In contrast to social insurance, where error rates in benefit calculation are typically 1 per cent or less, in the case of Income Support, error rates are now around 6 per cent and they have been over 10 per cent (HM Treasury, 1985, Table 3.12.11).

Third, there may be incomplete take-up by those eligible, with people not claiming their entitlement. That this should happen is often regarded with suspicion by economists. Why should people pass up what may be quite sizeable amounts of money or valuable benefits in kind? This behaviour scarcely accords with that assumed in other branches of public finance, such as the expected utility-maximizing tax evader. But there are a number of explanations for the non-take-up of transfers which are quite consistent with utility maximization. The simplest is the time required to file a claim. Where there is a time constraint as well as budget constraint, non-claiming may be a quite rational response. Once we allow for imperfect information, a variety of reasons for non-claiming arise. People may be unaware of the benefit, perhaps because they lack the skills of literacy or numeracy required to assimilate the information provided. They may be aware of its existence but not believe that they are entitled. This may happen where they have previously applied and have (correctly) been deemed ineligible but where there has been a subsequent change in the programme, or in their circumstances, which makes them eligible. They may be deterred by the way in which the benefit is administered and the treatment they receive from officials. Certainly there is evidence from a number of countries of incomplete take-up. In the Netherlands, for example, an analysis of administrative records for a means-tested supplement to the basic earnings-related benefit showed that 33 per cent of the unemployed did not claim and there is evidence of incomplete take-up for other benefits (Oorschot, 1991). In Ireland, Callan *et al.* (1989) found that in 1987 the take-up of Supplementary Welfare Allowance was less than 50 per cent.

Finally it has to be remembered that most of the statistical information relates to the *household population*. Those living in institutions may not be covered by the safety net. The payment of benefit to people without a fixed address is administratively more difficult, and Western societies have seen growing concern about the incidence of homelessness. People sleeping in the streets of cities like London, New York and Paris provide very real evidence of failure in the safety net.

3.3 Negative Effects of the Safety Net

We have also to consider the argument that the persistence of poverty in rich countries stems from the existence of the safety net itself. Conservative commentators suggest that people have taken advantage of the safety net, and not sought their own solutions. The proportion of the population with pre-transfer income below the poverty line has been augmented by the disincentive effect of the safety net provisions. People have been discouraged from seeking work and have not made private provision for old age. The effects may be expected to be greatest in the case of means-tested programmes, in view of the fact that any private income – from work or savings – tends to reduce the transfer payment by the same amount. There is typically a 100 per cent marginal tax rate. Where entitlement depends on categorical criteria, people have adapted their behaviour to satisfy these conditions.

That there are situations in which this happens cannot be denied. What can be debated, however, is the quantitative importance of the disincentive effects. This requires careful examination of the evidence about the many different decisions which may be affected. There is not space here to survey this evidence, but a number of such reviews have been undertaken in recent years, and I think that there is broad agreement that, to the extent that disincentive effects exist, they are

modest in size. Burtless (1990) summarizes the evidence from the US
Negative Income Tax (NIT) experiments:

> on average, studies based on the NIT experiments suggest that
> means-tested transfers have a statistically significant, but quantita-
> tively small, effect on the labour supply of low-income men and
> women who have children (p. 73).

Moffitt (1992) concludes that there is unequivocal evidence of an
effect of the US welfare system on labour supply, but that 'the
importance of these effects is limited in many respects' (p. 56).

It should also be remembered that the safety net may have positive
as well as negative effects on incentives. To give just one example, it
is frequently argued that people are too unwilling to leave wage
employment to set up as self-employed entrepreneurs. This decision
is likely to be affected at least in part by the costs of failure. The
existence of a safety net reduces these costs and may increase the
attractiveness of self-employment; it will reduce the probability of
success required to take the plunge; this will be further reinforced if
the benefit also serves to finance an initial period of unprofitable
operation before the business becomes successful.

4   CONCLUSIONS: THE INTEGRATION OF ECONOMIC AND SOCIAL POLICY

The discussion of incentives is illustrative of the interrelationship
between economic and social policy, two areas which are too often
treated as independent. This interrelationship has appeared at several stages in the argument. The extent to which cash assistance is
necessary depends on the degree of non-cash provision, which in turn
is influenced by decisions about price subsidies and public spending
which are usually debated in terms of their macroeconomic consequences. The categorical criteria for assistance depend on policy in
the labour market.

Economic policy, and programmes of economic reform, have implications for the role and scope of the safety net; and it is imperative
that these be taken into account in the design of this policy. Most
importantly, too much weight should not be placed on the safety net.
The experience of Western countries suggests that a safety net is not
easy to design and typically has only limited effectiveness. A safety

net cannot resolve all problems and it can easily become overloaded. Indeed the term safety net is itself misleading in suggesting a public good which cannot become overcongested. From asking people what image is conjured by this term, I know that most people think naturally of the safety net in the circus – a particularly appropriate response in this city – and in the case of the circus the establishment of the safety net costs the same whether it protects one trapeze artist or ten. It is a public good in that sense. But with a social security safety net the cost goes up with the number protected.

A better analogy may be with a *lifeboat*, which has a definite capacity. When the British liner *Titanic* struck an iceberg in the North Atlantic on her maiden voyage in 1912, the main reason for such a high loss of life was that the lifeboats on board could hold only 1178, whereas there were nearly twice as many (2201) people on board. After this disaster ships were required to carry sufficient lifeboats for all persons on board. But we have seen that the effective coverage of social safety nets in Western economies is considerably less than 100 per cent. That is why the avoidance of icebergs is of crucial importance, a factor which should in my view be given more weight in the design of economic reform and macroeconomic policy making.

Finally I have talked about safety nets at a national level, but we must not lose sight of the need at a world level. The sums spent by Western countries on safety net provision to their own citizens are too small to meet their needs, but these sums are much larger than those transferred to those in need outside their boundaries. The safety net spending in Britain represents 2.7 per cent of GNP; official development assistance is 0.27 per cent. There is a ratio of 10 to 1, or, on a per capita basis, of some 1000 to 1. As national boundaries come to have less significance, as is happening all over the world, there is less justification for such differences in generosity.

Notes

1. Presidential Address at the Tenth World Congress of the International Economic Association, Moscow, August 1992. I am grateful to Gary Burtless and Tim Smeeding for help with the United States statistics, although they should not be held responsible for the use I have made of them.
2. The programme may be subject to a test of income, in which case it is usually referred to as *income-tested*, or to a test of both income and assets, in which case it is said to be *means-tested*.

3. This series is known as the 'Blue Book' series, and was published for many years in the *United Kingdom National Accounts*. Recent references are given in Atkinson and Micklewright (1992), Statistical Appendix.
4. In these calculations the low income definition is maintained at 75 roubles a month for a single person, but applied on an equivalent adult basis to the families of different sizes. The results are only approximate, being linearly interpolated from the bottom interval for each family type.
5. Medicaid from Table 14, p. 1652; food stamps from the same source, Table 4, p. 1616; AFDC from Table 19, p. 654; SSI from Table 1, p. 779; earned income tax credit from Table 18, p. 1019; federal housing assistance from Table 29, p. 1681; 'other' includes the Women, Infants and Children Supplemental Food Program (Table 34, p. 1689), job training (Table 36, p. 1692), summer youth employment (Table 37, p. 1693), Jobs corps (Table 38, p. 1694), Head start (Table 39, p. 1696), low income home energy assistance (Table 41, p. 1701) and veterans' pensions (p. 1704). Figures for transfer programmes include administrative expenditures.
6. Although strictly we need to look at their effectiveness in helping those in poverty *after* non-means-tested transfers, in order to assess the incremental contribution of the means-tested programmes.
7. It is also possible that families qualify on income grounds but are excluded by the assets test.

References

Atkinson, A.B. (1991) 'The Social Safety Net', Welfare State Programme Discussion Paper 66, London School of Economics.
Atkinson, A.B. and Micklewright, J. (1992) *Economic Transformation and the Distribution of Income in Eastern Europe* (Cambridge: Cambridge University Press).
Beveridge, Sir W. (1942) *Social Insurance and Allied Services*, Cmd. 6404, (London: HMSO).
Burtless, G. (1990) 'The Economist's Lament: Public Assistance in America', *Journal of Economic Perspectives*, vol. 4, pp. 57–78.
Burtless, G. (1992) 'Public Spending on the Poor: Historical Trends and Economic Limits', paper presented at conference on Poverty and Public Policy, University of Wisconsin.
Callan, T., Nolan, B., Whelan, B.J. Hannan, D.F. and Creighton, S. (1989) *Poverty, Income and Welfare in Ireland* (Dublin: Economic and Social Research Institute).
Camdessus, M. (1992) 'Address to UN Economic and Social Council', *IMF Survey*, 3 August 1992, p. 255.
Committee on Ways and Means, US House of Representatives (1992) *1992 Green Book* (Washington, DC: US Government Printing Office).
Department of Health and Social Security (1988) *Low Income Families – 1985* (London: Department of Health and Social Security).

Eurostat (1990) 'Inequality and Poverty in Europe, 1980–1985', Rapid Report, 7, Eurostat, Luxembourg.

Goskomstat (1990) *Sostav sem'i, dokhody i zhilishchnve usloviia semei rabochikh sluzhashchikh i kolkhoznikov* (Composition of the family, incomes and living conditions of workers, employees and collective farm workers), Moscow.

Hauser, R. (1990) 'Socioökonomische Aspekte der Sozialhilfe' ('Socioeconomic aspects of social assistance'), in Kitterer, W. (ed.) *Sozialhilfe und Finanzausgleich* (Heidelberg: R v Decker's Verlag).

Hauser, R. and Semrau, P. (1990) 'Poverty in the Federal Republic of Germany' Sonderforschungsbereich 3, University of Frankfurt.

HM Treasury (1985) *The Government's Expenditure Plans 1985–86 to 1987–88* (London: HMSO).

HM Treasury (1992) *Public Expenditure Analyses to 1994–95* (London: HMSO).

IMF (1992) 'From the Executive Board . . .', *IMF Survey*, 17 August 1992, p. 267.

IMF, World Bank, OECD and EBRD (1991) *A Study of the Soviet Economy* (Paris: OECD).

Matthews, M. (1986) *Poverty in the Soviet Union* (Cambridge: Cambridge University Press).

Moffitt, R.L. (1992) 'Incentive Effects of the U.S. Welfare System: A Review', *Journal of Economic Literature*, vol. 30, pp. 1–61.

Oorschot, W. van (1991) 'Non-take-up of social security benefits in Europe', *Journal of European Social Policy*, vol. 1, pp. 15–30.

Sarkisyan, G.S. and Kuznetsova, N.F. (1967) *Potrebnosti i dokhod sem'i, uroven', struktura, perspektivy*, Moscow.

Saunders, P., Smeeding, T., Coder, J., Jenkins, S., Fritzell, J., Hagenaars, A.J.M., Hauser, R. and Wolfson, M. (1993) 'Non-cash Income, Living Standards and Inequality: Evidence from the Luxembourg Income Study', this volume, pp. 198–217.

Sen, A.K. (1981) *Poverty and Famines: An Essay on Entitlement and Deprivation* (Oxford: Clarendon Press).

Tinbergen, J. (1952) *On the Theory of Economic Policy* (Amsterdam: North-Holland).

Weinberg, D.H. (1987) 'Filling the "poverty gap", 1979–84', *Journal of Human Resources*, vol. 22, pp. 563–73.

8 Economics of Ageing

Dieter Bös[1]
UNIVERSITY OF BONN

1 INTRODUCTION

Demographic and economic research in population ageing may apply quite different definitions of ageing.[2] A typical demographic definition like that found in Billeter (1954) characterizes the age structure of a population by

$$D_1: = \frac{P_{0,\,14} - P_{50,\,+}}{P_{15,\,49}}$$

where $P_{a,\,b}$ is the number of people between a and b years of age and $P_{a,+}$ is the number of people aged a years and older. This measure differentiates age groups according to their reproductive abilities. The future development of the population is expressed in this measure by subtracting the old non-productive from the young non-productive part of the population. If the percentage of people over 50 is high, then D_1 is negative. An aged population is therefore characterized by a high negative value of D_1, and the demographic problems become worse if this negative value increases in absolute terms (ageing).

In economics, however, the differentiation of age groups has to follow economic criteria. Two economic measures of age structure are given in the following:

$$E_1: = \frac{P_{60,\,+}}{P_{0,\,+}} \,;\; E_2: = \frac{P_{0,\,20} + P_{60,\,+}}{P_{20,\,59}}$$

The first measure considers the relative number of persons over 60 years of age. This measure is of interest if 60 is the usual age of retirement and an investigation of old age pension schemes is at stake. According to this measure, an aged population is characterized by a high value of E and the economic problems become worse if this value is increasing over time (which is the most usual economic

140

definition of ageing). The second measure considers a dependency ratio which is of interest if the total burden of education and of pension financing which falls on the active population is investigated. This measure is influenced by ageing: *ceteris paribus*, any increase in the number of the elderly increases E_2. On the other hand, as an aggregate, E_2 gives no information about ageing. A higher E_2 may well be due to a larger number of the non-working young.

In both demographic and economic measures age groups are investigated. The alternative, that of characterizing an ageing population by its increasing average or median age, is not considered. Consequently ageing is identified as a change in the group composition of a population, where each group is characterized by specific economic behaviour. The exact number of age groups which must be distinguished depends on the objective of the relevant investigation. Aggregate economic conclusions can be adequately derived from theoretical models where, at a given point in time, two age groups live together, the young and the old, whose interdependence is treated in an overlapping-generations model. This is, for instance, a sufficient theoretical approach for investigating the long-run aggregate consequences of pension schemes where the young pay the contributions and the old reap the benefits. Other straightforward applications of the two overlapping-generations approach are given whenever the two generations exhibit dichotomous economic behaviour, for instance if the young save and the old dissave or if the young invest and the old enjoy the income from their previous investments. Further disaggregation into more than two age groups who live together does not change the basic qualitative results of the two overlapping-generations theoretical models, as the decomposition model of Balasko, Cass and Shell (1980) has shown.

However, if questions of economic practice are to be answered, and the year-to-year changes in economic policy variables over the next ten, twenty or thirty years are also to be considered, then it may be desirable to choose more than two overlapping generations. The best known example of such an approach is Auerbach and Kotlikoff's (1987) model, which considers 55 overlapping age groups (cohorts). This approach can well be applied to simulating alternative social security responses to demographic transition.[3] Moreover intermediate models which consider three or four overlapping generations are adequate if the life cycles of income, consumption, savings, etc. are divided into more than two different periods for which the economic characteristics are crucial for the investigation.[4] A good example is the short-run labour supply. As empirical investigations show, the youngest groups of employees are the most sensitive to business cycle fluctuations.[5] The middle-aged groups are less sensitive; however the higher age groups are once again more sensitive.[6] Similar problems arise with respect to intertemporal decisions on consumption and saving: the young save, the old dissave after retirement, but the very old once again save because of health- and age-dependent consumption constraints.[7] Another differentiation in empirical studies could refer to the differences in the behaviour of male and female age groups. The economic status of elderly widows, for instance, typically differs from the economic status of both elderly married women and elderly widowers. The female supply of labour, analysed for a typical course of life, can be contrasted with the lifetime profile of the male labour supply.[8] Retirement decisions of females differ from those of males. The empirical literature on the consequences of ageing carefully analyses these differences (for instance, Apps, 1991; Burkhauser and Duncan, 1991).

The most challenging theories on the consequences of ageing deal with the interplay of the various groups whose characteristics differ because of age. Of particular interest are cases of redistribution between groups, as in the case of old age pension insurance, treated in Section 2. However old age pensions are not the only important case where ageing influences (re)distribution. The relative size of the group of unemployed compared with the group of employed also depends on ageing, as does the respective process of redistribution (where the employed pay for the unemployed). Hence, Section 3 surveys theories on the influence ageing exerts on unemployment. Finally ageing leads to changes in the overall composition of the various income groups and hence influences the overall distribution of incomes. This is examined in Section 4.

This survey can be considered as a complement to Hurd's (1990) outstanding survey of the empirical research on the elderly. His survey concentrates on economic status, retirement, and consumption and saving.[9] Thus I omit these topics in my survey, and concentrate instead on reviewing some recent research on the theory of social insurance and on the influence ageing exerts on unemployment and on income distribution.[10]

2 AGEING AND SOCIAL INSURANCE

In the first two decades after 1945, it seemed natural in Europe to introduce and to expand pay-as-you-go systems of social insurance: the war-induced breakdown of funds and the postwar baby boom made unfunded systems most attractive. Currently, however, sufficient funds may be available for a funded social security system to be feasible. Moreover European populations are ageing. In ageing populations the sum of population and wage growth rates typically is lower than the interest rate, that is $n + w < r$. When this is the case, the returns on an unfunded pension scheme fall below the returns on a fully funded scheme.[11] This has led to intensive discussion about the optimality of alternative old age pension systems.

Although $n + w < r$ can be expected to hold in the future, this does not imply that a pay-as-you-go system is Pareto inefficient.[12] However this inefficiency was incorrectly assumed by Townley (1981). He suggested the following policy: retired people should receive pensions according to a pay-as-you-go system financed through government debt; working people should pay into a funded system, but the return on their contributions should be restricted to $n + w$, instead of r. The difference would then be used to repay the government debt. After a finite period of time, the total government debt would have been repaid and the return on the contributions could then be raised to r. No generation would be made worse off in the transition; however, after a finite period of time, all future generations would be made better off. Unfortunately, this policy cannot work, since the pay-as-you-go system is intergenerationally Pareto efficient, as long as the labour supply is inelastic or pay-as-you-go contributions have a lump sum character. As correctly shown by Verbon (1988, 1989) and by Breyer (1989), it is impossible to repay the government debt within a finite time, as proposed by Townley.[13]

Since the disbandment of a pay-as-you-go system requires that at least one generation loses in the process of transition, welfare-improving changes to pension systems have been investigated where welfare is measured by some kind of social welfare function. Most papers on this topic apply additive social welfare functions, where the individual utilities of the representative members of the various generations are added, either unweighted (the so-called 'Ramsey' approach, since the results are compatible with the golden rule) or weighted with the number of members of the generation (the 'Bentham' approach). Alternatively either altruistic utility or special forms of discounting of future utilities are considered. The relevant papers show welfare-optimal combinations of private savings and public pension systems where the payroll taxes of the pension scheme alternatively are lump sum or distortionary. Outstanding recent papers in this literature are Boadway, Marchand and Pestieau (1991) and Peters (1991a, 1991b).[14] If the class of welfare functions is restricted and the growth rate of the population constant,[15] then clear-cut qualitative results can be obtained in these theoretical models. However, if all kinds of welfare functions are allowed and combined in simulation studies with realistic scenarios of population growth,[16] then nearly every feasible mix of private savings and public pensions can be obtained from such a model. It may even be the case that the policy paths are time-inconsistent.[17] Blanchet and Kessler (1991) simulated the optimal policy mix between funding and pay-as-you-go pensions in order to cope with 'irregular demographic evolutions such as those expected in developed countries for the next century'. They assumed social welfare functions ranging from a log linear sum of individual consumption to a maximin policy. If optimal policy paths started in 1970, for example, private savings for pension funds in 2060 would lie between approximately 20 per cent of wage incomes (for a maximin policy) and − 8 per cent (for a policy with little concern for intergenerational equity). The corresponding contributions to the pay-as-you-go system are approximately 16 per cent and 42 per cent (!).[18]

Turning from theory to practice, let us make some tentative remarks on the transition of public pension systems in former communist countries.[19] Their present problems of financing old age pensions do not result from past problems of an ageing population. On the contrary, their fertility rates were formerly quite high and their life expectancy rates low. However this demographic pattern will soon change: life expectancies will increase. Moreover it will mostly be younger citizens who emigrate from these countries. Although ageing will be a problem only in the future, partial transitions to funded pension schemes have already been discussed in the former communist countries. These discussions arose as a by-product of mass privatization programmes. One of the main problems of mass privatization is the lack of effective control of privatized firms if all ownership shares are distributed among the general public. As a way out of the dilemma, some proposals for reform suggested giving a portion of the shares to pension funds which would be charged with controlling the firms.[20] Such a policy could achieve an instant transition to a partially funded pension scheme.

3 AGEING AND UNEMPLOYMENT

Young, middle-aged and elderly employees face age group-specific labour market conditions. Consequently ageing influences unemployment. Let us begin with a microeconomic general (dis)equilibrium model. In Pissarides (1989), the unions accord higher weights to older employees' wishes than to the younger workers' wishes. Therefore the co-operative Nash bargaining solution for firms and unions always gives the older workers the higher wages. However, if the older employees leave the firm, they are not entitled to a new job at a senior wage level. They must accept the same wages as younger employees. Even the unions cannot improve the low external pay options for older workers. However they can provide older employees with better protection against dismissal, which indirectly leads to lower unemployment rates for older employees. Consequently, in a general equilibrium, ageing reduces the overall unemployment rate (and the wage rate) of both groups of the population. Of course Pissarides bases his arguments on the seniority principle being the basis for unions' preferences. It should be mentioned, however, that there are many other possible explanations as to why ageing might reduce unemployment: older workers are less likely simply to quit their jobs. Moreover they may typically opt for early retirement instead of unemployment.

Hence it is not surprising that the favourable influence which ageing exerts on unemployment has also been deduced through macroeconomic models. These models investigate how the natural rate of unemployment depends on age. Best known are Johnson and Layard's (1986) calculations for the United States. To find an equilibrium rate of unemployment the authors do not estimate a Phillips curve, but follow the Lucas approach, which contends that actual unemployment deviates from the equilibrium rate owing to exogenous shocks. Hence for various age, gender and race groups unemployment is regressed against unanticipated money growth, lagged unemployment and time. The equilibrium unemployment rate is found by setting unanticipated money growth equal to zero. In all cases the equilibrium unemployment rate declines with age, except for the age group 65 and over. Since there are not too many would-be employees in this group, we can conclude that ageing would reduce the equilibrium unemployment rate in the US population.

Finally, in his West German study, Zimmermann (1991) arrives at long run conclusions which are compatible with Pissarides' and

Johnson and Layard's. In his model, ageing is represented by a decrease in the relative cohort size of the young, that is $P_{15,\,34}/P_{35,\,54}$. This decrease will not increase the unemployment of the young,[21] but will reduce the unemployment of the elderly.

4   AGEING AND INCOME DISTRIBUTION

The influence ageing exerts on the distribution of income[22] is a rather neglected area of theoretical and empirical research. Some discussions of this subject can be found in Atkinson (1983, p. 74) and in Bös and von Weizsäcker (1989, pp. 346–7) and a tentative modelling of the issue is presented in von Weizsäcker (1989). However a fully elaborated theory on the topic is still lacking. The basic problem is as follows. As is well known from empirical studies, people of the same age share a particular fate with respect to earnings, unemployment, retirement and savings.[23] Therefore a changing age pattern modifies the distribution of income. Ageing alone can be sufficient to bring about such changes, even if all individual lifetime profiles of income, including old age pensions, remain unchanged.

From a purely demographic point of view, ageing *increases* the overall inequality of annual net incomes. This is mainly due to the increased number of people in the more dispersed income groups of 45 to 60 years of age and to the increased number of old age retired people whose incomes are distributed even more unequally than the incomes of middle-aged families.[24] However this result is reversed if the government aims at achieving some equilibria in both its tax and pension budget (von Weizsäcker, 1989). In that case a pure demographic effect has to be traded off against two budget effects: an increase in the dependency ratio increases the contributions to the pension system, which reduces the coefficient of variation of net incomes. Similarly an increase in the dependency ratio increases the marginal tax rate because the tax-deductability of the increased pension contributions reduces the yields from income taxation and hence a given revenue from taxation can only be achieved by a higher tax rate. The higher tax rate, however, also reduces the coefficient of variation of net incomes. Von Weizsäcker (1989) shows that the two budget effects outweigh the pure demographic effect. Hence, in such a model, ageing *reduces* the overall inequality of net incomes.

Regardless of whether ageing decreases or increases inequality, any policy maker must be obliged to consider ageing explicitly when shaping redistributive policies. In particular the policy maker has to avoid considering only changes in inequality of the current period's annual incomes. Such a policy could well imply a cross-section fallacy, where only ageing is responsible for the change in inequality, although all individual lifetime income profiles have remained unchanged. Hence not only social security and unemployment operate in a framework of intertemporal value judgments and long term policy orientation; so too does the redistribution of incomes.

5 CONCLUSION

The economic theory of an ageing population is a mesoeconomic approach: it requires the distinction of groups whose behaviour differs according to age. The challenge of the economic theory of ageing, therefore, is the interdependence of cross-section and life cycle reasoning. This becomes clear in all three areas of research surveyed here. In social insurance models individual consumer decisions determine life cycle consumption and saving. As long as only funded pensions are at stake, with transfers between generations excluded, we are simply left with a life cycle problem. However the pay-as-you-go system requires the additional modelling of the cross-section interdependencies, typically in an overlapping-generations framework. The theory of income distribution shows how changes in the age group composition of the population may change the distribution of incomes, even if any individual life cycle of income and saving remains unchanged, so that a policy maker may commit a cross-section fallacy by thinking in the usual terms of a static theory of redistribution.

Whenever scenarios of an ageing society have been developed, the pessimistic view has prevailed (since Gulliver's travels into the country of the very old). The survey presented here shows that optimistic views are feasible.[25] Theories on the optimal mix between funded and pay-as-you-go insurance systems have proved that, in rich societies, old age pensions can be financed without exorbitant contributions. The surveyed theories on ageing and unemployment argue that overall unemployment will be reduced by ageing. Finally it has been shown that ageing could well reduce the overall inequality of incomes in spite of the widely held belief to the contrary.

Notes

1. The author gratefully acknowledges helpful comments by Günther Lang, Wolfgang Peters and Klaus F. Zimmermann and financial support by Deutsche Forschungsgemeinschaft (DFG).
2. For a good overview of various definitions of ageing see Dinkel (1989) pp. 245–56.
3. See Auerbach and Kotlikoff (1985).
4. Note that ageing typically also implies a reduction in the percentage of the young non-working individuals in the population. Even if this reduction is significant in theoretical models, a specific model of the decisions of young, non-working individuals is not necessary: economically speaking, these decisions are made by this group's parents. For such a model, see Wildasin (1991).
5. The young workers' high sensitivity is due to the newness of their career, which implies that they have less seniority and fewer voluntary job changes due to the job-matching process for men and family formation considerations for women (Ehrenberg, 1980).
6. However for West Germany a recent empirical study failed to give a statistically significant proof of such a U-shaped pattern of short run unemployment. See Zimmermann (1991) Tables 7 and 8. (Add the coefficients of the variables 'cycle', 'cycle (-1)' and 'cycle (-2)' to consider the influence of business cycles on unemployment.)
7. A theoretical model of the individual time paths of consumption constraints for the old is given in Börsch–Supan and Stahl (1991). They also contribute empirical evidence on the topic.
8. To my knowledge, Apps (1981) is one of the few exceptions of a theoretical, neoclassical analysis which explicitly differentiates female and male behaviour.
9. And so does the recent survey of Börsch-Supan (1991).
10. Many of the papers reviewed in this survey are collected in Bös and Cnossen (1991, 1992).
11. This comparison was first articulated by Aaron (1966) for the case in which $w = 0$.
12. For a general presentation of intergenerational Pareto efficiency, see Lang (1990, 1992).
13. Some further studies have recently appeared in Germany which show that efficiency gains can be obtained by a transition from distortionary payroll taxation to lump sum taxation (that is, government debt). From a theoretical point of view, this is hardly surprising. See Breyer and Straub (1991), Homburg (1990), Homburg and Richter (1990), Raffelhüschen (1991).
14. A political–economic model of the same type can be found in Verbon and Verhoeven (1992).
15. Boadway, Marchand and Pestieau (1991) allowed for cyclical fluctuations of population growth rates and productivity levels.
16. In Blanchet and Kessler (1991, p. 145), for instance, the net reproduction rate is taken to be 1.5 (1940–70), 0.833 (1970–2000), 0.8 (2000–30) and 1.0 (2030–90).

17. Compare, for instance, Figures 1 and 2 in Blanchet and Kessler (1991).
18. Most recent studies on social insurance deal with uncertain population development (Brandts and de Bartolome, 1992) and with endogenous fertility (Nishimura and Zhang, 1992).
19. For an overview see Holzmann (1991) which also provides many further references. See also Diamond (1992) for a particular case study.
20. For an overview of such proposals, see Borensztein and Kumar (1991).
21. Most of the respective coefficients of Zimmermann's econometric cointegration equations are not significant.
22. This section concentrates on the distribution of incomes. Needless to say, the distribution of wealth should also always be taken into account in such analyses.
23. See, for instance, Börsch-Supan and Stahl (1991) and Easterlin (1980).
24. See, for instance, Brotman (1977) and Mookherjee and Shorrocks (1982).
25. For particularly optimistic results of a political–economic model see Drissen and van Winden (1991). The trend towards a more optimistic view of ageing is also shared in Ng's (1992) paper with the provocative title 'The older the more valuable.'

References

Aaron, H.J. (1966) 'The Social Insurance Paradox', *Canadian Journal of Economics and Political Science*, vol. 32, pp. 371–4.
Apps, P. (1981) *A Theory of Inequality and Taxation* (Cambridge: Cambridge University Press).
Apps, P. (1991) 'Tax Reform, Population Ageing and the Changing Labour Supply Behaviour of Married Women', *Journal of Population Economics*, vol. 4, pp. 201–16.
Atkinson, A.B. (1983) *The Economics of Inequality*, 2nd edn (Oxford: Oxford University Press).
Auerbach, A.J. and Kotlikoff, L.J. (1985) 'Simulating Alternative Social Security Responses to the Demographic Transition', *National Tax Journal*, vol. 38, pp. 153–68.
Auerbach, A.J. and Kotlikoff, L.J. (1987) *Dynamic Fiscal Policy* (Cambridge: Cambridge University Press).
Balasko, Y., Cass, D. and Shell, K. (1980) 'Existence of Competitive Equilibrium in a General Overlapping-Generations Model', *Journal of Economic Theory*, vol. 23, pp. 307–22.
Billeter, E.P. (1954) 'Eine Maßzahl zur Beurteilung der Altersverteilung einer Bevölkerung' ('A measure for the evaluation of the age distribution of a population'), *Schweizerische Zeitschrift für Volkswirtschaft und Statistik*, vol. 90, pp. 496–505.
Blanchet, D. and Kessler, D. (1991) 'Optimal Pension Funding with Demographic Instability and Endogenous Returns on Investment', *Journal of Population Economics*, vol. 4, pp. 137–54.

Boadway, R., Marchand, M. and Pestieau, P. (1991) 'Pay-as-you-go Social Security in a Changing Environment', *Journal of Population Economics*, vol. 4, pp. 257–80.

Borensztein, E. and Kumar, M.S. (1991) 'Proposals for Privatization in Eastern Europe', *Staff Papers*, International Monetary Fund, vol. 38, pp. 300–26.

Börsch–Supan, A. (1991) 'Aging Population: Problems and Policy Options in the US and Germany', *Economic Policy*, vol. 6, no. 1, pp. 104–39.

Börsch–Supan, A. and Stahl, K. (1991) 'Life Cycle Savings and Consumption Constraints – Theory, Empirical Evidence, and Fiscal Implications', *Journal of Population Economics*, vol. 4, pp. 233–55.

Bös, D. and Cnossen, S. (eds) (1991) 'Economic Consequences of an Aging Population, Part I: Theory', *Journal of Population Economics*, vol. 4, pp. 87–175; 'Part II: Applications', *Journal of Population Economics*, vol. 4, pp. 177–255.

Bös, D. and Cnossen, S. (eds) (1992) *Fiscal Implications of an Aging Population* (Berlin, Heidelberg, New York, Tokyo: Springer Verlag). (Reprint of the papers published in the *Journal of Population Economics*, vol. 4, pp. 87–175, 177–255, 257–80.)

Bös, D. and von Weizsäcker, R.K. (1989) 'Economic Consequences of an Aging Population', *European Economic Review*, vol. 33, pp. 345–54.

Brandts, J. and de Bartolome, C.A.M. (1992) 'Population Uncertainty, Social Insurance, and Actuarial Bias', *Journal of Public Economics*, vol. 47, pp. 361–80.

Breyer, F. (1989) 'On the Intergenerational Pareto Efficiency of Pay-as-you-go Financed Pension Systems', *Journal of Institutional and Theoretical Economics*, vol. 145, pp. 643–58.

Breyer, F. and Straub, M. (1991) 'Welfare Effects of Unfunded Pension Systems when Labor Supply is Endogenous', mimeo, University of Konstanz, Germany.

Brotman, H. (1977) 'Income and Poverty in the Older Population', *Gerontologist*, vol. 17, pp. 23–6.

Burkhauser, R.V. and Duncan, G.J. (1991) 'United States Public Policy and the Elderly – The Disproportionate Risk to the Well-Being of Women', *Journal of Population Economics*, vol. 4, pp. 217–31.

Diamond, P. (1992) 'Pension Reform in a Transition Economy', mimeo, MIT, Cambridge, Mass.

Dinkel, R. (1989) *Demographie* (Munich: Vahlen).

Drissen, E. and van Winden, F. (1991) 'Social Security in a General Equilibrium Model with Endogenous Government Behavior', *Journal of Population Economics*, vol. 4, pp. 89–110.

Easterlin, R.A. (1980) *Birth and Fortune* (New York: Basic Books).

Ehrenberg, R.G. (1980) 'The Demographic Structure of Unemployment Rates and Labor Market Transition Probabilities', *Research in Labor Economics*, vol. 3, pp. 241–93.

Holzmann, R. (1991) 'Reforming Old-Age Pensions Systems in Central and Eastern European Countries in Transition: Necessity and Chance', in Felderer, B. (ed.) *Public Pension Systems* (Vienna: Institute for Advanced Studies).

Homburg, S. (1990) 'The Efficiency of Unfunded Pension Schemes', *Journal of Institutional and Theoretical Economics*, vol. 146, pp. 640–7.

Homburg, S. and Richter W. (1990) 'Eine effizienzorientierte Reform der GRV' ('An efficiency-oriented reform of the compulsory pension insurance'), in Felderer, B. (ed.) *Bevölkerung und Wirtschaft*, Schriften des Vereins für Socialpolitik 202 (Berlin: Duncker and Humblot) pp. 183–91.

Hurd, M.D. (1990) 'Research on the Elderly: Economic Status, Retirement, and Consumption and Saving', *Journal of Economic Literature*, vol. 28, pp. 565–637.

Johnson, G.E. and Layard, P.R.G. (1986) 'The Natural Rate of Unemployment: Explanation and Policy', in Ashenfelter, O.C. and Layard, P.R.G. (eds) *Handbook of Labor Economics*, vol. 2 (Amsterdam: North Holland) pp. 921–99.

Lang, G. (1990) 'Intergenerational Contracts and Their Decomposition: An Extension', *Journal of Economics/Zeitschrift für Nationalökonomie*, vol. 52, pp. 177–89.

Lang, G. (1992) 'Dynamic Efficiency and Capital Accumulation', *European Journal of Political Economy*, vol. 8, pp. 153–74.

Mookherjee, D. and Shorrocks, A.F. (1982) 'A Decomposition Analysis of the Trend in UK Income Inequality', *Economic Journal*, vol. 92, pp. 886–902.

Ng, Y.-K. (1992) 'The Older the More Valuable: Divergence Between Utility and Dollar Values of Life as One Ages', *Journal of Economics/Zeitschrift für Nationalökonomie*, vol. 55, pp. 1–16.

Nishimura, K. and Zhang, J. (1992) 'Pay-as-you-go Public Pensions With Endogenous Fertility', *Journal of Public Economics*, vol. 48, pp. 239–58.

Peters, W. (1991a) 'Public Pensions in Transition. An Optimal Policy Path', *Journal of Population Economics*, vol. 4, pp. 155–75.

Peters, W. (1991b) 'Public Pensions, Family Allowances and Endogenous Growth', in Felderer, B. (ed.) *Public Pension Systems* (Vienna: Institute for Advanced Studies).

Pissarides, C. (1989) 'Unemployment Consequences of an Aging Population', *European Economic Review*, vol. 33, pp. 355–66.

Raffelhüschen, B. (1991) 'Funding Social Security Through Pareto-Optimal Conversion Policies', in Felderer, B. (ed.) *Public Pension Systems* (Vienna: Institute for Advanced Studies).

Townley, P.G.C. (1981) 'Public Choice and the Social Insurance Paradox: A Note', *Canadian Journal of Economics*, vol. 14, pp. 712–7.

Verbon, H.A.A. (1988) *The Evolution of Public Pension Schemes* (Heidelberg: Springer).

Verbon, H.A.A. (1989) 'Conversion Policies for Public Pension Plans in a Small Open Economy', in Gustafsson, B.A. and Klevmarken, N.A. (eds), *The Political Economy of Social Security* (Amsterdam: North Holland) pp. 83–95.

Verbon, H.A.A. (1989) 'Conversion Policies for Public Pension Plans in a Small Open Economy', in Gustafsson, B.A. and Klevmarken, N.A. (eds) *The Political Economy of Social Security* (Amsterdam: North-Holland) pp. 83–95.

von Weizsäcker, R.K. (1989) 'Demographic Change and Income Distribution', *European Economic Review*, vol. 33, pp. 377–88.

Wildasin, D.E. (1991) 'The Marginal Cost of Public Funds with an Aging Population', *Journal of Population Economics*, vol. 4, pp. 111–35.

Zimmermann, K.F. (1991) 'Ageing and the Labor Market – Age Structure, Cohort Size and Unemployment', *Journal of Population Economics*, vol. 4, pp. 177–200.

9 Payment of Medical Providers and the Public Provision of Medical Care

Mark V. Pauly[1]
UNIVERSITY OF PENNSYLVANIA

1 INTRODUCTION

In all countries, governments provide assistance to citizens in paying for medical services. The form of this assistance varies widely, from full public provision (financing) *and* public production, in some countries, to subsidies to private insurance purchases for non-poor persons combined with public provision and/or production for poor persons, in others. In all cases the public sector has the ability to influence the quantities and the prices paid for medical services. Direct governmental control of or influence on prices paid to providers is not utilized in all circumstances, but such control or influence is almost always possible.

Normative theories to justify and, presumably, to explain the public provision of medical services usually do not emphasize the role of persons and firms that supply medical services, 'providers' in US terminology. Instead the rationale for such intervention is usually founded on some notion of altruistic externality (Pauly, 1971), or the closely related concept of goods-specific equity (Lindsay, 1969). The idealized welfare-maximizing government in these explanations takes into account the true social marginal cost of medical services in deciding on the allocation of resources to medical services.

An exception to this generalization is the positive theory of the socialization of commodities proposed by Usher (1977) and subsequent commentators (Wilson and Katz, 1983). In one version of this model, providers can be allies in proposals for 'socializing' medical care, in the sense of universal full and free public provision, because they expect income gains when reduction of the user price to zero increases the demand for their services. The precise mechanism by which increased demand translates into higher provider well-being is not treated in detail by Usher, but the notion presumably is that an increase in demand raises price and average provider welfare if the supply curve is upward sloping and the quantity of services provided is greater with socialization than without.

Usher's implicit model is one in which, despite full socialization, the government pays the competitive supply price at whatever point on the supply curve it chooses to settle. As a positive model, this theory seems incomplete in its treatment of two aspects of actual behaviour in medical markets. First, in at least some countries (the USA being the prime example), prices received by providers may include some monopoly rent. The evidence is not watertight; even the meaning of a competitive price or monopoly rent is obscure in the case of health professionals, who usually receive supply-limited publicly subsidized educational training, and who surely receive substantial quasi-rents once they enter their profession, regardless of the presence of monopoly rents. Second, governments use various devices, such as mandatory bargaining, buyer market power and direct price regulation to affect the prices they pay. Real-world governments frequently try to keep prices lower, or rising less rapidly, than would otherwise be the case. This does not *necessarily* mean that prices and quantities are not on the competitive supply curve, but it may well mean that the point on that curve that governments select is not the competitive equilibrium quantity.

Translations from market models to positive political models always limp a little, but the easiest descriptive model of government–provider relationships in many countries is that of a private monopoly cartel of sellers facing a public monopsony buyer – the model (such as it is) of bilateral bargaining. In those countries in which hospitals are government-owned and health professionals are government employees, this description may not literally hold, but even in this case suppliers of professional labour may have some market power, and there are frequently negotiations between governments and professional unions or professional associations.

If buyers affect input prices, total expenditures will be affected as well. One descriptive implication, and one which will be discussed in detail in this paper, is that total expenditures will be a very unreliable measure of real costs. Moreover monopsony in purchasing medical services or medical inputs has normative and positive connotations. What follows explores the implications of public monopsony power for (a) cross-national comparisons of medical expenditures; and (b) conventional welfare rationales for public provision of medical services.

2 THE BASIC MODEL

The basic normative model of public sector behaviour is reasonably straightforward. Medical services are assumed to be supplied according to a positively sloped aggregate supply curve. To keep things simple, it will be assumed that the number of suppliers or 'providers' is given, that all providers are identical, but that each provider firm supplies services (or work time) according to an upward-sloping marginal opportunity cost curve.

A normative formulation of the public *demand* for services can be based on the notion of altruistic externalities. The demand for services for any individual can be thought of as the vertical sum of that individual's demands for services for himself plus the altruistic or community demand for services by others for this person (Pauly, 1971). (There is some incompleteness here, since the level of community demand may depend not only on the aggregate quantity demanded by individuals but also on the position of each individual's demand curve.) The efficient quantity of services for any individual is the quantity at which this vertically summed demand intersects the supply curve.

An aggregate demand curve can then be derived by horizontally summing (across individuals) these vertically summed demand curves. Let this be represented by D_A in Figure 9.1. The efficient aggregate quantity of services is that quantity at which this demand curve intersects the supply curves. Thus Q^* is the Pareto optimal aggregate quantity, given the initial distribution of income, and it would sell at the price P^*. A welfare-maximizing government that accepted (or determined) the income distribution would presumably choose this quantity.

The basic positive model is based on the observation that, when government is the single buyer, it has the power to behave like a monopsonist. If consumers of care have sufficient political power, they will wish government to do so. This government would choose the quantity at the intersection of D_A (or some political approximation to it) with the curve *marginal* to the supply curve, MS, in Figure 9.1. The equilibrium will usually involve a smaller quantity at Q_{MS}

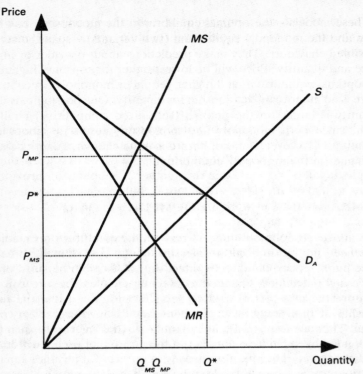

Figure 9.1   Alternative equilibria under competition, monopoly and monopsony

and a lower price at P_{MS} than at the welfare-maximizing optimum.

It is also possible to construct a (third) model in which providers obtain (or retain) market power and government does not try to affect market demand. Such a situation is surely possible if there is no government intervention, but it seems less plausible if the public sector is able to determine both private and public demand curves. One possible approach is to imagine that public provision consists solely of the provision of public insurance which lowers the out-of-pocket price, but leaves providers free to set gross prices as they choose. The equilibrium quantity and prices would be Q_{MP} and P_{MP} respectively. If, in addition, the amount of medical care patients obtain increased strongly once insurance covered it – the so-called 'moral hazard' of insurance – and if the socially desired insurance resulted in a low out-of-pocket price, the social demand curve could be shifted out further so that the equilibrium would be at an even higher price and quantity.

These models – the optimal equilibrium, the monopsony equilibrium and the monopoly equilibrium (two variants) – span the set of possible behaviours. They make predictions about provider or input price and quantity. Price will be lowest under monopsony, higher in the optimal equilibrium, and higher yet under monopoly. In contrast there is no monotonic relationship for quantity. One possibility is that quantity is largest in the optimal (subsidized competitive) equilibrium, since both monopoly and monopsony result in suboptimal quantities. However, if moral hazard is large enough, quantity could be higher in the monopoly equilibrium.

3   MEASURING THE COST OF MEDICAL CARE

The above observations suggest that total expenditure on medical care need not be an accurate measure of the cost of medical care, since public policy can directly affect the relationship between price and cost – indeed it is intended to affect price. We therefore want to measure the true cost of medical services and to consider the relationship of that true cost to the conventional measure of expenditures. Then we want to discuss possible reasons for variation in the divergence between expenditure and cost, since that reason will affect one's interpretation of policy options.

There has been considerable research directed at measuring and comparing the share of medical expenditures relative to GDP across countries (Culyer, 1989). The precise interest in or interpretation of this share is not clear. Its interpretation is considered in more detail below, but some initial observations may be appropriate here. To some extent, the share can be interpreted as reflecting variations in the *demand* for medical services. Newhouse's classic regression analysis (1977), for example, which showed that GDP per capita is highly predictive of expenditures (except for the USA) and that income elasticity is less than unity, was interpreted as demonstrating that demand is predominant in determining expenditures. Sometimes these figures are interpreted as measures of the relative *efficiency* with which different countries supply and produce medical services (Parkin, 1989). Since health indicators in developed countries are quite unresponsive to medical services (with the possible exception of some Eastern European countries) a high share is usually taken as evidence of inefficiency. Finally some are concerned that GDP shares have macroeconomic consequences; they feel that using resources for medical services reduces that level of aggregate investment or (in some vague sense) makes a country less competitive in international trade, all because it squanders its national treasure on medical care.

To analyse any of the three arguments properly, one should compare real opportunity costs relative to GDP, not money expenditures. It is therefore important to try to measure cost properly. If medical services inputs were sold in competitive markets that displayed neither monopoly nor monopsony, a proper measure of the cost of medical service (assuming no externalities) would be provided by the opportunity cost of those inputs – their value in their next best use. If the supply of some inputs is not perfectly elastic, total expenditure on inputs, even in a competitive market, will overstate total opportunity cost, since total expenditure contains some inframarginal rents. The more elastic the supply curves of inputs, the more closely total expenditure approximates to total opportunity cost.

In contrast, if sellers of inputs have monopoly power, price will exceed marginal (opportunity) cost. If aggregate public and private demand is relatively inelastic, as seems most likely, total expenditure will be higher under monopoly than under competition. The extent of divergence between price and marginal cost depends on firm-level demand elasticity. But, while total expenditure is probably greater under monopoly than under competition, opportunity cost can be *lower* (depending on the extent of moral hazard) because output is restricted below the competitive level.

The other possibility is that buyers (or the public sector, if it is the only buyer) have market power and bring about input prices that are at the monopsony level. This will result in expenditures and costs that are both *lower* than the competitive level. The degree of divergence between the optimal competitive and monopsony equilibrium depends on supply elasticity. In the monopsony case, total expenditure will usually still exceed opportunity cost at the level of inputs being hired. However observed payments to providers are still on the aggregate supply curve. The main difference under monopsony is that the *quantity* of inputs (and outputs) is lower than in the competitive equilibrium. Effects on price are related to (and may be caused by) effects on quantity.

These simple observations lead to some important implications:

1. The total opportunity cost of the medical services rendered in a country can be lower under either monopoly or monopsony than it is under optimal competition, since both non-competitive equilibria involve smaller quantities than the optimum and lower costs.

Competition is the least cost-constraining of the three institutional arrangements.
2. While the competitive equilibrium can be the most costly, it is also the one that maximizes overall welfare. Hence there is no direct connection between expenditures on medical care in a country and its well-being. Indeed, in two countries with the same GNP, the one with higher medical expenditures may well have a higher level of welfare.
3. The welfare of those users of medical services who are not providers will be highest under monopsony and lowest under monopoly, especially if the monopsony is exercised by government as a kind of buyers' cartel.

Without knowing the entire supply curve, it is not possible to calculate opportunity cost directly. What we can do, however, is to determine how levels of input prices affect the level of total spending. If the quantity of inputs used (adjusted for demand) is approximately the same in all settings, this can provide a measure of the impact of buyer market power relative to seller market power. If the quantity is lower when prices are lower, things are more ambiguous, since there is no way to distinguish between the monopsony case, in which the buyer restricts quantity *in order to* lower price, and a 'more efficient' managed care setting, in which the buyer lowers the quantity only to find that the price falls as well.

4 THE CONSEQUENCES OF ALTERNATIVE MEASURES OF THE MEDICAL GNP SHARE

If the share of GNP or GDP represented by national health expenditures can be affected by governmental pricing policies, how is this measure to be interpreted? Paradoxically although studies of health policy and health care reform are replete with references to the expenditures share – it is standard fare in the introduction to a discussion of health care reform in any country – the precise meaning or implication of the share has not been well defined.

If relative input prices were the same in all countries, and if one compared two countries with the same GDP or GNP per capita, then the share of GNP would measure the relative amount of resources devoted to medical services. In itself this comparison has no easy welfare interpretation: is a high share worse or better than a low share? If one has a measure of outcomes of the medical care system that is reliable, comparing spending per capita might shed light on the technology, in the broad sense, used in different countries; it could measure the productivity of each country's health care system. If better (or no worse) outcomes accompany lower cost, the conclusion might be that the lower cost country has a more efficient system. Parkin (1989) provides an example of such a study. This approach assumes, however, that medical care expenditures measure all of the inputs into or influences on health outcomes, which surely is not true. The initial health levels of the population, the provision of other public or private services, and the possibility of non-monetary costs are all potentially important. For example, the relatively high share in the United States could be attributable in part to (a) a larger poor (and non-white) population with socially generated health pathologies; (b) lower levels of other types of non-medical but health-related support, so much so that, if monetary sick leave benefits are added to direct medical expenditures, the USA spends a smaller proportion of its GDP on health than some other countries (BASYS, 1992); (c) shorter waiting and travel times for hospital and doctor services than in other countries (Danzon, 1992), offset by higher explicit provider prices.

The standard indicators of health outcomes that are collected in a reasonably reliable way across countries surely do not capture all dimensions of desirable outcomes. For example, in a careful comparison of US and Canadian physician expenditures, Fuchs and Hahn (1990) attributed much of the higher US spending to higher US levels of non-physician inputs per unit of physician service – higher cost, in the economic sense – but could not tell whether the additional inputs go to provide higher quality, greater convenience or simply represent departures from the efficiency frontier. It is possible that a particular health care system might be on the efficiency frontier and yet display higher total spending than some other system. For example, permitting providers to receive higher prices might translate into higher out-of-pocket payments for beneficiaries, which could discourage low-value care. Or, in a second-best sense, higher provider prices might avoid excessive reliance on other services which are substitutes. It is, for instance, widely believed that, in countries in which physicians are paid relatively poorly, they tend to substitute the issuing of a prescription for drugs for their own time in diagnosing and counselling patients.

Another reason for wanting to know about health care costs,

independent of the level of benefits from medical services, is based on the notion that alternative levels of spending may have macroeconomic consequences. It is widely alleged by vocal corporate executives in the USA, for example, that one of the impediments to the competitiveness of American products in international markets is the high relative level of medical care spending in the USA. This high level of spending, in their view, both raises corporate labour costs (because a large share of the health insurance premium is paid as an employer-provided fringe benefit) and displaces other, more economically productive, uses of GNP. To a considerable extent this view represents a misunderstanding (or denial) of some elements of basic economics: that the incidence of fringe benefits costs ultimately falls on workers, and that one type of consumption largely displaces another type of consumption, and does not impoverish or even displace savings to any great extent. However, with total medical spending (including drugs and sick pay) as high as 17 per cent of GNP (in Sweden), it is possible that such spending could reach levels that would affect both saving and the size of the basket of consumption goods and services available for non-medical purposes. And as populations around the globe age, the macroeconomic consequences become more serious.

If there is to be a proper debate about the share of medical costs in GNP, one obviously needs to measure real costs. For instance, transfers in the form of sick leave benefits, in the form of money, do not themselves represent real costs. To the great majority of citizens, such transfers probably represent net losses, since the distribution of illnesses and the known risk of illnesses are skewed. But they should have little economic impact. Transfers to medical care input suppliers may have a larger impact, especially if they represent transfers to professionals who would be in the upper part of the income distribution (doctors and dentists). One key issue for economic growth, then, is whether the marginal propensity to save of this group is above average. If it is, and if higher savings rates promote sustainable economic growth, then holding down medical care costs by holding down rents to providers may actually slow the rate of economic growth. Not that the effect would be substantial – it probably would not – but it might be at least as large as any other society-wide effects that might flow from health care reform.

In either setting, there is substantial value in trying to adjust measures of spending to more closely approximate real costs. Especially if the supply curve of medical services is relatively inelastic, there can be wide variations in total expenditures that accompany quite small variations in the extent of real resources devoted to medical care. Such misleading measures of what nations really forgo to provide medical services may lead to misleading policy. They may also lead to misguided attempts to influence the size of expenditures rather than real resource flows – either by manipulating payment policies or by substituting actions which are more costly in real terms but which save on explicit medical expenditures and put less pressure on prices. Modifying the thermometer rather than treating the fever is not likely to lead to good policy.

5   SOME ILLUSTRATIVE COMPUTATIONS

How important are the variations in pricing policy for inputs in different countries? No fully definitive answer can be given without the ability to measure opportunity cost directly, but a reasonable approximation can be provided by removing the input price variation from cross-national comparisons. We therefore used the OECD Health Data Programme, the best available data, to provide a rough measure of the extent of potential monopsony behaviour, and to provide a more accurate measure of the true cost of medical services. The results are set out in Table 9.1. We assume that the primary setting in which monopsony power would be exercised would be with regard to medical care labour, especially specialized labour, which makes up 50 to 60 per cent of personal health spending. Workers employed in research or in the production of drugs and materials are not included, and the supply of other inputs to the medical care sector is likely to be highly elastic.

We can distinguish three broad types of labour in the OECD data: doctors providing patient care, nurses, and all other health care workers. We subtracted the count of nurses and doctors from the total of all workers to get 'other medical care workers'. We were careful in classifying doctors to avoid double counting. For some countries in some years we also have estimates of total net incomes received by each of these labour groups. (Note that total *gross* revenue to doctors goes in part to office personnel; such costs are attributed to nurses and other labour in these calculations.) Column 2 of Table 9.1 shows that in 1986 actual expenditure on doctors' services relative to GDP was highest for Germany and the USA, much as the level of total health expenditure relative to GDP was also highest for the USA (last column). (The year 1986 is the one for which there is the best cross-national data; we also performed similar calculations for 1984 and 1988, with very similar results.) There is also a suggestion of the usual pattern of low shares for poorer countries, and a positive correlation of share and income per capita.

However these estimates all reflect 'local' prices, which may be affected by monopsony or monopoly behaviour. To construct a 'constant cost' alternative, we first used US annual 'wages' for a base. (The choice of base is arbitrary.) In the case of doctors, for instance, if we assume that the real marginal opportunity cost of producing a year of doctor work time is the same in all countries, we can obtain estimates of the relative real cost of doctor inputs by attributing the US doctor's income to each country's stock of doctors. We calculated the size of this number relative to each country's GDP measured in US dollars, converted at the purchasing power parity exchange rate.

The message, shown in column 3, is striking. Some poorer countries sacrifice much more for the work of doctors, relative to GDP, than do richer countries. The share in the USA is not unusually high, and is less than that in many other countries. The USA actually sacrifices about the same proportion of GDP as does Canada (in contrast to the 'local wages' estimates). All percentages increase, indicating that, relative to the USA, other countries engage in more monopsony or less monopoly behaviour. The jump is largest, relatively speaking, in Ireland and Turkey, and smallest in West Germany.

The approach taken here differs from the suggestion of Parkin (1989) that relative *output* prices (the so-called 'medical care purchasing power parity prices') be used to weight outputs. Output price variation does include variation due to profitability, local productivity and quality differences, whereas the input price calculations used here do not. In general, however, the implications of my calculations and Parkin's are roughly the same: using similar relative prices in all countries, the US health care cost share of GDP does not appear to be unusually high, relative to other countries of roughly the same GDP per capita. There are some important differences, however. Japan, for instance, has a lower share than the USA in my calculations, but would have a higher share using Parkin's. This is because the medical labour per unit of output is much lower in Japan than in the USA. Of course Japan's well-known brief doctor's office visits suggest that it may not be appropriate to interpret such differences as productivity differences in constant quality output.

We performed the same type of calculation for nurses and for other health care workers. The USA actually spends the second lowest proportion on nurses (second only to Turkey). Spending on other

Table 9.1 Comparisons of expenditures on medical care labour, 1986
(percentage of GDP)

Country	National income per capita PPP US$[a]	Total expenditure on doctors Local wages	Total expenditure on doctors US wages	Total expenditure on nurses Local wages	Total expenditure on nurses US wages	Total expenditure on 'other medical care workers' Local wages	Total expenditure on 'other medical care workers' US wages	Total expenditure on all medical care labour US wages	Total National health expenditure Actual
Australia	10 125	0.66	1.95	n.a.	2.30	n.a.	2.98	7.23	8.1
Canada	13 684	1.03	1.55	1.86	2.08	n.a.	1.08	4.70	8.8
Finland	9 878	0.46	1.85	0.75	1.53	2.81	4.01	7.39	7.4
France	10 655	0.76	2.33	n.a.	1.20	n.a.	2.93	6.46	8.5
Greece	5 558	n.a.	5.89	n.a.	1.13	1.16	1.47	8.49	5.4
Iceland	12 051	n.a.	2.18	n.a.	1.42	0.02	3.64	7.24	7.8
Ireland	5 623	0.40	2.72	1.40	2.68	n.a.	2.46	7.85	8.3
Italy	9 955	n.a.	1.33	n.a.	0.99	1.65	1.91	4.23	6.9
Japan	10 563	0.52	1.45	0.59	1.20	n.a.	0.75	3.40	6.7
New Zealand	9 241	0.68	1.99	n.a.	2.15	n.a.	2.71	6.84	6.8

Norway	12 441	0.43	1.83	2.09	3.17	2.82	3.14	8.14	7.1
Portugal	5 367	n.a.	5.43	n.a.	1.19	0.98	1.81	8.42	6.6
Sweden	11 484	n.a.	2.49	n.a.	1.78	3.14	4.88	9.15	8.5
Turkey	3 642	0.02	2.25	0.01	0.43	n.a.	0.51	3.20	3.5
United Kingdom	10 274	0.45	1.37	0.53	0.96	2.38	2.78	5.11	5.9
United States of America	14 773	1.56	1.56	0.85	0.85	2.11	2.11	4.51	10.9
West Germany	9 809	1.65	2.56	n.a.	1.01	1.54	2.45	6.03	8.7

Notes: n.a. = not available
 [a] Converted to US dollars at the purchasing power parity exchange rate

Sources: OECD Health Data Programme; *Socioeconomic Characteristics of Medical Practice 1987* (American Medical Association); *Survey of Current Business, July 1990* (US Department of Commerce).

workers is less affected by per capita GDP levels than is spending on doctors' services.

The overall pattern, in the next to last column, suggests that input price variation is substantial, and that removal of that variation gives a very different picture. Countries appear to differ substantially in the real cost of medical labour inputs relative to GDP. This proportion (in contrast to the more conventional health expenditure proportions) is not strongly related to GDP per capita, and it is not especially high for the USA. There is, it should be noted, an alternative explanation for input price variation to the one based on monopsony: it is possible that the position of the supply curve of specialized medical inputs may be different in different countries. While the real resource cost of educating and training a doctor or nurse may not differ substantially, the opportunity cost of time spent in providing medical services may vary. Specifically, in lower-income countries, less well endowed with capital relative to labour in the manufacturing or traded sector, skilled labour productivity will be lower and therefore the opportunity cost of providing medical services will be lower (Bhagwati, 1984). Alternatively productivity in the traded sector may simply be lower in poorer countries (Kravis *et al.*, 1978).

Since we have no independent measures either of 'true' opportunity cost or of relative monopsony power, it is difficult to distinguish these two theories empirically. The fact that the US share, when based on an estimate using uniform input prices, falls from extraordinarily high to about average for countries at the same level of economic development and income (and therefore the same opportunity cost) does suggest less use of monopsony power in the USA relative to other countries know to have more strictly governmentally controlled systems. It is difficult to define measures of the concept of 'extent of monopsony'. Explicit political decisions on the rate of growth of spending can occur even in systems with less extensive public financing. In West Germany, for instance, much of the financing is through self-governing sickness funds, but there is an explicit political choice about the rate of growth in doctors' services expenditures.

It is also instructive to construct a measure of cost which does not depend on the level of GDP per capita, that is, an 'absolute' measure. One such measure is the proportion of the population engaged in producing medical services. Since time spent in the medical care sector is time not spent in producing other goods and services, this calculation provides a measure of the real opportunity cost of medical services if the opportunity cost is proportional to GDP per capita. We constructed a crude measure to weight different kinds of medical labour by basing the weight for patient care doctors on their income relative to average non-doctor medical worker income; we calculated a population-weighted average of this measure across eight countries for 1986 (or the closest year for which data was available). On average, a doctor is assumed to be 4.27 times as productive as the average non-doctor medical worker.

The weighted proportion of the population is shown in the last column of Table 9.2; it varies from 0.47 medical workers per 100 persons to 5.36 workers. Some patterns are apparent. The highest ratios of this measure occur in the Scandinavian countries (and, to a slightly lesser extent, in Finland and Australia). Low ratios characterize lower-income countries: Turkey, Greece, Portugal and Ireland. The only high-income countries with low ratios are Japan, and, to a lesser extent, Italy. The remaining countries, including the USA, have averages close to each other. The US ratio is slightly above that in Canada and the UK, but virtually identical to the ratio in Germany and France. Beyond the observation that low ratios tend to characterize lower-income countries, this measure of real resource use is not strongly related to income. There is little regularity in real resource use per capita for medical services, in contrast to the money measure.

Under this assumption, the real relative cost of medical labour inputs is not unusually high in the USA. In real terms, it is the Scandinavian countries, not the USA, that are spending the most on medical services. Critics should know that it is those countries which would be impoverished by diverting the cream of the crop of their trained workers into medical services rather than into more productive uses.

If labour supply curves to the medical sector are also roughly the same in all countries, these results suggest that wages ought to be highest in those countries using the largest relative amounts of medical inputs. As noted, however, money wages appear to be higher in the USA than in the Scandinavian countries. This result implies either that there are monopoly rents or quasi-rents to medical labour in the USA, or that somehow suppliers in the Scandinavian countries are 'off their supply curves', supplying more labour at relatively low wages than one would have expected. The high prices in the USA may have provoked more aggressive economizing there than in Scandinavia.

Table 9.2 Weighted health workers as a percentage of total population, 1986

Country	Total population (Thousands)	Weighted number of doctors[a]	Total health employment excluding doctors (Numbers)	Total weighted health employment (Numbers)	Total weighted health employment as a percentage of total population
Australia	16 018	140 107	479 211	619 318	3.87
Canada	25 374	227 354	545 793	773 147	3.05
Finland	4 918	38 658	152 953	191 611	3.90
France	55 393	564 626	1 131 793	1 878 419	3.39
Greece	9 966	130 245	72 519	202 764	2.03
Iceland	243	2 701	8 268	10 969	4.51
Ireland	3 541	24 279	56 318	80 597	2.28
Italy	57 221	311 083	878 198	1 189 281	2.08
Japan	121 490	782 510	1 251 984	2 034 494	1.67
New Zealand	3 279	24 557	75 253	99 810	3.04

Norway	4 169	40 350	172 057	212 407	5.09
Portugal	9 716	109 799	77 304	187 103	1.93
Sweden	8 370	98 937	349 846	448 783	5.36
Turkey	51 731	159 990	84 179	244 169	0.47
United Kingdom	56 763	323 017	1 169 593	1 492 610	2.63
United States of America	249 600	2 327 930	5 805 200	8 133 130	3.26
West Germany	61 066	705 109	1 253 985	1 959 094	3.21

Note: [a] Number of doctors multiplied by weight of 4.27. Weight derived from salary data for the following countries for the year 1986, except where the year is shown in brackets: Australia (1983), Finland, West Germany, Italy (1981), Norway, Sweden (1983), United Kingdom and United States of America.

Source: OECD Health Data Programme.

6 THE EQUITY OF MONOPSONY

The review of the empirical evidence suggests that medical care expenditures in some countries are lower than those in others not because real costs are lower but because wages to suppliers of labour for medical services are depressed. We do not have concrete evidence that it is government policy which produces this result; however, since government makes almost all of the purchasing decisions in these countries, it is reasonable to suppose that they represent the results of policy decisions.

Is it inequitable for government to behave as a monopsonist in purchasing medical labour, and is it inefficient? An equity rationale supporting public monopsony behaviour is difficult to find. There seems to be no reason why it is just to reduce the rents of those whose talents are associated with supply of this service, as compared to people who are most skilled at supplying other services which are purchased in private markets. The same argument could be made with regard to people skilled at other activities that governments usually buy (for example, the military (Borcherding, 1971)).

On the other hand, in the countries in which governments depress net money incomes for health workers, they also tend to be more generous in subsidizing education for the skills that generate those incomes. For instance, medical education – for doctors, nurses and other health professionals – is financed in the USA by a combination of public and private funds, whereas in most European countries the explicit costs are fully covered by the state. Of course in both cases the most substantial cost is the opportunity cost of lost income, especially for doctors, which is generally borne privately, although there are stipends in some European countries to cover part of this. The relevant measure is not the income of a medical professional in any one year, but the net lifetime income, taking into account the opportunity cost of training. To some extent the lower medical services costs in European countries compared to the USA may be offset by higher public education costs, as medical education is more heavily subsidized. Definitive judgments about equity require better data on net lifetime income than is generally available.

However it does appear that monopsony behaviour violates the principle of horizontal equity. To be sure, in choosing a career, people in countries in which medical net incomes are depressed presumably know this fact, and choose their careers to equalize real incomes at the margin. However it is surely the case that monopsony behaviour depresses the lifetime net incomes of those whose talents are especially suited to providing medical services. There is no basis for justifying transfers from those with an aptitude for producing medical services.

All of this assumes that workers are on their supply curves. Are there ways to get workers to supply more labour, at a given wage, than would be utility-maximizing for them to do? The answer is 'Yes' – a monopsony purchaser can face suppliers with all-or-nothing options. Especially if this can be done in a discriminatory fashion, there can be a further extraction of producers' surplus. Paradoxically such quasi-coercive and discriminatory behaviour can improve efficiency.

7 WELFARE ECONOMICS OF MONOPSONY

Since at least some of the lower price in countries other than the USA appears to represent monopsony behaviour by buyers, one is led to ask whether monopsony behaviour is to be endorsed. Simple welfare economics is straightforward: compared to the competitive equilibrium, exercise of monopsony power reduces efficiency and moves away from Pareto optimality. While buyers of services are better off, sellers are worse off. The gains to buyers are less than the losses to sellers since total welfare is reduced. As usual, if the agent with market power could exercise that power in a perfectly discriminating way, the outcome would be efficient.

If the monopsony equilibrium is inefficient, that means that there is a potential change that can make everyone better off. This change could be accomplished by levying a lump sum tax on suppliers of medical inputs, using the tax to make lump sum transfers to buyers of care, and then paying the competitive price for medical inputs. The alternative method for achieving an efficient outcome is for the buyer to behave as a *discriminating* monopsonist, paying less for inframarginal units and less to inframarginal sellers. Alternatively, varying lump sum reductions in income may extract inframarginal rents.

While perfect discrimination is obviously impossible, some methods of distinguishing between those with different levels of producers' surplus may be possible. Differential levels of subsidy for new entrants into health professions is one version. At the personal margin, strategies of accompanying salaries with higher marginal payments for additional hours worked may make sense. These strategies are occasionally followed for non-doctor workers; for doctors, reverse strategies, in which the marginal price falls as volume rises, are more common. On balance it appears that monopsony behaviour by government reduces economic welfare, relative to the behaviour of an idealized public sector that is able to limit the quantities of services to those which are themselves optimal, so that there is no distortion from insurance coverage. This conclusion can be changed if moral hazard is taken into account. Insurance of the conventional sort, by lowering the user price, increases the quality of services demanded, compared to the no-insurance equilibrium. This means that the equilibrium quantity of services with competition but with no 'managed care' may be inefficiently high. One way to reduce the quantity consumed is to reduce the price to suppliers – to the level (approximately) consistent with the level that would have prevailed in the absence of insurance coverage. A buyers' cartel would surely set the price at least as low as that level, but would be motivated to push below that point, to the point at which the uninsured demand curve intersects the curve marginal to the supply curve.

As an institutionalized policy, is monopsony pricing efficient? Inefficient as it is, it may be superior to a competitive equilibrium with no managed care (that is, with only indemnity insurance). As managed care is introduced to limit quantities more precisely than would be the case under any pricing strategy – after all, pricing strategies can only make sure that the *aggregate* quantity is right, not that services go to the right people – monopsony becomes less defensible.

8   COMPETITIVE CONTROL OF MORAL HAZARD

Both competitive indemnity insurance markets and buyers' cartel monopsony markets are inefficient. Evaluating provider monopoly with indemnity insurance is more difficult, as Crew (1969) noted. With proportional co-insurance, higher than competitive provider prices might happen to lead to higher user prices that would ration care close to efficient levels. The efficiency gains would then go to providers, not consumers – and the achievement of this equilibrium would be a matter of coincidence. However even this fortunate arrangement also exposes buyers to much higher risk for out-of-pocket expenditures: they pay part of the gain to providers as a risky charge or tax. In effect this arrangement may lead to a closer approximation of the right quantities of services, but does so by generating potentially substantial and unnecessary financial risk for consumers.

There is, however, at least in principle, a first-best market alternative. The intuition behind it is reasonably straightforward. Imagine the creation of competing *health plans*. A plan (in contrast to an insurance policy) is an entity that both finances and controls the quantity of medical care services. It includes (but is not limited to) the Health Maintenance Organization (HMO) in the United States. Consider the most controlled form of HMO, the pre-paid group practice. This enterprise contracts exclusively with a set of doctors, nurses, other suppliers of inputs and hospitals. When there are many such competing plans, the utility level of the (assumed identical) input suppliers must be equal across plans. Since some individual suppliers have upward-sloping supply curves, the strategy of varying the marginal supply price is available to such plans, as are other strategies to control quantities directly on a patient-specific basis (for example, protocols, utilization review, case management and the like).

If such plans are to co-exist with indemnity insurance, equalization of provider real income may require a lump sum (salary) payment in the health plan setting as well as payments for each visit (Ellis and McGuire, 1990). Regardless of whether this is necessary, the outcome will be first-best optimal.

9 CONCLUSION

Much of the cross-national variation in medical care spending appears to reflect differences in the prices paid for inputs, not in the relative levels of real inputs consumed. There are empirical and theoretical reasons to believe that those prices in turn may often reflect different degrees of monopsony governments have or choose to use, rather than real costs. The issue of monopsony, though largely ignored (or mistreated) in discussions of health policy to date, does, I believe, demand more careful consideration. From the perspective of the beleaguered US systems – where we are sure something is wrong but we are not quite sure what it is – there should probably be a moratorium on cross-national comparisons until we can obtain reliable cost figures.

Note

1. I am very grateful to Doug Smink for assistance with the empirical data used in this paper.

References

BASYS (1992) 'Gesundheitsfinanzierunginternational', *BASYS Informationen* vol. 7, pp. 1–3.

Bhagwati, J.N. (1984) 'Why Are Services Cheaper in Poor Countries?', *Economic Journal* vol. 94, pp. 279–86.

Borcherding, T. (1971) 'A Neglected Social Cost of a Voluntary Military', *American Economic Review* vol. 61, pp. 195–7.

Crew, M. (1969) 'Coinsurance and the Welfare Economics of Medical Care', *American Economic Review* vol. 59, pp. 906–8.

Culyer, A. (1989) 'Cost Containment in Europe', *Health Care Financing Review*, Supplement, pp. 21–3.

Danzon, P. (1992) 'Hidden Overhead Costs: Is Canada's System Really Less Costly?', *Health Affairs*, Spring, pp. 12–43.

Ellis, R.P. and McGuire, T. (1990) 'Optimal Payment Systems for Health Services', *Journal of Health Economics*, vol. 9, pp. 375–96.

Fuchs, V. and Hahn, J. (1990) 'How Does Canada Do It?', *New England Journal of Medicine*, vol. 320, pp. 884–90.

Kravis, I. *et al.* (1978) 'Real GDP per Capita for More Than One Hundred Countries', *Economic Journal*, vol. 88, pp. 215–42.

Lindsay, C.M. (1969) 'Medical Care and the Economics of Sharing', *Economica*, vol. 36, pp. 351–62.

Newhouse, J.P. (1977) 'Medical Care Expenditures: A Cross-National Survey', *Journal of Human Resources*, vol. 12, pp. 115–25.

Parkin, D. (1989) 'Comparing Health Services Efficiency Across Countries', *Oxford Review of Economic Policy*, vol. 5, pp. 75–88; and in McGuire, A. Fenn, P. and Mayhew, K. (eds) (1991) *Providing Health Care: The Economics of Alternative Systems of Finance and Delivery* (Oxford: Oxford University Press) pp. 172–91.

Pauly, M.V. (1971) *Medical Care at Public Expense* (New York: Praeger).

Usher, D. (1977) 'The Welfare Economics of the Socialization of Commodities', *Journal of Public Economics*, vol. 8, pp. 151–69.

Wilson, L.S. and Katz, M.L. (1983) 'The Socialization of Commodities', *Journal of Public Economics*, vol. 20, pp. 347–57.

10 The Dynamics of Housing Prices: An International Perspective[1]

Peter Englund
UNIVERSITY OF UPPSALA

and

Yannis M. Ioannides
VIRGINIA POLYTECHNIC INSTITUTE AND STATE
UNIVERSITY and NBER

1 INTRODUCTION

Housing prices increased dramatically in many countries during the 1980s. Those increases accentuated differences across countries in the levels of housing prices. They have also attracted attention to the dynamics of housing prices more generally. In the USA the phenomenal price increases, some of which have been attributed to 'bubbles'.[1] in some regions and states during the mid- to late 1980s, have given way to price declines. The bubbles seem to have been burst throughout the USA from the North-Eastern states to the South and to California. Yet, as Poterba notes (Poterba, 1991, p. 178), housing prices do not appear to have declined as much as one would have expected if price increases were indeed due to bubbles and related phenomena.

Another interesting phenomenon that has attracted some attention is the fact that foreign investors, especially Japanese, borrowed heavily against real estate assets in their own countries in order to invest in assets in the USA, including real estate assets as well. Since real estate competes for finance with other investments, it is natural that the real estate boom would be related to more general investment or stock market booms. There seems to be virtually no formal analysis of these phenomena.

It is of particular interest to consider potential dependence in the dynamics of housing prices across different countries. In a financially integrated world economy, with the rate of return being determined internationally, one would expect prices of housing assets in different countries to move in concert with one another. The dual role of housing as an asset and a durable good providing shelter does have consequences for the long run equilibrium value of the capital stock. Housing markets are different from other asset markets in the sense that transactions costs and the non-equivalence between residential and owner-occupied housing impose frictions for arbitrage. This paper proposes a basic analytical model that may be used to examine the dynamics of housing prices in an international perspective. It involves a simple two overlapping-generations model with two sectors, one of which is producing a tradeable good and and the other housing, whose services are consumed only domestically. The choice of an overlapping-generations model is simply for ease of exposition. The model adopts a dynamic specific factors structure in the style of Eaton (1987, 1988). Housing is a produced durable and claims to it may be traded internationally. For symmetry, we allow for capital and land also to be traded internationally. With respect to land, in particular, which is a non-reproducible factor, we know from Eaton's work (Eaton, 1988) that its ownership by foreigners affects conventional wisdom in non-trivial ways.[2]

The dynamics of the model with foreign ownership of housing in addition to that of capital and land, discussed in Sections 3 and 4 below, are interesting in their own right. In addition the model allows further exploration of the importance of bubbles. Since bubbles have allegedly been detected in housing markets in various countries and regions of the USA, conditions which might rule out the existence of price bubbles on housing assets are of special importance. This is also important in view of the attention this topic is receiving at the present time in the empirical literature. An interesting result of Rhee (1991), itself a correction of Tirole (1985), overturned the conventional wisdom, invoked quite frequently and especially by macro theorists: that is, the presence of a fixed (that is, non-reproducible) factor of production (such as land) was thought to exclude the possibility of bubbles in the economy. We investigate this further in the present paper.

This study is to the best of our knowledge the first one to emphasize housing price dynamics in an international context. It is not, however, the first to take up the dynamics of housing prices as such. The work by Poterba (1984) has been decisive in explaining the complicated dynamics that might affect housing markets. In such models prices are sensitive to shocks in the short run because investment adjusts only sluggishly owing to adjustment costs.

After a discussion in Section 2 of some facts about the movements of housing prices internationally, we present the basic behavioural model in Section 3, and explore its dynamic properties in Section 4. The possibility of bubbles in land and housing prices is also explored there. Then in Section 5 we analyse a related model where the demand side is also affected by inertia due to the costs of moving from one dwelling to another. We use that model to study the dynamics of housing prices in the short run and to obtain predictions about the relationship between price volatility and the pattern of residential mobility across countries. Section 6 offers some brief conclusions.

2 FACTS ABOUT HOUSING PRICES IN AN INTERNATIONAL PERSPECTIVE

Poterba (1991) considers the traditional determinants of housing prices. He argues that the conventional view that real user costs, which were low during the 1970s, are an important determinant of housing prices is found wanting when confronted with data from the 1980s for the USA. Real user costs of housing increased during the 1970s but housing prices did not fall sufficiently. On the other hand, evidence from a large cross-section of cities provides support neither for the demography-based explanation for housing price dynamics, suggested for example by Mankiw and Weil (1989), nor for the real user cost theory. Variations in housing price appreciation do seem to be forecastable, which argues against the existence of arbitrage in housing markets. Finally, from some limited international evidence he takes up,[3] Poterba concludes that housing prices can be quite unstable even during relatively short periods, and may be subject to speculative bubbles.[4]

For the United States the most rapid increase was one of 20 per cent from 1976 to 1979. In contrast real house prices rose by 32 per cent in Canada between 1971 and 1973, by 37 per cent in the Netherlands between 1976 and 1978 and by 52 per cent in the United

Kingdom between 1971 and 1973. The most rapid decreases were 5 per cent for the USA (1981–3), 14 per cent for Canada (1977–9), 38 per cent for the Netherlands (1979–82) and 25 per cent for the United Kingdom (1974–7). Corresponding numbers for Sweden were +29 per cent (1986–9) and −31 per cent (1979–83).

Muellbauer (1992) emphasises the differences in housing market dynamics between Germany and the United Kingdom. Other evidence presented by Cutler *et al.* (1991) suggests that excess returns[5] to housing prices in the USA are positively autocorrelated at an annual frequency. This picture conforms to that for many other assets.[6]

An international comparison of returns to various assets during the 1980s is particularly interesting. From data reported by the Bank for International Settlements in a number of its annual reports (1986, 1989, 1990, 1991, 1992) we note a substantial correlation of house prices across countries, at least during the 1980s when capital markets became better integrated. During the earlier part of the decade, house prices fell in real terms in most countries or grew considerably more slowly than prices of financial assets like equities and bonds. During 1980–85, real price changes of houses sold in the USA, the United Kingdom and Italy fluctuated around an average of −1 per cent, 0.5 per cent and 0.5 per cent respectively. Whereas for the United States those fluctuations varied from a maximum of 2 per cent and a minimum of −3 per cent only, they were much wider in the United Kingdom: 6 per cent to −8 per cent respectively; and even more wide for Italy: 13 per cent to −9 per cent. Average real rates of return implied by the price of new houses sold in Germany, France and Canada similarly registered 0.5 per cent, −2.1 per cent and −4.1 per cent respectively, during that same period, with fluctuations being most pronounced for Germany and Canada. Japan, where urban land prices grew at an average of 3.7 per cent, was an exception. In contrast equities and bonds performed consistently much better during that same period.

The performance of housing in the second half of the 1980s all but made up for the lacklustre performance in the first half. Specifically, growth in urban land prices accelerated in Japan, with commercial properties leading the way and registering phenomenal increases. Housing prices moved upwards in most industrialized countries, but especially in North America and Western Europe. This housing boom exhibited substantial correlation across most countries, for example the USA, the United Kingdom, Canada, Australia, Sweden, France, Norway and Italy.

The performance since 1990 shows a sharp slowdown in growth or actual decline in real estate prices, thus completing a picture of a 'boom-to-bust' cycle in international housing markets. Urban land prices actually fell in Japan, for the first time in seventeen years and only the second time since the Second World War (Bank for International Settlements, 1992, p. 139). The overall picture does indeed tempt us to consider the extent of the internationalization of the housing cycle, making it more pressing to pursue a formal analysis of the dynamics of housing prices in an international perspective. In Section 5 below we offer some additional data, in order to contrast with varying patterns of residential mobility internationally.

3 THE MODEL

We assume an economy with a constant endowment of land, in amount T, and a constant labour force L. We allow for a growing labour force in Section 4.3 below. Without loss of generality, we shall set the quantity of land equal to 1. The model integrates housing into a specific factors model in the style of Eaton's. We assume two domestic sectors. Sector 1 produces a homogeneous output, using capital (K) invested in the previous period, K_{1t}, and labour employed in the current period, L_{1t}, according to a production function:[7]

$$Q_{1t} = F(K_{1t}, L_{1t}) \tag{1}$$

$F(\cdot)$ is assumed to yield output net of depreciation of capital,[8] satisfies the standard properties, and is homogeneous of degree one. Thus the producers operating in sector 1 hire capital and labour in competitive markets and earn zero profits at equilibrium. The output of sector 1 may be used for consumption and investment.

Sector 2 produces new housing stock, using capital and land, according to a production function:

$$Q_{2t} = G(K_{2t}, T_{2t}) \tag{2}$$

$G(\cdot)$ satisfies the standard properties and is homogeneous of degree one. Housing producers hire capital and land in competitive markets to produce housing. Once produced, new housing is added to the surviving housing stock in the following period. Once installed, housing stock is homogeneous and depreciates at a constant rate δ per period. Capital used in housing production depreciates fully. Land does not depreciate.

The model contains three assets, which may be used for transferring purchasing power over time: capital, land and housing. The difference between land and the other two is that land is nonreproducible. A novelty of the model is that foreign investment in all three of these factors is allowed. Let K^f_{t+1}, T^f_{t+1} and H^f_{t+1} be the respective amounts of foreign investment in those three factors, available at the beginning of period $t + 1$. The assumption of foreign holdings in housing, in particular, is made in response to some of the important stylized facts discussed in the introduction. It also simplifies the model considerably by allowing rather naturally for holdings of housing stock for consumption purposes to differ from those for investment purposes (Henderson and Ioannides, 1983).

The behaviour of individuals may be described as follows. Individuals live for two periods. Those born in period t work only when young, supplying their labour inelastically (one unit each), and consume output in both periods, in quantities c^y_t and c^o_{t+1}, respectively. We simplify the housing decision by assuming that housing is consumed only in the second period.[9] Let χ_{t+1} be the quantity of housing stock rented by a member of the generation born in period t during the second period of its life. The typical household's utility function is:

$$u = U(c^y_t, c^o_{t+1}; \chi_{t+1}) \tag{3}$$

Let k_{t+1}, ℓ_{t+1} and h_{t+1} be the holdings of assets acquired by a member of generation t when young, that is holdings of capital, land, and housing, respectively. Let w_t, r_t, q_t and x_t be the wage rate, rate of interest, price of land and price of housing stock, respectively. And let π_t and ρ_t be the rental rates of land and housing, respectively. All prices are defined in terms of the numeraire commodity, the output of sector 1.

An individual's decisions about how much to consume when young and old and how much housing to rent satisfy a lifetime budget constraint which, for convenience, may be written in two parts, as follows. Individuals save by investing in holdings[10] of capital, land and housing:

$$c^y_t = w_t - k_{t+1} - q_t\ell_{t+1} - x_t h_{t+1} \tag{5'}$$

They use the total returns from their investments in the second period of their lives to pay for consumption of housing and of the non-housing consumption good:

$$c_{t+1}^o + \rho_{t+1}\chi_{t+1} = (1 + r_{t+1})k_{t+1} + (q_{t+1} + \pi_{t+1})\ell_{t+1}$$
$$+ [\rho_{t+1} + (1 - \delta)x_{t+1}]h_{t+1} \tag{6'}$$

The determination of the consumption bundle may be analytically simplified as follows. In equilibrium, the returns to all assets are equalized.[11] Consequently by defining

$$s_t \equiv k_{t+1} + q_t\ell_{t+1} + x_t h_{t+1} \tag{4}$$

we may rewrite (5') and (6') above as follows:

$$c_t^y = w_t - s_t \tag{5}$$

$$c_{t+1}^o + \rho_{t+1}\chi_{t+1} = (1 + r_{t+1})s_t \tag{6}$$

We are now ready to close the model. Individuals maximize utility (3) subject to budget constraints (4) to (6) by choosing c_t^y, s_t, c_{t+1}^o, and χ_{t+1}.

Equilibrium in the market for capital is characterized as follows. The total supply of capital is equal to the demand for capital for investment purposes:

$$K_{t+1} = Lk_{t+1} + K_{t+1}^f \tag{7}$$

The total supply of capital is equal to the demand for capital for production purposes by the two sectors:

$$K_{t+1} = K_{1t+1} + K_{2t+1} \tag{8}$$

Equilibrium in the market for land is characterized as follows. The total supply of land, which has been normalized to 1, is equal to the demand for land for production purposes, which comes only from the housing producing sector (sector 2), $T_{2t} = T_t$. The total supply of land is equal to the demand for investment purposes. The demand for investment purposes has a domestic component $L\ell_{t+1}$ and a foreign component T^f_{t+1}. So for equilibrium we have:

$$1 = T_{t+1} = L\ell_{t+1} + T^f_{t+1} \tag{9}$$

Negative values for K^f_{t+1} and T^f_{t+1} imply net ownership of these assets abroad by nationals.

The supply of housing stock in every period satisfies:

$$H_{t+1} = Q_{2t} + (1 - \delta)H_t \tag{10}$$

This is the housing accumulation equation. Equilibrium in the market for housing stock for investment purposes implies:

$$H_{t+1} = L\,h_{t+1} + H^f_{t+1} \tag{11}$$

Equations (10) and (11) determine the price of housing stock x_t. Equilibrium in the market for housing stock for consumption purposes implies:

$$H_{t+1} = L\,\chi(w_t, r_{t+1}, \rho_{t+1}) \tag{12}$$

where $\chi(\cdot)$ is obtained from the solution for χ_{t+1} to the lifetime utility maximization problem.[12] Equations (10) and (12) determine the rental rate for housing stock, the price of housing services, ρ_{t+1}, in terms of the quantity of housing stock and its price in period t, H_t and x_t, respectively.

Employing the definition of savings (4) and substituting from the asset market equilibrium conditions (7), (9), and (11) we see that total asset values equal the sum of domestic and foreign savings:

$$K_{t+1} = Ls(w_t; r_{t+1}, \rho_{t+1}) - q_t - x_t H_{t+1} + \Phi_t \tag{13}$$

where $s(\cdot)$ is obtained from the solution to the individual's lifetime utility maximization problem and Φ denotes net foreign investment defined as

$$\Phi_t \equiv K^f_{t+1} + q_t T^f_{t+1} + x_t H^f_{t+1} \tag{14}$$

Further, in asset market equilibrium, the rates of return on invest-

ment in land and housing must equal the market interest rates; these
yield, respectively,

$$q_t = \frac{\pi_{t+1} + q_{t+1}}{1 + r_{t+1}} \tag{15}$$

$$x_t = \frac{\rho_{t+1} + (1 - \delta)x_{t+1}}{1 + r_{t+1}} \tag{16}$$

Standard marginal productivity conditions determine the wage rate
w_t, the rental rate for land π_t, and the rate of interest (rental rate of
capital, net of depreciation) r_t. The rate of interest is equal to the
marginal productivity of capital in both sectors. That is:

$$w_t = \frac{\partial F(K_{1t}, L_t)}{\partial L_t} \tag{17}$$

$$\pi_t = x_t \frac{\partial G(K_{2t}, T_t)}{\partial T_t} \tag{18}$$

$$r_t = \frac{\partial F(K_{1t}, L_t)}{\partial K_{1t}} \tag{19a}$$

$$r_t = x_t \frac{\partial G(K_{2t}, T_t)}{\partial K_{2t}} \tag{19b}$$

In analysing the equilibrium of the model we assume that we are
dealing with a small open economy where the rate of interest r_t is
exogenously given from the world market and equal to $\bar{r}_t$. For
simplicity we treat the interest rate as constant, $\bar{r}_t = \bar{r}$, although this is
not an essential assumption.

The factor demand conditions (17) and (19a), evaluated at the
exogenously given supply of labour, determine $K_1(\bar{r})$ and $w(\bar{r})$. Similarly conditions (18) and (19b) determine the capital stock and the
rental rate of land as functions of the price of housing stock, which is
determined elsewhere in the model: $K_2(x_t, \bar{r})$ and $\pi(K_2(x_t, \bar{r}))$.

The remainder of the equilibrium conditions are determined by a set of three dynamic equations, the accumulation equation for housing (10) and the two forward-looking asset demand equations (15) and (16). In analysing this system we note that the rental rate of housing may be expressed from the equilibrium condition in the housing market, by inverting (12):

$$\rho_{t+1} \equiv R(H_{t+1}, w(\bar{r}), \bar{r})$$

Furthermore it is convenient to write the output of the housing producing sector at equilibrium in terms of prices only:

$$g(x_t, \bar{r}) \equiv G(K_2(x_t, \bar{r}), 1)$$

We may now rewrite the dynamic system as:

$$H_{t+1} = g(x_t, \bar{r}) + (1 - \delta)H_t \tag{20}$$

$$q_t = \frac{\pi(x_{t+1}, \bar{r}) + q_{t+1}}{1 + \bar{r}} \tag{21'}$$

$$x_t = \frac{R(H_{t+1}, w(\bar{r}), \bar{r}) + (1 - \delta)x_{t+1}}{1 + \bar{r}} \tag{22'}$$

The system of equations (20), (21') and (22') yields the evolution of H, q and x over time, given initial conditions. Given this solution, the factor demand condition (19b) determines K_2. Since K_1 is already determined as a function of $\bar{r}$, this means that the path for K is determined. Finally the amount of foreign investment Φ is given from (14).

4 DYNAMICS

Dynamic equilibrium in this model is subject to the basic indeterminacy of equilibrium in overlapping-generations models. The equilibrium conditions do not yield initial conditions for q_t and x_t. Given initial conditions for capital and the housing stock, K_0 and H_0, and with arbitrary initial values for the price of land and housing, we may solve equations (20), (21') and (22') for the values of the state variables in period 1 and successive periods.[13]

When the rate of interest is endogenous, the dynamic system is fully simultaneous, exhibits no block structure and is thus very complicated to analyse. This is one reason for examining the case of an exogenous rate of interest in some detail. We then return to the general case in order to examine the possibility of bubbles.

4.1 Dynamics with an Exogenous Rate of Interest

The dynamic analysis is simplified by substituting for H_{t+1} from (20) in (22') and from (22') in (21'). After solving for q_{t+1} and x_{t+1} we obtain the counterparts of (21') and (22'):

$$q_{t+1} = (1 + \bar{r})q_t - \pi \left[\frac{1 + \bar{r}}{1 - \delta} x_t - \right.$$

$$\left. \frac{1}{1 - \delta} R[g(x_t, \bar{r}) + (1 - \delta)H_t, \bar{r}], \bar{r} \right] \qquad (21)$$

$$x_{t+1} = \frac{1 + \bar{r}}{1 - \delta} x_t - \frac{1}{1 - \delta} R[g(x_t, \bar{r}) + (1 - \delta)H_t, \bar{r}] \qquad (22)$$

By linearizing around the steady state in the standard fashion we obtain a linear system of first order difference equations in terms of the deviations of the endogenous variables (H_t, q_t, x_t) from their steady state values:

$$\begin{bmatrix} \Delta H_{t+1} \\ \Delta q_{t+1} \\ \Delta x_{t+1} \end{bmatrix} = \begin{bmatrix} 1 - \delta & 0 & g_x \\ \pi_x R_H & 1 + \bar{r} & -\dfrac{1 + \bar{r} - g_x R_H}{1 - \delta} \pi_x \\ -R_H & 0 & \dfrac{1}{1 - \delta}(1 + \bar{r} - g_x R_H) \end{bmatrix} \begin{bmatrix} \Delta H_t \\ \Delta q_t \\ \Delta x_t \end{bmatrix} \qquad (23)$$

All entries in the right-hand side of (23) are evaluated at the steady state values of all variables. The characteristic equation corresponding to the above system is

$$(1 + \bar{r} - \lambda)\left[\lambda^2 - \left[1 - \delta + \frac{1}{1 - \delta}(1 + \bar{r} - R_H g_x)\right]\lambda \right.$$

$$\left. + 1 + \bar{r} \right] = 0 \qquad (24)$$

Equation (24) has three distinct roots, the eigenvalues of the system (23). One is equal to $1 + \bar{r}$ and thus positive and greater than 1. The other two are given by the roots of the quadratic equation:

$$\lambda_{2,3} = \frac{1}{2}(1 - \delta + \frac{1}{1 - \delta}(1 + \bar{r} - R_H g_x)$$

$$\pm \frac{1}{2}\left[(1 - \delta + \frac{1}{1 - \delta}(1 + \bar{r} - R_H g_x))^2 - 4(1 + \bar{r}) \right]^{\frac{1}{2}}$$

The roots of equation (24) are always real and both are positive.[14] One of these roots is greater than 1 and the other is less than 1. We conclude that the system exhibits saddlepoint stability.

4.2   Properties of the Steady State Equilibrium

The system of equations (20), (21′), and (22′) in the steady state yield:

$$\delta H^* = g(x^*, \bar{r}) \tag{25}$$

$$\bar{r}q^* = \pi(x^*, K_2(x^*, \bar{r})) \tag{26}$$

$$(\bar{r} + \delta)x^* = R(H^*, w(\bar{r}), \bar{r}) \tag{27}$$

Equations (25) and (27) give conditions for producers and consumers to be at equilibrium. They are represented in Figure 10.1 by the curves PP and DD, which jointly determine H^* and x^* as functions of the world market rate of interest. The equilibrium price of land follows recursively from (26).

We may refer to Figure 10.1 to illustrate how steady state equilibrium is affected by an increase in the world interest rate. Such an increase may be represented by a shift to the right of the PP locus to $P'P'$. At a higher interest rate producers will hire less capital and supply less housing at given house prices. The effect on the DD curve as it shifts to $D'D'$ is ambiguous, however. We explore that by differentiating (27) to get:

$$\frac{dx^*}{d\bar{r}} = \frac{1}{\bar{r} + \delta}\left(\frac{\partial R}{\partial \bar{r}} - x^* \right)$$

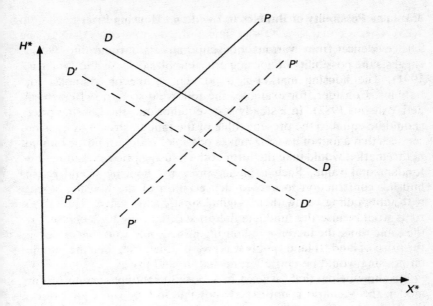

Figure 10.1 Steady state equilibrium

where

$$\frac{\partial R}{\partial \tilde{r}} = -\frac{(\partial \chi/\partial w \times \partial w/\partial r) + \partial \chi/\partial \tilde{r}}{\partial \chi/\partial \rho}$$

Since $\frac{\partial \chi}{\partial w} > 0, \frac{\partial w}{\partial \tilde{r}} < 0, \frac{\partial \chi}{\partial \tilde{r}} > 0$ and $\frac{\partial \chi}{\partial \rho} < 0$, the sign of $\frac{\partial R}{\partial \tilde{r}}$ is ambiguous. Rents may go either up or down, depending on the relative strength of two factors. On the one hand, an increase in $\tilde{r}$ lowers the discounted price of housing and increases housing demand; this tends to increase rents. On the other hand, an increase in $\tilde{r}$ lowers wages and hence has a negative income effect on housing demand. If the negative income effect is sufficiently strong, then the net effect on the house price x^*, given H^*, is unambiguously negative. Finally we note that the effect on the land price q^* is ambiguous. If the effect on x^* is sufficiently small, then the effect on q^* is clearly negative.

4.3   The Possibility of Bubbles in Land and Housing Prices

The evidence from various housing markets around the world suggests the possibility of housing price bubbles (Meese and Wallace, 1991). The housing market is a popular source of examples for bubbles. Consider, for example, the following scenario (Blanchard and Watson, 1982). In a steady state equilibrium, the housing price should be equal to the present value of the infinite stream of housing services that a unit of housing makes possible. A deterministic bubble in this market would take the form of the housing price exceeding this fundamental value. Such a higher price for housing would cause housing construction to exceed depreciation of the housing stock, with rents falling below their original steady state value. The fall in rents would cause the fundamental price of housing to decrease. At the same time, the increase in housing price would cause increases in the price of land. If land supply was entirely inelastic, then the bubble on housing would be entirely reflected in land prices.

We show below that, at least in a closed economy version of our model, this scenario is not exactly possible in long run equilibrium. Such a bubble, if it starts, must burst. We see that, whereas a bubble on the asset price of land is possible, this is not the case on the asset price of housing. These results depend on some of our specific assumptions, namely that housing is produced with land and capital under constant returns to scale. A bubble on the asset price of housing would cause, as we shall see, the per capita value of housing stock held in portfolios to become infinitely large. In contrast, this is not the case for land. The per capita amount of land held in portfolios tends to zero. If the share of land in housing production does not vanish asymptotically, then indeed a bubble on the price of land but not on that of housing is perfectly possible in long-run equilibrium. This result confirms the importance of the reconsideration of conventional wisdom on this matter by Rhee (1991).

Let prices q_t and x_t be decomposed into a fundamental component and a bubble component:

$$q_t \overset{\text{def}}{=} \psi_t^q + \beta_t^q$$

$$x_t \overset{\text{def}}{=} \psi_t^x + \beta_t^x$$

The fundamental components must be particular solutions of the difference equations (15) and (16), which we rewrite here in the standard form:

$$q_{t+1} = (1 + r_{t+1})q_t - \pi_{t+1} \tag{15'}$$

$$x_{t+1} = \frac{1 + r_{t+1}}{1 - \delta} x_t - \frac{1}{1 - \delta} \rho_{t+1} \tag{16'}$$

The bubble components must satisfy the respective homogeneous equations. Therefore, if bubbles exist, they must grow at the equilibrium rate of interest. To make the problem meaningful we assume that the economy is growing and that the rate of interest is endogenous. We also assume for convenience that the economy is closed.

Let population grow at a constant rate η: $L_t = L_0(1 + \eta)^t$. The constancy of land implies that the amount of land held by a young person in period t, ℓ_{t+1} satisfies $T_t = L_t\ell_{t+1} = 1$, and evolves over time according to $\ell_{t+2} = \frac{1}{1+\eta}\ell_{t+1}$. The fundamental law of motion for this economy is (13), which we rewrite in our new notation as follows:

$$L_t q_t + L_t x_t h_{t+1} + L_{t+1}k_{t+1} = L_t s(w_t; r_{t+1}, \rho_{t+1}) \tag{28}$$

The question of existence of a 'bubbly' equilibrium reduces to whether (28) admits a steady state equilibrium at which the rate of interest is equal to the rate of population growth, and the steady state (total) capital–labour ratio k_b and 'aggregate bubble' b satisfy:

$$(1 + \eta)\hat{k}_b + \hat{b} = S(\hat{w}; \eta, \hat{\rho})$$

We now take up the issue of whether such an equilibrium exists, and if it exists, whether $\hat{b}$ contains both land and housing. If a bubbly equilibrium exists, then $\hat{b} = \lim_{t \to \infty} \psi_t^q \ell_{t+1} + \beta_t^q \ell_{t+1} \psi_t^x h_{t+1} + \beta_t^x h_{t+1}$. It is straightforward to see that the component of the aggregate bubble that corresponds to a bubble on housing would tend to ∞. That is, at the steady state, with $\ell_t \to 0$, the amount of housing produced per capita is equal to $G(k_{2b}, 0)$. If this is non-zero, which would indeed be the case with a constant elasticity of substitution (CES) production function $G(K, T) \equiv (K^{\sigma_h} + T^{\sigma_h})1/\sigma^h \ 0 \leq \sigma_h \leq 1$, then so is the total amount of housing stock per capita. Therefore there cannot be a bubble on the asset price of housing.

The case of land is quite different, on the other hand, because ℓ_t tends to 0 as $t \to \infty$. This makes the fundamental component of the aggregate bubble tend to 0. As for the bubble component, a non-zero value is possible provided that the share of land in the production of housing does not vanish as the amount of land per capita vanishes.

This follows directly from Rhee (1991) and may be demonstrated easily by means of a CES production function like the one invoked above. In that case, $\lim_{t \to \infty} \beta_t \ell_{t+1} = \beta_0 L_0$. Specifically for the CES example above, it suffices to assume that $0 \geq \sigma_h$.

This result clearly depends on the assumption that housing production exhibits homogeneity of degree one. Otherwise, if it exhibited decreasing returns to scale, then housing per capita would tend to zero in long-run equilibrium and a bubble on housing could in principle be sustained. This case requires a major revision of our basic framework and will not be pursued further here.

5   DYNAMICS AND TRANSACTIONS COSTS

In previous sections we have dealt with the long-run tendencies of house prices. In particular we assumed housing demand to adjust instantaneously to changes in market prices. But households can only alter their housing consumption by moving, and moving entails large transactions costs. Hence, when prices or other economic factors change, most households will not adjust their housing consumption. Only if the change is big enough will they find it worthwhile to move, given the transactions costs. This suggests that in analysing price determination it is important to recognize that prices are set to equate supply and demand from those households that actually trade in the market. Taking this into account should be important in understanding what drives housing prices in the short run. We pursue this here by means of a model of short-run dynamics that emphasizes mobility[15] by heterogeneous households.

The degree of mobility varies across countries. Americans move much more often than most others. The annual mobility rate for US home owners between 50 and 60 years of age is 10 per cent, while the corresponding number for Germany is as low as 2.5 per cent (Börsch-Supan, 1992). Only 2 per cent of all Japanese and 4.5 per cent of all Swedish home owners move in any year (Seko, 1992; Edin and Englund, 1991). Relating these differences to the differences in price volatility noted in Section 2 suggests that there may be a negative correlation. The model considered in this section explains why this may be so.

We now sketch a partial equilibrium model that allows us to throw some light on the relation between transactions costs and price volatility. The model is related to the standard asset price model employed by Poterba (1984), Mankiw and Weil (1989) and others to study house prices. It departs from that model in assuming an overlapping structure of households living for two periods and having the choice of whether or not to move between the first and second period of their life.

Consider a household living for two periods and consuming housing (h^y, h^o) and other goods (c^y, c^o) in both periods of life. The budget constraint is given by

$$p_t h^y + \zeta p_{t+1} h^o + c^y + \zeta c^o = w - \alpha \tag{29}$$

where $\alpha = 0$ if $h^y = h^o$. Here ζ is equal to the discount factor $\frac{1}{1+r}$, w is lifetime endowment and α is transactions costs. We do not take a stand as to whether transactions costs are a fixed sum or whether they are related to the amount of housing consumed in the first or second period.[16] The prices of housing consumption p_t are user costs, defined by

$$p_t = x_t + \zeta(1 - \delta)x_{t+1} \tag{30}$$

It is easy to recognize that the choice of whether to move or not depends on the transactions costs α. That is, there exists a critical value α^* such that the household moves if $\alpha < \alpha^*$, and stays in the same house in both periods otherwise. The critical value depends on the utility gain from moving, which is related to the relative preferences for housing consumption when young and old and on relative prices, p_t and ζp_{t+1}.

In a population of heterogeneous households transactions costs and preferences will vary. This implies that at any set of prices a fraction ξ will choose to move and a fraction $(1 - \xi)$ will choose to stay. In general these fractions depend on relative prices. Assume that prices are such that the marginal household, which is indifferent between moving and staying, would choose $h^o > h^y$ if it were to move. Then the effect of an increase in the first period price, p_t, would be to increase the fraction of movers ξ, whereas an increase in the second period price ζp_{t+1} has the opposite effect.

The discussion above refers to the problem of a young household making its optimal lifetime plan. Our model is one of perfect foresight, but we will in standard comparative-static fashion consider the effects of sudden unforeseen changes. This leads to the problem of replanning in the middle of life; under what conditions would a household that planned to be a mover (stayer) reverse its plans, if prices turned out to be different from those originally anticipated? This is an interesting issue which we will pursue further in another paper. For now we conjecture that such replanning will not occur as a result of marginal price changes.[17]

Let us now regard the market equilibrium in an economy of overlapping generations facing the decision problem outlined above. L_t denotes the size of a generation born at t, and H_t is the demand per household. There are three categories of households acting in the market: young movers (ym), stayers (s) and old movers (om). In this economy the equilibrium prices are determined not by equating the *stock* of housing supplied with some measure of the aggregate demand for housing, but by equating the *flow* of demand by the young generation and old movers to the supply coming from old movers, and from old houses put on the market by the retiring generation and from new investment, I_t. Investment is assumed to be an increasing function of the market price of houses. The condition for market equilibrium is

$$L_t \xi_t H_t^{ym} + L_{t-1} \xi_{t-1} H_{t-1, t}^{om} + L_t (1 - \xi_t) H_t^s$$
$$= L_{t-1}(1 - \delta)\xi_{t-1} H_{t-1}^{ym} + L_{t-2}(1 - \delta)\xi_{t-2} H_{t-2, t-1}^{om}$$
$$+ L_{t-2}(1 - \delta)^2(1 - \xi_{t-2})H_{t-2}^s + I_t \qquad (31)$$

Here subscripts refer to the date when relevant decisions were taken with double subscripts indicating that second period demand for movers depends on decisions taken both when young and when middle-aged. This equilibrium depends on decisions taken back in period $t - 2$ and while looking two periods ahead until $t + 2$. Assuming perfect foresight it is hence described by a fourth order difference equation.

In order to come to grips with the price dynamics we now make two simplifying assumptions. First, the proportion of movers and stayers is fixed over time. This may be justified by strong idiosyncratic preferences that divide the population into two distinct groups where no households are marginal with respect to moving or staying.[18] Second, there are no cross-price effects. Income and substitution effects cancel exactly as under a logarithmic utility function. The local dynamic properties may then be obtained by linearizing around the stationary solution for a constant population. It can be shown that two of the characteristic roots corresponding to the resulting equation

Table 10.1 The dynamic response of the market price of houses to a
demographic shock at time *t*
(percentage deviation from steady-state values)

	Period					
	t	*t+1*	*t+2*	*t+3*	*t+4*	*t+5*
H^{ym}=0.8; H^{om}=1.2						
ξ=0.25	+2.91	+0.59	−1.53	−0.08	−0.05	−0.02
ξ=0.50	+2.74	+1.06	−1.68	−0.14	−0.06	−0.02
ξ=0.75	+2.62	+1.45	−1.77	−0.23	−0.05	−0.02
H^{ym}=1.2; H^{om}=0.8						
ξ=0.25	+3.20	+0.09	−1.32	−0.07	−0.09	−0.05
ξ=0.50	+3.26	+0.18	−1.35	−0.14	−0.08	−0.08
ξ=0.75	+3.33	+0.26	−1.38	−0.20	−0.06	−0.06

are outside and two are inside the unit circle. Hence the equilibrium
is a saddle point.

We now ask how the price sensitivity to shocks depends on transactions costs as reflected in the share of movers. To investigate this we
look at a demographic shock where it is learned at time *t* that the size
of generation *t* is 20 per cent larger than all previous and following
generations. We solve for the stable adjustment path by multiple
shooting methods. Some numerical results are given in Table 10.1.
These are based on the assumption that demand price elasticities are
unity for all categories of households while the supply elasticity is
five, values which are in line with those previously used in the
literature. There is little firm knowledge, however, particularly about
the supply elasticity. A lower value would obviously give a larger
price response; lowering the supply elasticity to three would increase
the initial price response by approximately 50 per cent.

Several patterns emerge from Table 10.1. First, we find that there
are strong 'echo' effects. The price in the initial period is around 3 per
cent above its long-run value, but the price in period *t* + 2 is around
1.5 per cent below. The reason is of course that the initial price rise is
accompanied by increased building and a larger housing stock, but
that demand from *t* + 2 and onwards falls back to its initial value.
Second, it matters whether mover demand typically is larger in the
first or second period of life. The upper section of the table reports
the empirically more plausible case where demand from the old is
larger (by 50 per cent) than demand from the young. This gives an

immediate price response which is some 20 per cent lower than in the opposite case where the young demand more housing, reported in the lower section. The reason is simply that the immediate demand shock is smaller in the former case. On the other hand, the price impact in period $t + 1$, when the larger generation is middle-aged, is larger in the upper section, where middle-age demand exceeds young demand, than it is in the lower section. Third, we see that the fraction of movers in the population matters. In the upper section of Table 10.1, where movers move to larger houses, the initial price response is some 10 per cent larger in the case of a majority of stayers, $\xi = 0.25$, than with a majority of movers, $\xi = 0.75$. The reason is that with many stayers there are fewer households that react immediately to the higher housing prices by lowering their demand, thereby mitigating the price increases.

We conclude that accounting for transactions costs and the fact that most households should not be expected to react at all to price changes has potential effects on the degree of price volatility. Quantitatively the effects do not appear to be all that large. Nevertheless they suggest that countries with low mobility should exhibit high price volatility, just as seems to be the case empirically.

6 CONCLUSIONS

During the late 1980s the world economy experienced a considerable amount of foreign investment in real estate-related assets. At the same time economists have been paying considerably more attention to the consequences for the dynamics of exchange rates of international movements of assets. It may even be said that economists may have rediscovered that asset movements are a key determinant of exchange rates.

In view of these observations the present paper proposes a model for the dynamics of housing prices. Both long run and short run dynamics are examined. They correspond neatly to two senses in which an international perspective is invoked by the paper. One is that foreign investment is allowed in all assets of the economy, that is physical capital, land and housing. We examine the long-run dynamics of such an economy. The importance of the saddle point property of long-run equilibrium is reaffirmed. We then consider the possibility of bubbles on land and housing prices. We show that, whereas under the right conditions a bubble on the asset price of land is possible, this is not the case with the asset price of housing.

The second perspective emphasizes potential consequences of international differences in patterns of residential mobility. We show that allowing for transactions costs and for the fact that housing demand does not adjust instantaneously to changes in prices affects the degree of price volatility. Even though the underlying effect does not appear to be quantitatively important, it does nonetheless suggest that countries with low mobility should exhibit high price volatility. This appears to be in accordance with casual empiricism.

Notes

1. The authors are grateful to Dieter Bös for comments and corrections, to Philippe Weil for useful references, to Rita Maurice for editorial assistance and to Linda Dobkins for excellent research assistance.
2. For example, Eaton (1988) shows that a permanent increase in net foreign investment can reduce steady state welfare if a consequence is higher land prices.
3. Poterba uses data for real house prices for Canada, 1950–89, for the United Kingdom, 1970–91, and for the Netherlands, 1965–85.
4. See also Case and Shiller (1988) and Meese and Wallace (1991).
5. Excess returns are defined as $R_t = \ell n \frac{P_t}{P_{t-1}} - \ell n(1 + i_{US\,t})$, where P_t are constant-quality house prices and $i_{US\,t}$ is the nominal rate in US Treasury bills. This calculation abstracts from economic fundamentals for housing.
6. Cutler *et al.* (1991) list four regularities in asset returns: first, asset returns are positively serially correlated at high frequencies; second, returns are negatively serially correlated at lower frequencies; third, there is a tendency towards fundamental reversion in asset prices; fourth, when short term interest rates are high, the excess returns on other assets are low.
7. It would be straightforward to augment the model and allow for land to be used in production by sector 1.
8. This is equivalent to writing gross output minus capital depreciation.
9. This may be justified since housing consumption reaches a peak late in the life cycle.
10. Note that the time subscripts for asset holding refer to the period in which they yield returns.
11. See equations (14) and (15) below.
12. We think it is necessary to impose the restriction $H_t^f{}_{+1} \geq 0$. That is, housing services may not be imported, but foreigners may own claims to the domestic housing stock. Equations (11) and (12) imply that the investment demand for housing may not exceed the consumption demand, in the terminology of Henderson and Ioannides (1983).
13. This fundamental indeterminacy was first noted by Calvo (1978), who also considered specifically the case of land. Azariadis (1991) provides the latest and clearest statement on this issue.

14. The discriminant may be written as $\left(\frac{1+\hat{r}}{1-\delta}\right)^2 - 2R_H g_x \left(\frac{1+\hat{r}}{1-\delta} + 1\right)$.

15. Mobility is also emphasized by Hardman and Ioannides (1991), who solve for the frequency of moves by finitely lived households in continuous time and analyse the steady state of an infinite overlapping-generations model.

16. Different specifications of transactions costs are studied in Englund (1986).

17. Some intuition in support of this conjecture is as follows. Consider a household that was originally indifferent between being a mover and a stayer but that chose to be a mover and purchased a relatively small house h^y anticipating to move to a larger house h^o. In the middle of life it turns out that p_{t+1} is slightly higher than anticipated. Had the household known about this it would have chosen to be a stayer and to consume $\bar{h}(h^y < \bar{h} < h^o)$ in both periods. But the household being in a position of already having chosen a low quantity h^y, the stayer alternative is less attractive than it would otherwise be, because it implies a second period housing consumption far below the desired level. This intuitive argument may be formalized for this and other possible cases. It leads us to conclude that as long as we are considering the impact of small changes we are entitled to disregard the possibility that households change their plans in mid-life.

18. Taking the endogeneity of the fraction of movers into account turns out to have little quantitative impact.

References

Azariadis, C. (1991) 'The Problem of Multiple Equilibrium', Vilfredo Pareto Lecture, Southern European Association for Economic Theory and Econometrics (ASSET) Conference, Athens, November.

Bank for International Settlements (1986, 1989, 1990, 1991, 1992) *Annual Report*, Basle.

Blanchard, O.J. and Watson, M.W. (1982) 'Bubbles, Rational Expectations, and Financial Markets', in Wachtel, P. (ed.) *Crises in the Economic and Financial Structure* (Lexington, Mass.: Lexington Books).

Börsch-Supan, A. (1992) 'Housing and Living Arrangement Choices', mimeo, Department of Economics, University of Mannheim.

Calvo, G. (1978) 'On the Indeterminacy of Interest Rates and Wages with Perfect Foresight', *Journal of Economic Theory*, vol. 19, pp. 321–37.

Case, K.E. and Shiller, R.J. (1988) 'The Efficiency of the Market for Single Family Homes', *American Economic Review*, vol. 78, pp. 125–37.

Cutler, D.M., Poterba, J.M. and Summers, L.H. (1991) 'Speculative Dynamics', *Review of Economic Studies*, vol. 58, pp. 529–46.

Eaton, J. (1987) 'A Dynamic Specific-Factors Model of International Trade', *Review of Economic Studies*, vol. 54, pp. 325–38.

Eaton, J. (1988) 'Foreign-Owned Land', *American Economic Review*, vol. 78, pp. 76–88.

Edin, P.A. and Englund, P. (1991) 'Moving Costs and Housing Demand: Are Recent Movers Really in Equilibrium?', *Journal of Public Economics*, vol. 44, pp. 299–320.

Englund, P. (1986) 'Transactions Costs, Capital Gains Taxes, and Housing Demand', *Journal of Urban Economics*, vol. 20, pp. 274–90.

Hardman, A.M. and Ioannides, Y.M. (1991) 'Moving Behavior and Housing Market Reform in General Equilibrium', working paper, Department of Economics, Virginia Polytechnic Institute and State University, October (revised September 1992).

Henderson, J.V. and Ioannides, Y.M. (1983) 'A Model of Housing Tenure Choice', *American Economic Review*, vol. 73, pp. 98–113.

Mankiw, N.G. and Weil, D.N. (1989) 'The Baby Boom, the Baby Bust, and the Housing Market', *Regional Science and Urban Economics*, vol. 19, pp. 235–58.

Meese, R. and Wallace, N. (1991) 'Determinants of Residential Housing Prices: Effects of Economic Factors or Speculative Bubbles?', Working Paper No. 91–193, Center for Real Estate and Urban Economics, University of California, Berkeley.

Muellbauer, J. (1992) 'Anglo–German Differences in Housing Market Dynamics: The Role of Institutions and Macroeconomic Policy', *European Economic Review*, vol. 36, pp. 539–48.

Poterba, J.M. (1984) 'Tax Subsidies to Owner-Occupied Housing', *Quarterly Journal of Economics*, vol. 99, pp. 729–52.

Poterba, J.M. (1991) 'Housing Price Dynamics: The Role of Tax Policy and Demography', *Brookings Papers on Economic Activity*, no. 2, pp. 143–83.

Rhee, C. (1991) 'Dynamic Inefficiency in an Economy with Land', *Review of Economic Studies*, vol. 58, pp. 791–7.

Seko, M. (1991) 'Residential Mobility in Japan', mimeo, College of Economics, Nihon University, Japan.

Tirole, J. (1985) 'Asset Bubbles and Overlapping Generations', *Econometrica*, vol. 53, pp. 1071–1100.

11 Non-cash Income, Living Standards and Inequality: Evidence from the Luxembourg Income Study[1]

Peter Saunders
UNIVERSITY OF NEW SOUTH WALES

Timothy M. Smeeding
SYRACUSE UNIVERSITY
and LUXEMBOURG INCOME STUDY

John Coder
BUREAU OF THE CENSUS

Stephen Jenkins
UNIVERSITY OF SWANSEA

Johan Fritzell
UNIVERSITY OF STOCKHOLM

Aldi J.M. Hagenaars
ERASMUS UNIVERSITY

Richard Hauser
UNIVERSITY OF FRANKFURT
and

Michael Wolfson
STATISTICS CANADA

1 INTRODUCTION

The economic well-being of households is determined by their re-sources relative to their measurable economic needs. Economic resources include both cash and non-cash income. While after-tax cash income is the most widely employed measure of household economic well-being, it may exclude considerable amounts of resources received in a non-cash form. These include health care, education, housing, food and other subsidies from governments; production for own consumption by farmers, peasants and other individuals living mainly in rural areas and small towns; and in-kind transfers received from relatives, friends and others in the form of food, clothing and/or shelter. Moreover the distribution of these non-cash resources may vary systematically by population subgroup, thus affecting measures of relative economic well-being within and between households. They may also differ systematically by country. They almost certainly differ by regime, for example in the post-communist reforming socialist economies (RSEs) as compared with Western European and other Western nations.[2]

The omission of non-cash income from micro data-based measures of economic well-being is not purely unintentional. In most countries, aggregate income in kind is measured by systems of national income and/or social accounting. But the problems inherent in the measurement, valuation and imputation of non-cash income to individual households on the basis of micro data files are formidable for any one country. While a few countries (for example the USA and The Netherlands) have partially accomplished this task with some difficulty, and while others have achieved at least some limited micro data accounting of selected non-cash income sources (Australia, Germany, Switzerland, United Kingdom and many RSEs), some countries (Canada and Sweden) have never before systematically attempted such a task. Moreover none of these countries has ever attempted a joint project aimed at producing measures of non-cash income which are internationally comparable among such nations.

A group of researchers has been working on such a project in Western nations for the past several years under the auspices of the Luxembourg Income Study (LIS). This paper presents a summary of the methodology and results of this project as they relate to living standards and income inequality for several types of families. Additional detail is available in a longer paper, available on request, by Smeeding, Saunders, Jenkins *et al.* (1992).

The remainder of this paper discusses the importance of non-cash income in Western nations, and our conceptual and empirical approach to measuring the size and impact of non-cash income in seven of the countries participating in the LIS project. The results reported here are restricted to non-cash incomes associated with education (schooling) and health services. The paper encompasses non-cash benefits accruing to individuals as a result of direct (subsidized) public provision, tax concessions and provisions subsidized by employers. After explaining the methodology and data sources, the paper discusses and analyses the results, focusing specifically on comparisons of the distribution of non-cash income across family types and across countries. Particular attention is given to comparisons of the distributions of final (cash plus non-cash) income in each country. A classification according to family type allows the results to be analysed more thoroughly and highlights the role of non-cash income in redistribution both across and within the life course of individuals and families and its impact on the living standards of such families.

2 THE LUXEMBOURG INCOME STUDY PROJECT

Comparative research on the distribution of economic well-being has made considerable progress in recent years. That progress has been facilitated by advances in both methodological procedure and data availability. Methodologically, recent income distribution research has achieved greater clarity on questions relating to the appropriate unit of analysis, the basis for ranking those units and their weighting in deriving aggregate measures of inequality (Atkinson, 1983). These developments have permitted analysis of the distribution of income among households to translate more readily into the distribution of economic well-being among individuals. Much, though not all, of the empirical application of this new methodology has been undertaken within a comparative context. That, in turn, has been made possible by advances in data availability, specifically by the production of micro data sets which generally conform to agreed and standardized concepts and definitions.

At the forefront of this research effort has been the Luxembourg Income Study (LIS), an international, co-operative research endeavour which began in 1983 with the aim of improving comparative measures of economic well-being. There are, in fact, three distinct components of the research undertaken as part of the LIS project. The first involves the reorganization of national micro data sets in order to conform to a standard conceptual and definitional framework. The second involves the use of the data thus generated to analyse various aspects of economic well-being and inequality within a comparative framework. The third is to make the standardized data sets easily available to the international research community, in order that researchers within national boundaries can utilize them, confident in the knowledge that national differences in data concepts and definitions have, as far as possible, been eliminated. The LIS data base currently covers more than twenty countries with data covering various periods from 1969 to 1989. Several volumes and over 75 working papers have been published by LIS so far.

Analysis of the effect of cash transfers and benefits on income distribution for the countries included here can be found in Smeeding, O'Higgins and Rainwater (1990). Other recent research utilizing the LIS data includes Buhmann *et al.* (1988); Smeeding, Torrey and Rein (1988); Mitchell (1991) and Smeeding (1992). It is noticeable that all of the research undertaken so far as part of the LIS project has been based on measures of cash income. The income concepts around which the LIS data base has been constructed – factor income, gross income, disposable income and equivalent income – are all based on a conception of income expressed in terms of cash only. Non-cash elements which form part of income in its broader meaning have, with few exceptions, been excluded.[3] This segregation was inevitable in the early phases of the LIS project, but its continuation has become increasingly problematic, for at least two reasons. First, because economic well-being is, in fact, determined by more than just receipts of cash income, there is a need to begin to expand cash income measures to reflect a broader range of non-cash components. Second, studies based on cash income may give a distorted picture of the impact of government budgetary policies because within this limited framework government (cash) transfers and (direct) taxes do not balance – even in the remote sense which characterizes the actual overall fiscal situation – and also because governments may seek to achieve their redistributive goals through programmes which provide non-cash benefits rather than just through tax transfer mechanisms. This means that measures of economic well-being based on disposable cash income are subject to the vagaries of the overall fiscal structure within countries, and that comparisons of both the level and distribution of well-being between countries are dependent upon the existing fiscal structures.

3   THE SIGNIFICANCE OF NON-CASH INCOME

Knowledge about the distributional impact of non-cash benefits is essential adequately to understand the distribution of well-being in modern industrial societies. Non-cash income may be provided to private households by governments, by private third parties such as employers, or by the household itself, as in the case of imputed return from durables such as owned housing or motor cars. By far the largest amounts of non-cash benefits are provided by governments. Governments tax and transfer large amounts of total personal (factor) income – ranging from 20 per cent (in the USA) to over 40 per cent (in Sweden) – in going from market-determined factor income to disposable income. In most countries, cash income transfers constitute less than half of government expenditures. Hence not all of the income taxed away by governments, even counting only direct taxes, emerges as contributing to the post-tax, post-transfer cash or disposable income of households. Most of the amounts taxed but not transferred in cash constitute non-cash income components. While not all such components can be measured, valued and imputed to households, large parts of public non-cash income transfers in the form of health care, education and housing can be so imputed, at least in principle.

Not only is the size of non-cash income important (OECD, 1985), but its distribution may also have considerable effects on the distribution of well-being between different classes of households. Consider, for example, public health and education benefits. Most would argue that health benefits provided by governments and insurance companies are most valued by older citizens who are more likely to make use of medical services. Similarly children (and/or families with children) are most likely to enjoy the benefits from education subsidies in a given year. One would thus expect differential gains and losses to be realized across different household types. Because the value of non-cash benefits is likely to be disproportionate to net (cash) income, these income components might also have large distributional effects by income class, as well as by demographic group.

For all of these reasons, the distribution of disposable cash income may yield misleading inferences about the relative well-being of various types of households both within and across countries. If we accept the axiom that the more comprehensive the definition of income used the better is the measure of welfare, then measuring, valuing and imputing non-cash income will give a more complete picture of well-being than that afforded by cash income alone.

4 CONCEPTUAL, METHODOLOGICAL AND EMPIRICAL ISSUES

4.1 Conceptual Approach

In practice the range and type of non-cash income to include in a project such as this is enormous. It has already been noted that, although important, government is not the only source of non-cash income to private households. The goods and services from which non-cash income is derived may also be provided by private third parties such as employers or charitable organizations, or by the household itself in the form of home-grown food or implicit rent on owner-occupied housing. These items may be delivered and subsidized directly or, in the case of government provisions, indirectly via tax expenditures or regulatory policies. Employer-provided benefits such as health care insurance in the USA may also attract government support if they, or employee contributions, receive concessionary tax treatment. Thus our first task was to agree on a set of criteria for selecting non-cash benefits. The jointly determined goals and criteria which have guided our project should therefore be made explicit.

Our primary goal was to improve upon measures of economic well-being and the size distribution of well-being within and between countries by adding quantitatively important and practically measurable components of non-cash income to the LIS cash income data base. Moreover, in selecting components of non-cash income for imputation, we sought to measure the flow from those sources of non-cash income which have a deliberate (large) and differential impact on private incomes within or between countries. Conceptually acceptable but quantitatively insignificant non-cash income components (for example transportation subsidies) were for this reason deliberately ignored. It is important to emphasize that the principle of international comparability was our *sine qua non*. Because one of our main objectives was the improvement of the LIS data base, it was important to produce measures of non-cash income components which were robust across countries. Following this prin-

ciple we sometimes chose to abandon preferred measurement tech-
niques available for practical implementation in only one or two
countries and adopted instead less accurate but wholly comparable
approaches to non-cash income measurement across all countries
included in the study.

For instance, we were forced to exclude those goods and services
for which we did not have the requisite data needed to impute a value
to them (for example, tertiary education subsidies) and/or which
were not of great overall significance at the time of the income
surveys with which we were working (child care services). We also
excluded, reluctantly, non-cash income in the form of chronic (long
term) health care subsidies – provided in the form of both domiciliary
and institutional care – for the frail elderly and for younger people
with disabilities. This was partly due to lack of reliable comparative
data on the cost of these services, but also because the institutional
population is excluded from most household survey data sets.

Two broad classes of non-cash benefits are reported on here:
education (schooling) and health care.[4] Tertiary education spending
and its associated non-cash income was excluded because the LIS
tapes did not permit those studying in tertiary institutions to be
identified. Although cash scholarship support of living expenses for
tertiary education was identifiable for those who received such support, these are a very small minority of such students in most of the
countries studied, so that this was not a feasible identification approach in practice. This study thus estimates non-cash income provided by government and employers in most of the health and
education areas. Non-cash income provided through tax expenditures
are also included, although these are implicitly incorporated into the
LIS cash income framework because they affect taxable income and
are thus allowed for when deriving disposable income from gross
income. In a limited sense, therefore, the project can lay claims to
incorporate all three elements of Titmuss's social divisions of welfare
spending (public, occupational and fiscal) at least within the education and health areas (Titmuss, 1963).

4.2   Imputation Rules

Having described the scope of non-cash income, the next set of issues
relates to the identification and valuation of non-cash benefits necessary for the imputation of non-cash income. Again it is only possible

here to describe our methods in general terms. Our imputation procedures were based on the following four general principles:

1. In order to impute non-cash income, account must be taken of both benefits and costs, with only the resulting net subsidy being imputed to households. Thus the benefits associated with a partial subsidy are included as non-cash income, just as any costs (whether third party charges or taxes) must be subtracted from total (gross) benefits. If there is no net subsidy, households pay market prices and thus receive no non-cash income.[5]
2. The total (gross) value of non-cash benefits is assumed equal to the amount of money a government (or employer) spends on each item. No attempt has been made to estimate the recipient or cash equivalent value of non-cash benefits. This implies that the recipient's value of non-cash income may be overstated in some cases, particularly for those families on low incomes who might well have chosen to spend the monetary value of non-cash subsidies in other areas, had they been provided as cash transfers.
3. The household which directly receives each non-cash benefit is assumed to be the only household to benefit. We thus disregard all general (social) or specific (private) externalities, largely because of the practical impossibilities of estimating them.
4. We include both operating and capital outlays when allocating public non-cash benefits for education and health care. Annual capital outlays have been estimated where data on interest and depreciation were available; where they were not, five-year averages of actual capital expenditures have been used.

We now turn to describing the specific imputation procedures which we have followed. In the field of *education subsidies*, our analysis has been restricted to public elementary (primary) and secondary schooling. The benefits of current (operating) and capital outlays have been allocated to families with children in education. Our estimation methods involve calculating, for each level of education, average outlays per student from data on total outlays and student enrolments, and imputing these averages as non-cash income to families with children participating in each level of education. Adjustment for early leavers ('drop-outs') have been made and public subsidies for private education (which are important in Australia) have been allocated on a randomized basis. Apart from Australia, because the resulting non-cash incomes are allocated to all students, whether they attend public (government) or private schools, we assume that subsidies to government schools are of value and thus also provide benefits to those with children in private schools, and likewise that government subsidies to private schools are of value to those with children in government schools. In contrast families whose children 'drop out' of school are assumed to place a zero value on their forgone opportunity of school attendance. Finally we have deducted property tax payments from home-owners in order to arrive at a net subsidy figure. This is because property taxes are the major financing mechanism for local schools in most countries in the study.[6]

In the field of *health care subsidies*, our imputations have been based on a risk-related insurance premia approach. That is, we view health care as an insurance benefit received by all those covered, independently of their actual use of health care benefits, and also that the benefits (and hence premia) differ by age and gender in line with differences in need. According to this line of argument, insurance premia should be actuarially adjusted (age- and sex-related) to account for differences in the need-related value of being covered by health insurance. Thus benefits received are estimated by age- and sex-specific outlays spread over all those covered in each age–sex cell of the population. The actual cells used to estimate benefits and the method for allocating non-tax (user) charges for health insurance are derived from national data sources on utilization rates for different elements in the health care system, differentiated by age and gender, and national data on the incidence of any tax or user charges. In cases where freely available public health insurance is all that exists (for example, in Sweden), gross benefits only are imputed, the taxes to support them already being deducted. In cases where public and private third party charges are levied on households and employers (The Netherlands, USA and West Germany) an allocation of costs is also specified. In the case of direct payments to providers (for example, out-of-pocket charges and deductibles), no imputation of costs or benefits is undertaken. Finally, in cases where total third party premia equal expected benefits (that is, no subsidy is realized), no imputation is made. Thus only subsidized and insured benefits and payments to insurers are taken into account.

In summary, our imputation methods have involved combining the existing LIS data set with additional national data on non-cash expenditure aggregates and on the utilization rates of education and health services. In order to achieve this we have had to combine familiarity with the existing LIS data with detailed knowledge of the national data sources which comprise LIS, an understanding of the structure and operation of the education and health insurance schemes in each country and expertise in bringing other national data sources to bear on the way the detailed allocation of non-cash benefits was to be imputed.[7]

4.3 Other Measurement Issues

There are a number of additional issues that have to be discussed before turning to our results. Again these are dealt with only briefly, in order that readers may gain a basic understanding of our actual procedures. The first such issue relates to our choice of the basic *unit of analysis*. Non-cash benefits have to be imputed to income units, that is to individuals, families or households. Our emphasis is on the distribution of non-cash benefits between families defined to include either a group of two or more related persons living together as a family and sharing their housekeeping, or single persons who are assumed to keep independently their own housing units. This definition implies that two unmarried individuals (without children) sharing the same living quarters are treated as independent families. The bias implicit in this treatment is to ignore economies of scale in housing (and other domestic arrangements) among unmarried people living together.

The major exceptions to these general rules are in The Netherlands and Sweden, where unmarried persons living together in a marriage-like relationship (that is sharing living quarters, facilities and expenses) are counted as a single family and in Canada, where related generations of families (for example elderly mother and adult children) are treated as separate economic units, even where they live together. In general, while these procedures treat some households or families differently from others, they come closest to the preferred and usual definition of families within each country.

Having defined families for the purposes of analysis, the next step is to specify a number of different *family types* for measuring the impact of non-cash subsidies on different families. The results presented in the next section of this paper disaggregate families in two different dimensions, according to eight family types. In relation to this disaggregation, we adopted the following exclusive and exhaustive categorization which was chosen in part because of its relevance for both analytical and policy purposes.

1. *Families with children* (children aged 17 or younger):
   (a) non-aged couples (head under 65, couple may or may not be married),
   (b) non-aged single parents (one adult only under 65, plus children),
   (c) other families with children (including a few units with head 65 or over).
2. *Elderly families* (head 65 or over):
   (a) single elderly persons (one person unit 65 or over),
   (b) elderly couple (head 65 or over).
3. *Non-aged families without children*.
   (a) single persons,
   (b) childless couples,
   (c) other childless families (more than two adults or families with young adults aged 18 or over).

As already noted, the basic *income concepts* we have used are those developed as part of the LIS project and other research in the area (Smeeding, O'Higgins and Rainwater, 1990). However to the familiar (cash income) concepts of factor income, gross income and disposable income we now add the concept of full income, which is equal to the sum of disposable income and imputed non-cash income in the form of education and health care.

5 LEVELS OF NON-CASH INCOME AND LIVING STANDARDS

5.1 The Level of Non-cash Income

The overall mean amounts of (unadjusted disposable) cash and non-cash income are presented for each country in Table 11.1. The figures in the top section for each country are expressed in national currencies, while the figures in the lower section are standardized relative to each country's mean disposable income. It is important to remember that the non-cash incomes shown in Table 11.1 are net of all costs and charges, including only the *net* subsidy from government and/or employers. Overall, non-cash health and education income averages 16.6 per cent of disposable income, ranging from 13 per cent in the USA and West Germany to almost 22 per cent in the United Kingdom and Sweden. The health component of non-cash income is

Table 11.1   Overall average amounts of cash and non-cash income by
country

Country and year (1)	Disposable income (2)	Education (3)	Health (4)	Health and education (3)+(4) (5)	Final income (2)+(5) (6)
Amounts in national currency					
Australia, 1981–2	14 669	948	1 124	2 072	16 741
Canada, 1981	21 505	1 631	1 537	3 168	24 673
Netherlands, 1983	31 377	2 502	3 037	5 539	36 916
Sweden, 1981	64 283	5 399	8 653	14 052	78 335
United Kingdom, 1979	5 290	638	509	1 147	6 437
United States of America, 1979	14 338	1 091	774	1 865	16 203
West Germany, 1981	31 302	1 573	2 497	4 070	35 327
As a percentage of disposable income					
Australia	100	6.5	7.7	14.1	114.1
Canada	100	7.6	7.1	14.7	114.7
Netherlands	100	8.0	9.7	17.7	117.7
Sweden	100	8.4	13.5	21.9	121.9
United Kingdom	100	12.1	9.6	21.7	121.7
United States of America	100	7.6	5.4	13.0	113.0
West Germany	100	5.0	8.0	13.0	113.0
Simple average	100	7.9	8.7	16.6	116.6

greater than the education component in all countries except Canada,
the United Kingdom and the USA. In the United Kingdom this
mainly reflects the high level of non-cash education income, while in
the USA it reflects the relatively low net subsidy to health care. The
difference between these categories in Canada is fairly small.

5.2   Living Standards

The effect of non-cash income on the average income levels of family
types – the effect on living standards of different family types – is
shown in Table 11.2. The living standard impact was calculated by
comparing overall average group income – unadjusted disposable
income and final income – with the national average. Net differences
in impact by family type are shown at the bottom of the table.

The bottom section of Table 11.2 indicates that, relative to average
incomes, non-cash income is greatest for families with children and

Table 11.2 Effect of non-cash income on living standards: net benefits as a proportion of overall average income by family type and country

Family type	Australia	Canada	Netherlands	Sweden	United Kingdom	United States of America	West Germany
				Disposable Income (1)			
Families with children							
(a) non-aged couples	119	119	115	159	122	126	125
(b) non-aged single parents	50	58	69	99	71	55	93
(c) other[a]	163	151	127	128	176	146	149
Elderly[b]							
(a) single person	37	42	56	56	31	41	50
(b) couple	66	80	82	100	58	87	87
Non-aged without children							
(a) single	60	59	58	68	58	61	65
(b) couple	117	119	118	140	120	125	119
(c) other[c]	154	135	120	n.a.	135	135	139
				Final Income (2)			
Families with children							
(a) non-aged couples	125	126	121	167	137	133	131
(b) non-aged single parents	61	71	79	114	91	70	100
(c) other[a]	170	158	147	153	176	158	159

	(1)	(2)	(3)	(4)	(5)	(6)	(7)
Elderly[b]							
(a) single person	39	47	56	69	33	43	48
(b) couple	68	84	84	111	57	86	86
Non-aged without children							
(a) single	55	53	51	59	52	55	60
(b) couple	108	108	104	124	104	114	112
(c) other[c]	147	126	115	n.a.	119	126	133
Difference ((2) minus (1))							
Families with children							
(a) non-aged couples	6	7	6	8	15	7	6
(b) non-aged single parents	11	13	10	15	20	15	7
(c) other[a]	7	7	20	25	0	12	10
Elderly[b]							
(a) single person	2	5	0	13	2	2	-2
(b) couple	2	4	2	11	-1	-1	-1
Non-aged without children							
(a) single	-5	-6	-7	-9	-6	-6	-5
(b) couple	-9	-11	-14	-16	-16	-11	-7
(c) other[c]	-7	-9	-5	n.a.	-16	-9	-6

n.a. = not available.

Notes: [a] Other families with children include those with at least one parent age 65 or over or children living with more than two adults.

[b] Elderly are families with head or spouses age 65 or over.

[c] Other families without children include those with three or more adults.

211

the elderly. The biggest relative losers in most countries are non-aged single people and families without children, including younger, recently married couples and older couples approaching retirement age. The size of the relative gains for families with children are greater than those for the elderly in all countries. Amongst families without children, relative losses are generally greater for couples than for the other groups. The effects on the elderly are generally more modest than one would have thought, given their relatively higher benefits from health care. The differences in health subsidy for the aged versus other groups (adults, children) are clearly less than the differences in education which benefit only one group, that is families with younger children.

Before the addition of non-cash income, single parents with children, single adults – aged and non-aged – and aged couples had below-average disposable incomes. Non-aged married couples, with and without children, and larger families – generally those included under 'other' – had higher incomes. Because of our not adjusting these incomes for family size, we clearly create upward bias in the measured well-being of the 'other' categories. Despite this, the addition of non-cash income in the form of health and education most improves the position of single parents with children in most countries. Single aged persons gain a small amount and aged couples hold their own (except in Sweden, where the gains are large for the aged). The childless non-aged lose in relative terms – both the couples and others who already had above-average incomes, and also non-aged single persons whose cash incomes were initially below-average.

If one were to double the living standards of the singles (or halve the incomes of the couples), they would be much closer to each other, indicating that overall living standards per capita are higher for these people than is shown in Table 11.2. Single parents with children – the least well-off group in cash terms in several of these nations – appear to gain most from this exercise. Their full incomes remain below-average (except in Germany and Sweden), but they are higher once income in kind is added than they were before.

6   INEQUALITY

The effect of non-cash benefits on the overall size distribution of income is captured most simply in Table 11.3. In interpreting these results it is important to remember that no adjustments are made for

Table 11.3 Effects of non-cash income on the overall income distribution, by country

Quintile share of income	Australia	Canada	Netherlands	Sweden	United Kingdom	United States of America	West Germany
Disposable Income (1)[a]							
Lowest	5.4	5.4	6.9	8.3	5.9	4.7	7.0
Second	11.7	12.0	13.2	13.2	11.4	11.3	13.1
Middle	18.0	18.2	18.0	17.6	18.2	17.7	17.7
Fourth	24.9	25.0	23.7	24.3	25.0	25.5	24.1
Highest	40.0	39.4	38.2	36.7	39.5	40.7	38.1
Total	100.0	100.0	100.0	100.0c	100.0	100.0c	100.0
Final income (2)[b]							
Lowest	5.7	6.1	7.6	8.6	6.2	5.3	10.2
Second	11.8	12.4	13.2	13.0	11.6	11.6	15.7
Middle	17.9	18.4	18.3	17.2	18.6	17.7	18.8
Fourth	24.9	25.0	23.8	24.4	25.4	25.4	22.7
Highest	39.7	38.1	37.2	36.8	38.2	40.0	32.6
Total	100.0	100.0	100.0c	100.0	100.0	100.0	100.0
Difference ((2) minus (1))							
Lowest	0.3	0.7	0.7	0.3	0.3	0.6	3.2
Second	0.1	0.4	0.0	-0.2	0.2	0.3	2.6
Middle	-0.1	0.2	0.3	-0.4	0.4	0.0	1.1
Fourth	0.0	0.0	0.1	0.1	0.4	-0.1	-1.4
Highest	-0.3	-1.3	-1.0	0.1	-1.3	-0.7	-5.5

Notes: [a] Disposable income includes all forms of cash income net of income and payroll taxes.
[b] Final income adds the market value of health and education benefits to disposable income.
[c] Column does not add up to the total because components have been rounded independently.

family size or type, implying that the results have limited relevance to the distribution of individual economic well-being. The bottom section of the table again captures the difference due to non-cash benefits. For the most part, non-cash benefits from health and education are equalizing, increasing the income share at the bottom and decreasing it at the top, particularly in the top quintile. In all countries except Sweden, the Lorenz curve for the distribution of final income lies entirely outside that for the distribution of disposable income.

The distributional effects are largest by far in Germany, followed by Canada and the United Kingdom. The effects are least in Australia, followed by Sweden and the USA. Interestingly, non-cash income has a slight unequalizing effect at the top of the income distribution in Sweden, even though the biggest gainers are those in the bottom quintile. The rank order of nations in terms of the income shares of the lowest quintile are unaffected by the addition of health and education benefits, with the exception of Germany, which jumps to the highest, with Sweden second. In all nations, the bottom quintile does better with non-cash benefits included. The USA still has the lowest share for the bottom quintile, but it is now much closer to Australia (second lowest) than before. Effects on the top quintile are generally small, except in Germany: here rank order changes slightly, with Germany again becoming the most equal (lowest upper quintile share) and Sweden moving to second most equal. The rest of the rankings remain intact.

7 SUMMARY AND CONCLUSIONS

The main aim of this paper has been to summarize the impact of non-cash income – health and education benefits – on living standards and income distribution. Non-cash income is an important source of well-being in all countries, and comparisons of living standards and inequality must recognize that and take account of it wherever possible. Although our valuation methods are open to criticism and may overstate the value of non-cash benefits for those on low (cash) incomes, the results are nonetheless interesting and informative.

The impact of non-cash income is best viewed within a life cycle context. Education benefits accrue to families with school-age children, while health care benefits – though received by all – are disproportionately high for the elderly, particularly the very old. The inclusion of non-cash income thus has the largest impact on the final incomes, and hence average living standards, of families with children and the elderly. In contrast non-elderly single people, particularly young single people, and non-aged families without children find their relative income positions are worsened by the inclusion of non-cash income. Because single elderly persons and single parents on average have low living standards, non-cash benefits have a large impact on their well-being.

Overall, although the results in this paper show that non-cash income has distributional consequences within nations, they do give rise to a pattern of national differences in living standards or income inequality which are markedly different from those to emerge from previous LIS research based on cash income alone. It thus appears that non-cash income reinforces the redistributive impact of conventional (cash) tax transfer mechanisms rather than acting to offset them in any major way.

Notes

1. This paper summarizes a six-year project which was conducted in conjunction with, and under the auspices of, the Luxembourg Income Study (LIS). Sponsors have included the United States National Institute on Aging, the United States National Science Foundation, and the LIS member countries. The authors would also like to thank various individuals who helped as project participants. These include Grant Cameron, Wolfhard Dobröschke–Kohn, Flip de Kam, Peter Hedstrom, Brigitte Buhmann, Michael O'Higgins, Uwe Warner, Julie Tapp and Inge O'Connor. However the authors accept responsibility for all errors of commission and omission.
2. Non-cash income does not include off-the-books cash income (in the grey economy) and hence this topic is not discussed in this paper. While we do not include any of the RSEs, it should be noted that many such countries, including Poland and Hungary, have elaborate systems of national accounts, consumption studies and income distribution estimates which include a wide range of goods and services provided in kind. Yet even these nations exclude large portions of such items. For more on this topic, see Smeeding and Torrey (1991) and Teglarsky and Struyk (1990).
3. 'Near-cash' income – that is, payments made in flexible currency denominations, such as food stamps in the United States, or cash benefits contingent on meeting certain needs, for example university scholarships or housing allowances in Sweden or the United Kingdom – are already included in LIS disposable income on the grounds that these benefits are denominated in money terms and are thus very nearly equivalent to an equal cash transfer in the eyes of the recipient.

4. For five of the seven countries studied it was also possible to impute non-cash housing benefits in the form of imputed rent to owner-occupiers. These results are summarized in Smeeding, Saunders, Jenkins *et al.* (1992).
5. The indirect effects of government subsidies or taxes on market prices were also excluded. The implicit counterfactual is therefore that the market price is the price which would prevail in the absence of any government intervention via taxes or subsidy.
6. Where property taxes are not used in this way (for example in Australia), the deduction of property taxes from non-cash education benefits was not undertaken.
7. Thus, while the focus of our research effort has been explicitly comparative, what we have attempted would almost certainly not have been possible except as a joint venture undertaken by a group of national researchers committed to such a task.

References

Atkinson, A.B. (1983) *The Economics of Inequality*, 2nd edn (Oxford: Clarendon Press).
Buhmann, B., Rainwater, L., Shmaus, G. and Smeeding, T. (1988) 'Equivalence Scales, Well-Being, Inequality and Poverty: Sensitivity Estimates across Ten Countries Using the Luxembourg Income Study (LIS) Database', *Review of Income and Wealth*, vol. 34, June, pp. 115–42.
Mitchell, D. (1991) *Income Transfer in Ten Welfare States* (Aldershot, UK: Avebury Press).
OECD (1985) *Social Expenditure 1960–1990. Problems of Growth and Control* (Paris: OECD).
Smeeding, T.M. (1992) 'Why the U.S. Anti-Poverty System Doesn't Work Very Well', *Challenge*, January–February, pp. 30–35.
Smeeding, T. and Torrey, B. (1991) 'Goldmines and Minefields. A Summary of the LIS Conference: The Changing Structure of Income and Social Policy in Eastern Europe: A Comparative Focus', Working Paper no. 68, Luxembourg Income Study, Walferdange, Luxembourg.
Smeeding, T.M., O'Higgins, M. and Rainwater, L. (eds) (1990) *Poverty, Inequality and Income Distribution in Comparative Perspective. The Luxembourg Income Study* (Hemel Hempshead: Harvester Wheatsheaf).
Smeeding, T.M., Torrey, B. and Rein, M. (1988) 'Patterns of Income and Poverty: The Economic Status of Children and the Elderly in Eight Countries', in Palmer, J.L., Smeeding, T. and Torrey, B.B. (eds) *The Vulnerable* (Washington, DC: The Urban Institute) pp. 89–119.
Smeeding, T., Saunders, P., Jenkins, S. *et al.* (1992) *Noncash Income, Inequality and Living Standards in Seven Nations* mimeo, Luxembourg Income Study, Walferdange, Luxembourg.
Teglarsky, J. and Struyk, R. (1990) *Toward a Market-Oriented Housing Sector in Eastern Europe: Developments in Bulgaria, Czechoslovakia,*

Hungary, Poland, Romania and Yugoslavia (Washington, DC: Urban Institute Press).
Titmuss, R.M. (1963) 'The Social Division of Welfare: Some Reflections on the Search for Equity', in Titmuss R.M., *Essays on the Welfare State*, 2nd edn (London: George Allen & Unwin) pp. 34–55.

12 Gender Inequality and Economic Development

Jane Humphries
CAMBRIDGE UNIVERSITY

1 INTRODUCTION

Inequality between men and women has been associated with economic backwardness. Although the causes of gender inequality were disputed, in the 1950s and 1960s, it was widely held that forces unleashed in economic development would lead to a convergence in the status and well-being of men and women.[1] For example, modernization theorists argued that increasing reliance on impersonal markets to allocate economic resources was incompatible with discrimination. Moreover structural changes, associated with development, such as the increasing relative importance of manufacturing and at a later stage the rapid growth of the service sector, were thought to facilitate women's involvement in production and therefore to increase their economic value. In turn women's economic usefulness was seen as a key determinant of their relative status and well-being.[2] But current research has questioned the spontaneity of links between the level of development and women's relative status. Behind this retreat from easy generalizations has been an accumulation of evidence suggesting significant differences in the extent, pattern and terms of women's involvement in paid work in countries at similar levels of development. If the comparative static fit between gender roles and economic structure looks less than tidy, the implication is that there may be only a weak correspondence between women's relative well-being and economic development.

Section 2 below describes how comparative analyses have been the main source of evidence against a universalist view of women's roles in high income economies, while case studies have demonstrated that economic development is neither necessary nor sufficient for improvements in women's relative well-being. Missing are international comparisons of the status of women and the level of economic development. This is surprising in that such studies are common in the

218

general literature on the standard of living (see Dasgupta and Weale, 1992, for a recent review). Section 3 provides an exploratory analysis of this kind and the final section underlines the implications.

2 DIFFERENCES WITHIN THE SIMILARITIES AND THE RETREAT FROM ECONOMISM

In the 1970s several influential studies which focused directly on women's experience during economic development heralded a retreat from the optimistic orthodoxy of modernization theory. Although these studies did not share the optimistic perspective of the modernization school, nor its vision of linear progress, they retained a powerful causal role for economic forces. Boserup (1970), for example, argued that the changes in economic structure associated with economic development promoted a distinct 'U'-shaped pattern in women's economic participation. Tilly and Scott (1978) linked the evolution of the economic functions of the family, and derivatively the forms of women's economic involvement, to macroeconomic structure in the context of European industrialization. Closer to modernization theory, neoclassical economics did not see distinct gender roles as the result of economic processes. Differences between men and women were either disequilibrium phenomena or the outcome of gendered differences in tastes. In either case improvements in the integration of markets, the elimination of pre-market discrimination driven by the need to use labour efficiently and non-discriminatory state policies implied a convergence in the labour market behaviour of men and women. Bargaining within the household then equalized access to resources.

In many models the extent and terms of women's participation in production were viewed as intermediate variables which themselves changed systematically, though perhaps not monotonically, as development occurred, enhancing or reducing women's social status and economic well-being according to whether women were being integrated or marginalized. All too often difficulties in measuring women's well-being pushed researchers to concentrate instead on the changes in women's involvement in production, with the link to living standards remaining implicit. Alternatively the extent of female involvement in production was seen as governing women's status and well-being directly and independently of the level of development.

The 1970s saw a rapid growth in the literature on the political economy of women as a second generation of researchers sought to apply these influential models. Comparative-static studies traced the ways in which different economic structures had an impact on women's lives and dynamic studies showed how economic changes could transform women's access to resources and derivatively their relative well-being. These studies suggested that the links between economic changes and changes in gender roles were more complicated than the original theories had suggested. Institutions, customs and practices proved important filters through which the economic forces had to operate. The trend was against simple economism. Nonetheless at this stage empirical research on gender continued to stress the similarities in the position of women among countries at similar levels of development: the tendency to occupational segregation, both vertical and horizontal; the low pay that women command in the labour market and the differences between men and women in participation rates and working hours associated with domestic commitments in relatively high-income economies; and the tendency to exclusion from capitalist development and industrialization in relatively low-income economies both historically and contemporaneously.

Current work on gender exhibits a further withdrawal from economism. Empirical researchers have backed away from the simple propositions implicit in stage or convergence theories. Recent comparative studies of the relationship between women's status and economic structure have discovered differences within the similarities both in the pay and participation of women in advanced economies and in the marginalization of women in the third world. Thus in introducing a collection of essays on women's economic role in seven OECD economies, Jane Jenson wrote recently: 'There is a great deal of diversity in women's actual experience. No clear trend has emerged that could adequately characterise the present status or future of the female labour force' (1988, p. 4; see also Rubery, 1988, p. 254; Meulders *et al.*, 1991, p. 1). If occupational segregation, pay differentials and working time are not structured to match universal gender requirements and the characteristics of production at certain levels of GNP, then even the loose links between women's economic integration and economic development are undermined and the determination of women's well-being floats free of its economic moorings.

Comparative analyses of pairs or small groups of countries at similar levels of development have been the primary means used to establish the heterogeneity of women's experience among high-income economies. Examples include Garnsey (1984), Walters and

Dex (1992), Proctor and Ratcliffe (1992) and David and Starzec (1992) on Britain and France; Dale and Glover (1990) on Britain, France and the USA; Jenson *et al.* (1988) on seven OECD countries; Rubery (1988) on Britain, France, Italy and the USA; Koistinen and Ostner (1992) and Pfau-Effinger (1992) on Finland and Germany; Bettio and Villa (1992) on Mediterranean and Anglo-Saxon economies; Dex and Shaw (1988) on the USA and Britain; and Meulders *et al.* (1991) summarizing the work of the Expert Group on Women and Employment of the European Commission.

The same move away from universalist propositions is evident in recent writings on women in development. The primary vehicle here has been case studies of responses to particular economic development strategies. While earlier studies emphasized women's marginalization from modern manufacturing employment, more recent studies focus on the integration of women into manufacturing employment and their marginalization within employment through segregation into labour-intensive and low-pay sectors (Humphrey, 1985; Joekes, 1985; Hein, 1984; Anchor and Hein, 1985; Elson and Pearson, 1981; Safa, 1981; Nash, 1983; Lim, 1983; Berik and Çağatay, 1992).

But development economists retain a direct interest in the relationship between economic development and women's relative well-being. Evidence that women's relative mortality, widely taken as an index of well-being, varied greatly among poor countries suggested that economic growth was neither a necessary nor a sufficient condition for improvement. Attention turned to what had often been seen as an intermediate variable: the economic usefulness of women and girls (Preston, 1976; Miller, 1981; Kynch and Sen, 1983; Bardhan, 1984; Kumar, 1989). Sex differentials in mortality have not been thought of as explicable by economic factors not mediated by cultural perceptions of the 'value' of female life, or as mechanically linked to industrialization or urbanization (Kynch and Sen, 1983). Consistent with the new emphasis on heterogeneity of experience, authors have been careful to see economic pressures as funnelled through institutions, customs and practices.

Despite the centrality of these issues to gender analysis and the revisionist thrust of recent writings, international comparisons of the relative status of women and the level of economic development are rare (Allèn, 1992). The Population Crisis Committee (1988) publication 'Poor, Powerless and Pregnant', represents a significant exception.[3] An obstacle to such analyses is that conventional data are often not ideally suited to a focus on gender.[4] The next section presents a first attempt at an international cross-section comparison which is intended to complement the comparative and case study research in questioning economistic approaches to the determination of women's relative well-being.

3   THE RANKING OF COUNTRIES BY WOMEN'S WELL-BEING

Well-being is difficult to measure even without distinguishing between males and females. Economists have recognized that living standards involve more than disposable income per capita. As long ago as 1954, a United Nations Expert Group recommended that, in addition to real per capita income, use should be made of quantitative measures in the fields of health, education, employment and housing to assess a country's standard of living. Today the *World Development Report* (World Bank, 1991), and UNICEF's *State of the World's Children* contain large numbers of cross-country socioeconomic indicators. There is an emerging consensus that at the aggregate level, real national income per capita, infant and child survival rates, life expectancy at birth and adult literacy rates comprise the optimum package of indicators. Questions about the distribution of well-being, whether it be on gender or other lines, should concern the distribution of these indices.

Attempts to redefine these variables on a gendered basis meet with mixed success. It is impossible to measure the per capita income of a country separately for males and females. Alternative indices of relative command over purchasing power based on activity rates and relative wages are feasible, but they conflate the indicators of well-being with those of women's relative importance within a national economy, whereas we are interested in looking at the relationship between these variables. Data on infant mortality, life expectancy, and educational attainment are available for males and females separately. Estimates of relative mortality rates, relative life expectancy and numbers of female students per 100 male students at different levels of education are readily constructed from World Bank data for a number of rich and poor countries. In addition, maternal mortality was added to the series as representing another dimension of women's relative living standards.

These variables constitute the basis of my index of women's well-being. Two points must be made. First, decisions about what to include in such an index are obviously subjective. I have begun here with the variables suggested in the mainstream literature on living standards generally and added maternal mortality. But there is scope for widening the coverage. For example, one obvious omission is of an indicator of women's relative political freedom. Another omission is that of any indicator of access to contraception. Including variables which cover these gaps runs into both conceptual and measurement problems. Neither, it is hoped, is insurmountable. Second, there are conceptual difficulties in looking at the mortality, life expectancy and access to education of women relative to men. The problem is how to define 'equality' (see Preston, 1976). In the absence of a convincing theory of what constitutes 'natural' differences in death rates, life expectancy and educational enrolment between the sexes, we use ratios of attainments for women relative to men even though these sometimes exceed unity and are sensitive to the levels of the variables (see Preston, 1976).

The quality of these data makes it unwise to rely on cardinal values. Comparisons are usually made of ordinal measures which are unaffected by systematic biases in claims about achievements across countries. Table 12.1 shows the rankings of a sample of low-income countries by each of these indicators. The countries are listed in ascending order of their GNP per capita in 1989. The Borda Rule was used to aggregate over the ordinal measures.[5] The Borda score and rank according to that score are given in the final two columns. Table 12.2 provides the corresponding rankings for a sample of high-income countries. Again the countries appear in ascending order of their GNP per capita. Rankings range from the worst score of 1, to the best score of 28 in the low-income sample and 24 in the high-income sample.

Looking first at the sample of low-income economies, the rankings appear consistent with other findings. Other work has suggested that Islamic countries rank poorly according to indices of this kind and studies which concentrate on mortality and health indicators would broadly confirm our ranking (Allèn, 1992). What about the relationship between gender inequality and economic development? Again our results seem consistent with other findings. Allèn, for example, found that 'Among the 12 countries with the lowest living standards of women and the greatest inequalities between men and women, there are five of the world's poorest countries' (Allèn, 1992, p. 108). But if, as Allèn says, 'The "positive correlation" between the level of GNP and gender inequalities in economic, social and political variables seems to be evident' (1992, p. 108) it is not *so* evident.

Table 12.1   Rankings of women's relative living standards: low-income economies[a]

	GNP per capita 1989	Relative mortality under 5 1989	Relative life expectancy 1989	Maternal mortality per 100 000 live births 1980	Females per 100 males in primary school, 1985	Borda score[b]	Borda score ranking
Mozambique	1	9	14	15	15	53	12
Ethiopia	2	7	16	1	9	33	3
Tanzania	3	15	24	19	28	86	25
Somalia	4	14	16	4	3[c]	37	6
Bangladesh	5	2	1	9	14	26	2
Malawi	6	4	4	23	17	48	10
Chad	7	8	19	8	1	36	4[d]
Sierra Leone	8	6	27	17	10[c]	60	17
Madagascar	9	11	6	21	26	64	20
Nigeria	10	16	28	3	11[c]	58	15
Uganda	11	21	14	21	19	75	22
Zaire	12	19	12	6	15[c]	52	11
Niger	13	10	26	18	5	59	16
Burkina Faso	14	5	16	9	6	36	4[d]
Rwanda	15	12	24	24	27	87	26

India	16	1	3	14	20	38	7
China	17	28	5	28	21	82	23
Haiti	18	22	8	20	12[c]	62	18[d]
Kenya	19	25	21	13	25	84	24
Pakistan	20	3	2	9	2	16	1
Benin	21	17[d]	23	2	4	46	8[d]
Central African Republic	22	17[d]	13	9	7	46	8[d]
Ghana	23	23	9	5	12	54	13[d]
Togo	24	20	10	16	8	54	13[d]
Zambia	25	24	22	26	22	94	28
Sri Lanka	26	27	11	27	23	88	27
Indonesia	27	26	7	6	23	62	18[d]
Mauritania	28	13	19	25	13	70	21

Notes: [a] Rankings vary from 1 (worst) to 28 (best).
[b] See note 5. The sum of the four previous columns.
[c] Estimates.
[d] Equal ranking and score to that of another country.

Source: World Bank (1991).

Table 12.2 Rankings of women's relative living standards: high-income economies[a]

	GNP per capita 1989	Relative mortality under 5 1989	Relative life expectancy 1989	Maternal mortality per 100 000 live births 1980	Females per 100 males in primary school 1985	Borda score[b]	Borda score ranking
Saudi Arabia	1	4	2	1	1	8	1
Ireland	2	16	12	14	14	56	20
Spain	3	6	7	11	14	38	4
Israel	4	18	1	16	24	59	21
Hong Kong	5	9	3	21	18	51	12[c]
Singapore	6	9	11	6	13	39	5[c]
New Zealand	7	18	9	6	9	42	7[c]
Australia	8	20	19	6	10	55	18[c]
United Kingdom	9	16	8	14	6	44	9
Italy	10	15	17	4	3	39	5[c]
Netherlands	11	9	13	16	22	60	22
Kuwait	12	23	5	2	2	32	3
Belgium	13	5	17	11	16	49	11
Austria	14	24	20	6	4	54	16[c]
France	15	20	24	4	21	69	23

Canada	16	9	13	24	5	51	12[c]
Germany	17	20	20	6	8	54	16[c]
Denmark	18	6	9	21	19	55	18[c]
United States	19	3	20	13	6	42	7[c]
Sweden	20	1	3	21	20	45	10
Finland	21	13	20	16	23	72	24
Norway	22	6	13	16	16	51	12[c]
Japan	23	2	6	3	10	21	2
Switzerland	24	13	13	16	10	52	15

Notes: [a] Rankings vary from 1 to 24.
[b] See note 5. The sum of the four previous columns.
[c] Equal ranking and score to that of another country.

Source: World Bank (1991).

Economic development has only a loose relationship, if it has a relationship at all, with women's relative status. Of the ten poorest countries in the world, only four would appear in the bottom ten countries from the relative perspective of women. Things are not so different for the better off countries in this group which also includes a large number whose ranking according to the Borda index is less than its ranking according to GNP per capita. Pakistan, which ranks twentieth according to GNP per capita, is the worst ranked according to the relative well-being of women. Summarizing the relationship in terms of a Spearman rank correlation, although the correlation is indeed positive, it is low and insignificant ($R = 0.323$, $t = 1.74$).

But if economic development appears poorly correlated with women's relative well-being, what about the alternative hypothesis which sees their involvement in economic activities as the key to emancipation? Unfortunately we do not have comprehensive data for these countries on the productive roles of women, but it is possible to look at specific individual cases where there are significant gaps between their Borda ranking and their rank in terms of GNP per capita. Pakistan has the biggest negative rank difference (worst on the Borda index, twentieth according to GNP per capita). The female activity rate in 1989 was 6.8 per cent, compared with a male rate of 49.4 per cent. Symmetrically we can find examples of countries which rank higher according to the Borda index than they do according to GNP per capita, such as Malawi, which also have relatively high female activity rates. Women in Malawi apparently make up more than half the labour force. However countries which fall into this category (higher Borda index than rank according to GNP per capita) such as Tanzania, Malawi, Kenya, China, Nigeria, Sri Lanka and Zambia may have other things in common, or indeed their relatively good performance on the gender front may be explained by individual factors. Government policy may play a role, in particular a good performance on general living standards relative to income levels appears positively correlated with women's relative well-being (see for example, Dasgupta and Weale, 1992, p. 123).

As far as high-income economies are concerned, although several countries rank roughly the same by GNP per capita and by women's relative living standards, again there are some spectacular differences. Japan performs poorly on gender, given its income ranking, while, surprisingly, Ireland does well.[6] Again the Spearman rank order correlation coefficient though positive is not significant ($R = 0.15$, $t = 0.71$). Data are available (ILO, 1991) to rank the sample of high-income countries according to women's relative activity rates. Here the correlation is again positive (though not large) and insignificant ($R = 0.32$, $t = 1.82$). So although women's involvement in paid work does appear positively correlated with their relative well-being, this relationship too is weak, the implication being that other factors can (and do) have effects.

4 CONCLUSIONS

The exploratory comparison of women's relative well-being and both GNP per capita and women's relative activity rates over samples of very poor and very rich countries confirms, from a different direction, the conclusions evident in much recent work on gender. Women's relative status and well-being appear only loosely linked to the level of development. This has important implications. It undermines complaisant and sceptical attitudes about policies designed to advance and assist women. There is no justification for the view either that economic growth will automatically 'trickle down' to women, or that policy makers have no degrees of freedom to influence the situation of women independently of economic growth. Although this study has been limited in its range and design, there is clearly scope to develop both a better and more comprehensive index of women's relative well-being and to explore more systematically the reasons for its variation across countries.

Notes

1. This view is associated with the modernization school of social scientists writing in the 1950s, 1960s and early 1970s. Thus W.J. Goode, often cited as a representative figure, suggested that economic development, and industrialization in particular, 'is accompanied by a trend towards "equalitarianism" between the sexes, mainly derived from the needs of an industrialising system – specifically, the demand for skill wherever it may be found. Racial, ethnic and sex barriers weaken before this requirement, which gains added force from a long ideological debate about equal rights and opportunities' (1963, p. 21). Janet Thomas (1988) locates the optimistic views of the modernization school in a wider literature.
2. For the classic sociological statement of the argument that domestic authority and command over family resources is dependent on an individual's contribution to those resources, see Blood and Wolfe (1960). Several theoretical approaches recently developed in orthodox economics

are discussed in Pollak (1985). For a recent critical survey, see Pahl (1989).
3. This study provides a survey of twenty variables measuring women's status according to five dimensions – health, marriage and children, education, employment and social equality – for 99 countries representing 2.3 billion women (92 per cent of the world's female population). However the inclusion of employment status as a component of well-being is inappropriate. Work itself may not be constitutive of welfare though as suggested in this literature, involvement in economic life may well be positively correlated with social status and command over resources, which may, in turn, enhance well-being. The study also conflates measures of absolute and relative well-being in the same index. The emphasis here is on relative welfare. It is obvious that the absolute condition of women, as well as of men, will be positively correlated with economic development in the long run. Finally the study compares the absolute scores achieved by countries rather than their ranks, which is the focus here, and does not systematically investigate the relationship between country performance on the one hand and per capita income or women's economic value on the other. Indeed the latter is not possible because employment status has been incorporated directly into the status of women index.
4. The same is also true of standard methodology and orthodox theory. Acknowledgment of these problems constitutes another theme of recent gender research (Bergmann, 1987; Folbre and Hartmann, 1988).
5. The Borda Rule provides a method of rank order scoring. The procedure is to award each country a point equal to its rank in each criterion of ranking (here relative mortality, relative life expectancy, maternal mortality and number of girls in primary or secondary education per 100 boys), add each country's score and then rank countries on the basis of their aggregate scores. To illustrate, suppose a country has the ranks i, j, k and l for the four criteria. Then its Borda score is $i + j + k + l$. The rule invariably yields a complete ordering of countries. The strengths and weaknesses of the Borda Rule have been investigated by Goodman and Markowitz (1952), Smith (1973) and Fine and Fine (1974). In the context of this preliminary investigation the attractions of the Borda Rule are its simplicity and transparency.
6. Clearly a product of the narrowness of the standard of living indicators.

References

Allèn, T. (1992) 'Economic Development and the Feminisation of Poverty' in Folbre, N. *et al.* (eds) *Issues in Contemporary Economics Volume 4: Women's Work in the World Economy* (London: Macmillan) pp. 107–19.

Anchor, R. and Hein, C. (1985) 'Why Third World Urban Employers Usually Prefer Men', *International Labour Review*, vol. 124, no. 1, pp. 73–90.

Bardhan, K. (1984) *Land, Labour and Rural Poverty: Essays in Development Economics* (Oxford: Oxford University Press).

Bergmann, B. (1987) 'The Task of a Feminist Economics: A More Equitable Future', in Farnham, C. (ed.) *The Impact of Feminist Research in the Academy* (Bloomington: Indiana University Press).

Berik, G. and Çağatay, N. (1992) 'Industrialisation Strategies and Gender Composition of Manufacturing Employment in Turkey', in Folbre, N. *et al.* (eds), *Issues in Contemporary Economics Volume 4: Women's Work in the World Economy* (London: Macmillan) pp. 41–60.

Bettio, F. and Villa, P. (1992) 'Is There a Mediterranean Path to Female Integration into the Labour Market?', paper presented at the International Working Party on Labour Market Segmentation Conference, Cambridge, UK.

Blood, R.O. and Wolfe, D.M. (1960) *Husbands and Wives* (New York: Free Press).

Boserup, E. (1970) *Woman's Role in Economic Development* (New York: St Martin's Press).

Dale, A. and Glover, J. (1990) *An Analysis of Women's Employment Patterns in the UK, France and the USA: The Value of Survey-Based Comparisons*, Research Paper No. 75, Department of Employment, London.

Dasgupta, P. and Weale, M. (1992) 'On Measuring the Quality of Life', *World Development*, vol. 20, no. 1, pp. 119–31.

David, M.G. and Starzec, C. (1992) 'Women and Part-time work: France and Great Britain Compared', in Folbre, N. *et al.* (eds) *Issues in Contemporary Economics, Volume 4: Women's Work in the World Economy* (London: Macmillan) pp. 180–94.

Dex, S. and Shaw, L. (1988) 'Women's Working Lives: A Comparison of Women in the United States and Great Britain', in Hunt, A. (ed.) *Women and Paid Work* (London: Macmillan) pp. 173–95.

Elson, D. and Pearson, R. (1981) 'The Subordination of Women and the Internationalization of Factory Production', in Young K. *et al.* (eds) *Of Marriage and the Market* (London: Conference of Socialist Economists) pp. 144–66.

Fine, B. and Fine, K. (1974) 'Social Choice and Individual Rankings, I and II', *Review of Economic Studies*, vol. 44, nos 3 & 4, pp. 303–22.

Folbre, N. and Hartmann, H. (1988) 'The Rhetoric of Self-Interest: Ideology and Gender in Economic Theory' in Klamer, A. *et al.* (eds) *Consequences of Economic Rhetoric* (Cambridge: Cambridge University Press) pp. 184–203.

Garnsey, E. (1984) 'The Provision and Quality of Part-time Work: The Case of Great Britain and France', Report to the Equal Opportunities Office of the European Community, Brussels.

Goode, W.J. (1963) *World Revolution and Family Patterns* (New York: Free Press).

Goodman, L.A. and Markowitz, H. (1952) 'Social Welfare Functions based on Individual Ranking', *American Journal of Sociology*, vol. 58, November, pp. 257–62.

Hein, C. (1984) 'Jobs for the Girls: Export Manufacturing in Mauritius', *International Labour Review*, vol. 123, no. 2, pp. 251–65.

Humphrey, J. (1985) 'Gender, Pay and Skill: Manual Workers in Brazilian Industry', in Afshar, H. (ed.) *Women, Work and Ideology in the Third World* (London: Tavistock) pp. 214–31.

ILO (1991) *Yearbook of Labour Statistics* (Geneva: International Labour Office).

Jenson, J., Hagen, E. and Reddy, C. (eds) (1988) *Feminisation of the Labour Force* (Cambridge: Polity Press).

Joekes, S. (1985) 'Working for a Lipstick? Male and Female Labour in the Clothing Industry in Morocco', in Afshar, H. (ed.) *Women, Work and Ideology in the Third World* (London: Tavistock) pp. 183–213.

Koistinen, P. and Ostner, I. (eds) (1992) 'Women in the Markets: Learning of the Differences in the Finnish and German Labour Markets', unpublished manuscript.

Kumar, G. (1989) 'Gender, Differential Mortality and Development: A Perspective on the Experience of Kerala', *Cambridge Journal of Economics*, vol. 13, no. 4, pp. 517–39.

Kynch, J. and Sen, A. (1983) 'Indian Women: Well-being and Survival', *Cambridge Journal of Economics*, vol. 7, no. 4, pp. 363–80.

Lim, L. (1983) 'Capitalism, Imperialism and Patriarchy: The Dilemma of Third World Women Workers in Multinational Factories', in Nash, J. and Fernandez-Kelly, M.P. (eds) *Women, Men and the International Division of Labour* (Albany: State University of New York).

Meulders, D., Plasmar, R. and Vander Stricht, V. (1991) 'Position of Women on the Labour Market: Developments between 1983 and 1989–90', Report to the Commission of the European Community, Department of Applied Economics, Free University of Brussels.

Miller, B. (1981) *The Endangered Sex: Neglect of Female Children in Rural North India* (Ithaca, NY: Cornell University Press).

Nash, J. (1983) 'The Impact of Changing International Division of Labour on Different Sectors of the Labour Force', in Nash, J. and Fernandez-Kelly, M.P. (eds) *Women, Men and the International Division of Labour* (Albany: State University of New York).

Pahl, J. (1989) *Money and Marriage* (London: Macmillan).

Pfau-Effinger, B. (1992) 'Socio-cultural Differences and the Labour Market Behaviour of Women in European Countries: The Example of Germany and Finland', paper presented at the International Working Party on Labour Market Segmentation Conference, Cambridge, UK.

Pollak, R.A. (1985) 'A Transaction Cost Approach to Families and Households', *Journal of Economic Literature*, vol. 23, June, pp. 581–608.

Population Crisis Committee (1988) 'Country Rankings of the Status of Women: Poor, Powerless and Pregnant', Briefing Paper No. 20, Washington, DC.

Preston, S. (1976) *Mortality Patterns in National Populations* (New York: Academic Press).

Proctor, I. and Ratcliffe, P. (1992) 'Employment and Domestic Work: A Comparison of Samples of British and French Women', in Arber, S. and Gilbert, N. (eds) *Women and Working Lives: Divisions and Change* (London: Macmillan) pp. 71–88.

Rubery, J. (ed.) (1988) *Women and Recession* (London: Routledge & Kegan Paul).

Safa, H. (1981) 'Runaway Shops and Female Employment: The Search for Cheap Labour', *Signs*, vol. 7, no. 2, pp. 418–33.

Smith, J.H. (1973) 'Aggregation of Preferences with Variable Electorate', *Econometrica*, vol. 41, no. 6, pp. 1027–42.

Thomas, J. (1988) 'Women and Capitalism: Oppression or Emancipation? A Review Article', *Comparative Studies in Society and History*, vol. 30, pp. 534–49.

Tilly, L. and Scott, J. (1978) *Women, Work and Family* (New York: Holt, Rinehart & Winston).

UNICEF (annual) *State of the World's Children* (New York: United Nations).

Walters, P. and Dex, S. (1992) 'Feminisation of the Labour Force in Britain and France', in Arber, S. and Gilbert, N. (eds) *Women and Working Lives: Divisions and Change* (London: Macmillan) pp. 89–103.

World Bank (1991) *World Development Report 1991* (Oxford: Oxford University Press).